Shots in the Dark

Shoji Yamada

Translated by Earl Hartman

BUDDHISM AND MODERNITY

A series edited by Donald S. Lopez Jr.

NICHIBUNKEN MONOGRAPH SERIES
No. 9

Shots in the Dark

Japan, Zen, and the West

The University of Chicago Press
Chicago and London

International Research Center
for Japanese Studies
Kyoto

SHOJI YAMADA is associate professor at the International Research Center for Japanese Studies, Kyoto. He is the author of ten books, most recently of *"Kaizokuban" no shisō: jūhasseiki eikoku no eikyū kopīraito tōsō* (Reasoning about "pirate editions": battles over perpetual copyright in eighteenth-century Britain; 2007), *CD-ROM ban kuzushiji kaidoku yōrei jiten* (The CD-ROM dictionary of Japanese historical characters; 2007), *Bunka to shite no terebi komāsharu* (Cultural perspectives on television commercials; 2007).

EARL HARTMAN is a licensed kyudo instructor and professional translator based in California.

The University of Chicago Press, Chicago 60637
The University of Chicago Press, Ltd., London
© 2009 by The University of Chicago
All rights reserved. Published 2009
Printed in the United States of America

Originally published as *Zen to yū na no Nihon-maru* by Kobundo Publishing Co., Ltd.
© 2005 Shoji Yamada.

English translation © 2009 International Research Center for Japanese Studies, Kyoto.

18 17 16 15 14 13 12 11 10 09   1 2 3 4 5

ISBN-13: 978-0-226-94764-8   (cloth)
ISBN-10: 0-226-94764-5   (cloth)

Library of Congress Cataloging-in-Publication Data
880–01 Yamada, Shoji, 1963–
    [880–02 Zen to iu na no Nihon Maru. English]
    Shots in the dark : Japan, Zen, and the West / Shoji Yamada ; translated by Earl Hartman.
        p. cm. — (Buddhism and Modernity)
    Includes bibliographical references and index.
    ISBN-13: 978-0-226-94764-8 (cloth : alk. paper)
    ISBN-10: 0-226-94764-5 (cloth : alk. paper) 1. Herrigel, Eugen, 1884–1955. Zen in der Kunst des Bogenschiessens—Influence. 2. Herrigel, Eugen, 1884–1955—Criticism and interpretation. 3. Zen Buddhism—Study and teaching—Europe. 4. Civilization, Western—20th century—Japanese influences. 5. Archery—Japan—Religious aspects. 6. Ryoanji Teien (Kyoto, Japan) 7. Rock gardens, Japanese—Religious aspects. I. 880–03 Kokusai Nihon Bunka Kenkyu Senta. II. Title. III. Series: Nichibunken monograph series ; no. 9.
    GV1188.J3Y3313 2009
    799.3′2—dc22

                                                                2008042071

Contents

Preface to the American Edition

It is said that Japanese "soft power"—such as *manga* and *anime*—is overwhelming the world. Many foreigners become interested in and familiar with Japanese culture through them. However, Japanese culture has been popularized in the West not only by *manga* and *anime*, but also by Zen.

In the 1980s, many foreigners became interested in Japan because of its economic power. Times, however, are changing: even though Japan went through a deep depression in the mid-1990s, Japanese culture still retains a powerful attraction for foreigners, who see it as embodying a sense of spiritual exoticism. What has happened in the recent quarter of a century could be described as a shift from "yen to Zen." While we find only a slight difference between "yen" and "Zen" in terms of alphabetic order, they represent vastly dissimilar value systems. This book presents some of my research on the process of how the value system surrounding Zen has changed, based on an analysis of information transmission between Japan and the West. I hope that readers of this book will enjoy sharing the intellectual interest that I have had for nearly twenty years.

It is a great honor for me to have my book translated and published in English as the first copublishing project between the University of Chicago Press and the International Research Center for Japanese Studies (Nichibunken) in Kyoto. Earl Hartman, my friend and a skilled practitioner of Japanese archery, kindly undertook the difficult task of translation. I have adapted and expanded his original translation by incorporating corrections to the Japanese edition, adding new footnotes, and modifying some of the Japanese expressions to make the text more understandable to an English-speaking audience. As a result, this book is not a word-for-word translation of the original Japanese volume, but a completely revised edition. All mistakes and inadequacies in this book are mine.

I am grateful to Patricia Fister, editor of the Nichibunken monograph series, and to Alan Thomas, the editorial director for humanities and sciences at the University of Chicago Press, for their editorial expertise and cooperation throughout the copublication process; Hans-Peter Rodenberg, who kindly undertook the German-English translation of the text of Herrigel's Defense; and my Nichibunken colleagues Markus Rüttermann and Frederik Cryns, who graciously checked the German and French citations, respectively.

In addition, I wish to thank the following people for their support and encouragement: James C. Baxter, William Bodiford, Inaga Shigemi, Katakura Motoko, Kawakatsu Heita, Donald S. Lopez Jr., Nakamura Norio, Sakamoto Yasuyuki, Mieko Akisawa-Schamoni, and Wolfgang Schamoni.

I would also like to express my gratitude to the colleagues and members of my project room: Iwai Shigeki, Okaya Junko, and Chavalin Svetanant, who always cheered me on as I was engaged in working on this English edition. Finally, I thank my helpmate, Yamada Kazue, from my heart.

Shoji Yamada
Kyoto, June 2008

Introduction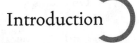

Everyone knows this fairy tale:

"Mirror, mirror on the wall, who is the fairest of them all?"
"Why, you are, of course."

In a corner of their hearts, everyone is looking for a magic mirror. If there was a mirror that would reflect the image of them as they fervently wished to be, surely everyone would treasure such a mirror for as long as they lived.

On the other hand, there are mirrors that don't do that, such as concave mirrors and convex mirrors. For a long time there have been two full-length fun-house mirrors on the observation deck of the Tsūtenkaku tower in Osaka. For people from other parts of Japan who are not familiar with Osaka's fun-loving and idiosyncratic culture, why such things are in that particular place is a complete mystery; but in any case, it is amusing to play with them.

When you stand in front of the concave mirror, you appear stretched out as though you are being pulled up and down by your head and your toes—as though you have been transformed into a toothpick. In front of the convex mirror it is the reverse: you look short and fat as though you have been squashed in a mechanical press. Unsightly and with short legs, you look like a comic book character. Tourists look at their distorted appearances and laugh. But how can they laugh at such warped reflections? Is it because they can relax knowing that they could not possibly look like the twisted images in the mirror? People do not believe they really look like the grossly distorted images in fun-house mirrors, so they laugh them off. However, when a magic mirror reflects an image distorted in a beautiful way, people want to think: yes indeed, this is how I really look.

All of you astute readers should understand by now. The image reflected in the mirror that I am talking about in this book is the image of Japan drawn by foreigners. However, this brings up a question. What kind of a distorted image would a Japanese accept as being him or herself? What sort of a distorted image would he or she laugh off? Where exactly is the boundary between the two?

On February 25, 1936, with the Nazi swastika flag flying over Germany, a lecture called "Die Ritterliche Kunst des Bogenschiessens" (The chivalrous art of archery) was given at the Berlin branch of the Germany-Japan Association. The name of the lecturer was Eugen Herrigel (1884–1955), a tenured professor of philosophy at the University of Erlangen in southern Germany. Herrigel had taught at Tōhoku Imperial University in Sendai, Japan, from May 1924 to July 1929. In the lecture, Herrigel spoke about the lofty spirituality of Japanese archery, which he had come to know during his stay, and related the astonishing details of the training he had undergone.

The text of the lecture was published immediately in the German magazine *Nippon* (Japan).[1] In the same year, a translated version was featured in the magazine *Bunka* (Culture) published by Tōhoku Imperial University,[2] and in 1941 Iwanami Shoten published a revised translation under

---

1. Eugen Herrigel, "Die Ritterliche Kunst des Bogenschiessens," *Nippon, Zeitschrift für Japanologie* 2:4 (1936): 193–212.

2. Eugen Herrigel, "Kyūjutsu ni tsuite,"*Bunka* 3:9 (1936): 1007–34.

3. Eugen Herrigel, *Nihon no kyūjutsu*, trans. Shibata Jisaburō with an essay (1940) by Komachiya Sōzō (Tokyo: Iwanami Shoten, 1941). Several Japanese words that refer to Japa-

the title *Nihon no kyūjutsu* (Japanese archery).[3] The popularity at that time of Tōhoku Imperial University and the arbiters of culture associated with Iwanami Shoten can be inferred from the rapid succession of publications of this text.[4]

However, the translation was problematic. When it was revised, there were inconsistencies in the Japanese expressions used to explain some vital concepts. The people responsible for the translation were all close to Herrigel and his archery teacher, Awa Kenzō (1880–1939). They were all in a position to understand Awa's archery instruction better than Herrigel, whose Japanese language skills were weak.

It seems that Herrigel's translators and Japanese friends, while praising what he had written, were confused about the discrepancies between his writings and Awa's teachings. Did Master Awa really say things like this? Why did Herrigel come to understand Japanese archery in this way? This confusion can be seen in the inconsistencies among the translations.

In 1948, Herrigel published *Zen in the Art of Archery*,[5] which can be considered the definitive version of the chronicle of his archery training in Japan. In his book, Japanese archery is described in even more mystical terms, and not only archery, but all of Japanese culture, is presented as being synonymous with Zen.

Zen in the Art of Archery was translated into more than five languages and became a worldwide bestseller. The Japanese version was published in 1956.[6] Hand in hand with the Zen and New Age booms in Europe and the United States, it was very fashionable as a trendy kind of "wisdom" from the 1950s through the 1970s. There is a surprisingly large number of foreigners who have said they formed their image not only of Japanese archery, but of Japanese culture itself, from reading *Zen in the Art of Archery*.

---

nese archery appear in the present volume. *Kyūjutsu, kyūdō, and shadō* can be translated as traditional Japanese archery, the Way of the Bow, and the Way of Shooting, respectively. *Kyūjutsu* is a somewhat archaic term; *kyūdō* is a modern term that came into widespread use after World War II; and *shadō* was Awa Kenzō's personal term originally used in Daishadōkyō, a school founded by Awa, which I describe later.

4. Iwanami Shoten, one of Japan's most prestigious publishing houses, was founded in 1913 by Iwanami Shigeo (1881–1946) and influenced the opinions of the Japanese intelligentsia in the twentieth century. Herrigel had many friends at Tōhoku Imperial University with connections to Iwanami Shigeo.

5. Eugen Herrigel, *Zen in der Kunst des Bogenschiessens* (Muenchen-Planegg: Otto Wilhelm Barth-Verlag, 1948).

6. Eugen Herrigel, *Yumi to zen*, trans. Inatomi Eijirō and Ueda Takeshi (Tokyo: Kyōdō Shuppan, 1956).

The book became a widely discussed topic among the Japanese cultural elite as well. It is not an exaggeration to say that it was accepted as a central text in the discussion of "Japaneseness" which took place from the 1960s through the 1970s. Proclaiming that the book presented the ideal image of Japanese culture and believing in Herrigel's writings 100 percent, countless numbers of people took it as the starting point for the development of their theories of Japaneseness.[7] I do not know of any other document on the theory of Japaneseness that has been accepted this uncritically. *Zen in the Art of Archery* was a magic mirror that, for Japanese people, reflected the ideal image they had of themselves.

One day I was reading an authoritative book about Awa Kenzō, written by a specialist in the field, and I came upon the following statement:

> While Kenzō used the phrase "the bow and Zen are one" and employed the philosophical language of Mahayana Buddhism in particular to describe *shadō* (the Way of Shooting), he did not approve of Zen unconditionally.

To be honest, I was shocked. If this is true, it cannot be overlooked. The man who supposedly taught the bow to Herrigel as Zen did not approve of Zen unconditionally? If that is the case, then the book that Herrigel wrote—what was it, exactly? What kind of a mistake did he make to come up with a book like that and where did he make it?

I should mention that there was a period in my life when I spent a considerable amount of my free time practicing *kyūdō* (the Way of the Bow / Japanese archery), and Herrigel was always floating vaguely around in the back of my mind. I started my scholarly career as a research associate at a three-year engineering college, but it so happened that I later transferred to an institute that researches Japanese culture from an international perspective and so I was blessed with an environment that allowed me to deepen and expand my research and contemplation of this question. I compared *Nihon no kyūjutsu* (Japanese archery) and *Zen in the Art of Archery* in great detail, surveyed related documents, and discovered a great deal of unpublished material in museums and universities on my trips to Germany. Through doing this I came to see how the myth of *Zen in the Art of Archery* was born and how it was imported back into Japan—that is, I

---

7. For example, Terada Tōru, *Dō no shisō* (Tokyo: Sōbunsha, 1978) and Kawai Hayao, *Kage no genshōgaku* (Tokyo: Shisakusha, 1976).

came to see the process by which the Japanese found and polished a magic mirror that reflected a beautiful image of themselves.

In this book I want to discuss an additional topic: the rock garden at the temple of Ryōanji in Kyoto. I am a complete amateur when it comes to gardens, so perhaps it might be considered rash of me to venture an opinion on this subject. However, Ryōanji also illustrates the "magic mirror effect" and so I think it is worthy of discussion.

Today, the rock garden at Ryōanji is one of the most well-known examples of the Japanese garden. If one asks foreign Japan experts, "What is the most beautiful garden in Japan?" a large number of them would probably reply "the rock garden at Ryōanji."

However, I heard the following story from a foreigner who was an expert on Japanese gardens. He had lived in Kyoto for a number of years and had gone to many different gardens, but he simply could not bring himself to visit Ryōanji. He confessed to me that he was afraid: what would he do if he went to Ryōanji, saw the rock garden, and did not like it? Just exactly what kind of a rock garden is it that can intimidate a foreigner to such an extent?

Leaving aside foreigners for the moment, how much do the Japanese themselves value the rock garden at Ryōanji? Of course, to professional gardeners, its beauty and importance are self-evident. But do regular tourists really think it is beautiful? I have visited the rock garden any number of times. But to be perfectly honest, not once did I think that it was pretty. What a frightening confession to make! Just like the above-mentioned foreign expert on Japanese gardens, the fact that I think this is a frightening confession shows that I, too, have been thoroughly intimidated by the supposed beauty of this rock garden.

Having admitted that, I think I should make a full confession: I prefer gardens where one can experience the subtle moment-to-moment changing of nature from month to month throughout the year. The rock garden at Ryōanji is nothing but an abstraction of nature. One cannot feel the seasons. Not only that, it is always packed with tourists, and as a final indignity, a loudspeaker is always blaring the message: "View the garden quietly, please!" I am reduced to having to leave the rock garden behind and go to the Kyōyōchi pond elsewhere on the grounds to catch my breath.

The fact that I do not like the rock garden at Ryōanji is probably just a matter of personal taste. It is also not really fair to dislike it just because it is always crowded with tourists. However, I am confident in my speculation that those who are moved by its beauty when they see it for the first time are rare. It is not difficult to find documents that support my speculation from a historical perspective. Prior to the beginning of the Shōwa period (1926–1989), few people visited the rock garden at Ryōanji, and within Japan itself, aside from a few professionals, there were not very many people who said that it was particularly beautiful. Moreover, praise from foreigners did not come to be dominant until after the Zen boom in Europe and the United States started in the 1950s. As a Japanese, it is somewhat gratifying to know that Japan has a garden that foreigners praise and travel all the way across the ocean to visit. But this, again, is just a magic mirror that reflects a beautiful image of me.

I know that there are passionate devotees of both Herrigel and rock gardens all over the world, and I am sure that some of you will be angry with me for writing this sort of thing. However, I want you to stop and think for a moment. If you are angry at this book, what is the source of that anger?

Just exactly how many magic mirrors do we have? What kind of an image must a mirror reflect for us to love it? What kind of an image must a mirror reflect for us to laugh it off as a fun-house mirror? And what kind of an image must a mirror reflect for us to hate it? Where is the boundary between these mirrors?

It is on this boundary line that we can find the visage of what we believe to be the ideal Japan as well as the form of Japanese culture that we ourselves arbitrarily create. And it is also on this boundary line that we can see how the Japanese have created Japanese culture while actively selecting their self-image from among the various images of Japan that come from foreign countries. With archery, rock gardens, and Zen as our clues, let us begin our voyage of self-discovery.

1

Between the Real and the Fake

THE KITSCHY WORLD OF "ZEN IN/AND THE ART OF . . ."

In researching Eugen Herrigel's *Zen in the Art of Archery*, I discovered that this book has exerted an influence in unexpected directions. There are a large number of books with titles like *Zen in/and the Art of . . .* that seem to be playing on the title of Herrigel's original book. Before going into the actual contents of *Zen in the Art of Archery*, I would like to discuss this baffling social phenomenon.

The most famous book of this kind is probably *Zen and the Art of Motorcycle Maintenance* by Robert M. Pirsig (1928–).[1] This book is an autobiographical account written by a former university professor who lost his memory as a result of electric shock therapy. It is one of the best-selling New Age books, so I am sure most people have heard of it. Pirsig does not discuss Japanese Zen Buddhism, but his book had a big influence on the so-called Zen boom in Europe and the United States.

Regarding the question of what connection there is between Zen and motorcycle maintenance, Pirsig says the following:

1. Robert M. Pirsig, *Zen and the Art of Motorcycle Maintenance* (New York: Morrow, 1974).

Zen Buddhists talk about "just sitting," a meditative practice in which the idea of a duality of self and object does not dominate one's consciousness. What I'm talking about here in motorcycle maintenance is "just fixing," in which the idea of a duality of self and object doesn't dominate one's consciousness.[2]

Riding with his young son on the back of his motorcycle as he slowly regains his memory, the hero of *Zen and the Art of Motorcycle Maintenance* ponders his personal philosophy of "quality," which transcends the duality of subject and object. Regardless of whether this is Zen or not, there is no doubt that many people in the West felt a great spiritual connection to this book.

In Zen training, people do work such as cutting grass and cleaning toilets. Sometimes they experience enlightenment as they concentrate single-mindedly on this manual labor. Therefore, one cannot say that it is impossible to experience enlightenment while fixing a motorcycle. The idea that the practice of manual labor can illuminate profound philosophical questions is similar to the theory of applied art expounded by Yanagi Muneyoshi (1889–1961).[3]

However, there are probably many Japanese who have doubts about how real the Zen in *Zen and the Art of Motorcycle Maintenance* is. Why is this, exactly? Looking at the title, it is obvious that Pirsig was conscious of Herrigel's *Zen in the Art of Archery*. Pirsig's book was born out of *Zen in the Art of Archery*. However, Pirsig's *Zen and the Art of Motorcycle Maintenance* was such a bestseller that many of the books that followed got their inspiration not from Herrigel, but rather from Pirsig. One can say that books with title beginning *Zen in the Art of . . . .* take after Herrigel, and books with title *Zen and the Art of . . .* take after Pirsig. Having said that, though, since Pirsig himself was almost certainly influenced by Herrigel, one can probably consider all books with the title *Zen in/and . . .* published after *Zen and the Art of Motorcycle Maintenance* to be Herrigel's grandchildren, so to speak.

One such book is called *Zen in the Art of Writing* (1989).[4] It is a collection of essays for aspiring writers written by the science-fiction writer Ray

2. Ibid., 296–97.

3. Yanagi Muneyoshi was a theologian and philosopher who devoted himself to promoting Japanese folk crafts.

4. Ray Bradbury, *Zen in the Art of Writing* (Santa Barbara, CA: Joshua Odell Editions, 1989).

Bradbury (1920–), who is famous as the author of *Fahrenheit 451*. Bradbury has this to say:

> Now—are you surprised?—seriously I must suggest that you read ZEN IN THE ART OF ARCHERY, a book by Eugen Herrigel. Here the words, or words like them, WORK, RELAXATION, and DON'T THINK appear in different aspects and different settings. I knew nothing of Zen until a few weeks ago. What little I know now, since you must be curious as to the reason for my title, is that here again, in the art of archery, long years must pass where one learns simply the act of drawing the bow and fitting the arrow. Then the process, sometimes tedious and nerve-wracking, of preparing to allow the string, the arrow, to release itself. The arrow must fly on its way to a target that must never be considered.[5]

Since Bradbury put "Zen" in the title of his book, it appears that he felt that writing a novel is quite similar to what Herrigel was talking about in *Zen in the Art of Archery*. Leaving aside the question of whether he is right or not, however, the word "Zen" was removed from the title of the Japanese version of *Zen in the Art of Writing*. In Japan the book is called *Buraddoberi ga yatte kuru* (Bradbury this way comes).[6]

There is another book where the word "Zen" disappeared from the Japanese title. This book is *Shoshinsha no tame no intānetto* (The Internet for beginners) by Brendan P. Kehoe (1970–). The original title is *Zen and the Art of the Internet: A Beginner's Guide* (1992).[7] While it has a provocative title, it is just an explanation of Internet technology for beginners, written in a decidedly conservative style. Among the large number of similar books available, it seems to have sold well. Kehoe is a hacker who works at the well-known IT company Cygnus Solutions. He does not appear to be particularly enamored of Zen, and there is not a single mention of Zen anywhere in the book. The Japanese title appears to be an attempt to convey the meaning of the book's contents.

The question is: why was the word "Zen" omitted from the Japanese

---

5. Ibid., 151.

6. The Japanese title is a play on the title of Bradbury's novel *Something Wicked This Way Comes*, published in 1962. I am grateful to Professor Tatsumi Takayuki of Keio University for pointing out this connection.

7. Brendan P. Kehoe, *Zen and the Art of the Internet : A Beginner's Guide* (Englewood. Cliffs, NJ: PTR Prentice Hall, 1992).

title of both Bradbury's *Zen in the Art of Writing* and Kehoe's *Zen and the Art of the Internet*? Was it because the publishers thought that Japanese readers would get a strange impression? Or was it perhaps more likely that the translators and the editors felt that there was a gap between the image that Bradbury and Kehoe have of Zen and what Japanese people would understand by the term "Zen"? They probably thought that including "Zen" in the title would make the books appear a bit disreputable in the eyes of Japanese readers, and that there was a danger that they would think that the books were written by foreigners who had weird ideas about Zen.

In a field related to *Zen in the Art of Writing*, there is a book called *Zen and the Art of Screenwriting: Insights and Interviews* (1996).[8] The author is a professor emeritus at the University of California at Los Angeles and is the creator of UCLA's movie and television scriptwriting program. The book discusses the vital points in writing screenplays for film and television and has interviews with ten well-known scriptwriters. The contents have nothing to do with Zen.

Let me give one more example from the field of art and literature: the mystery novel *Zen and the Art of Murder* (1998).[9] The hero of the book is a tough female private detective who is still hooked on cigarettes even after surviving lung cancer. The author names her Zen Moses. This book was nominated for the Seamus Prize for Best Debut Novel in 1999. The author, Elizabeth M. Cosin, also published *Zen and the City of Angels* in 1999.[10]

In the field of books about living, there is a book called *Zen and the Art of Making a Living: A Practical Guide to Creative Career Design* (1993).[11] At more than six hundred pages long, this tome is full of Zen wisdom and studded with iconic Zen sayings. Its aim is to teach self-realization through success in business, but wouldn't a Japanese think, rather, that the pursuit of material gain has nothing to do with Zen?

Zen fits well with the world of sports. Under the general rubric of "mental training," in recent years top athletes have taken to practicing Zen-like methods for concentration and relaxation. Although I do not play golf my-

8. William Froug, *Zen and the Art of Screenwriting: Insights and Interviews* (Los Angeles: Silman-James Press, 1996).

9. Elizabeth M. Cosin, *Zen and the Art of Murder* (New York: St. Martin's Press, 1998).

10. Elizabeth M. Cosin, *Zen and the City of Angels* (New York: St. Martin's Minotaur, 1999).

11. Laurence G. Boldt, *Zen and the Art of a Making Living: A Practical Guide to Creative Career Design* (New York: Arkana, 1993).

self, when I watch golf on television it looks as though the states of mind of the players are similar to those of Zen practitioners, and according to the author of *Zen in the Art of Golf* (1991), "all these things are one thing."[12] In the field of exercise and recreation books, there are titles like *Zen in the Art of Mountain Climbing* (1992)[13] and *Zen in the Art of Street Fighting* (1996).[14] Books like *Zen in the Art of Stickfighting* (2000),[15] written by a person claiming to be a Grand Master with a tenth-degree black belt, are also amusing.

In English, there is a saying that "travel broadens the mind." According to *Zen and the Art of Travel* (2000),[16] the "Zen" mind can enrich the experience of travel and if you travel you will come to better understand "Zen." A beautiful pocket book with full color plates of scenes from around the world accompanying the text, *Zen and the Art of Travel* explains that travel preparations, destinations, food and lodgings, precautions, and homecomings are all connected to "Zen" wisdom. The same publishing company has also published a series of books with titles like *Zen and the Art of Gardening* (2000),[17] *Zen and the Art of Cooking* (2001),[18] and *Zen and the Art of Well-Being* (2001).[19] For Japanese, the word Zen is imbued with an aura of stoicism, but for Westerners, pleasure is apparently also "Zen."

Roulette, craps, baccarat, blackjack, slot machines, video poker: according to *Zen and the Art of Casino Gaming* (1995),[20] casino gaming involves complex player psychology and strategies for winning. The author, who is a professional gambler, claims to transmit the know-how needed to be successful at gambling. There is also another gambling and Zen book called *Zen and the Art of Poker* (1999).[21] On the subject of game centers, there is

12. Joseph McLaughlin, *Zen in the Art of Golf* (New Philadelphia, OH: Pale Horse Press, 1991).

13. Neville Shulman, *Zen in the Art of Climbing Mountains* (Rutland, VT and Tokyo: Tuttle, 1992).

14. Jack M. Sabat, *Zen and the Art of Street Fighting* (Berkeley, CA: Frog Ltd., 1996).

15. Stephen F. Kaufman, *Zen and the Art of Stickfighting* (Lincolnwood, IL: Contemporary Books, 2000).

16. Eric Chaline, *Zen and the Art of Travel* (Naperville, IL: Sourcebooks, 2000).

17. Gill Hale, *Zen and the Art of Gardening* (Naperville, IL: Sourcebooks, 2000).

18. Jon Sandifer, *Zen and the Art of Cooking* (Naperville, IL: Sourcebooks, 2001).

19. Eric Chaline, *Zen and the Art of Well-Being* (Naperville, IL: Sourcebooks, 2001).

20. Miron Stabinsky and Jeremy Silman, *Zen and the Art of Casino Gaming: An Insider's Guide to a Successful Gambling Experience* (n.p.: Summit Publishing, 1995).

21. Larry W. Phillips, *Zen and the Art of Poker* (New York: Plume, 1999).

an interesting book called *Zen and the Art of Foosball* (2002),[22] which explains the secret to winning foosball, a table soccer game where players spin numerous handles mounted in a table to kick the ball towards a goal.

Not only gambling, but comedy is "Zen" too. According to *Zen and the Art of Stand-Up Comedy* (1998),[23] "Zen" is defined as "your guess is as good as mine." It talks about how "Zen" accepts that which is unpredictable and lives life just as it is in the present moment. If that is true, is not stand-up comedy nothing other than "Zen"? English-language stand-up comedy is usually delivered in an incredibly rapid-fire style and so I have great difficulty understanding it. However, is there really "Zen" there of which Japanese people are unaware? The same author has also written a book in the same category called *Zen and the Art of the Monologue* (2000).[24]

I would also like to mention two books that, simply from the unexpectedness of the juxtapositions in the titles, are really amusing. *Zen in the Art of Close Encounters* (1995)[25] is a critical anthology concerning things like UFOs and crop circles. According to the book, these phenomena can be understood if you expand your concept of reality. Just like in "Zen." There is also *Zen and the Art of Changing Diapers* (1991).[26] This book was self-published by the author, a female journalist and poet. It is a book of poems expressing love for a child written from the point of view of the father. While I stand in a certain kind of flabbergasted awe at her ability to bring Zen into a discussion of diaper changing, as a parent who has raised children there is something strangely convincing in the author's statement that "a baby, too, is a kind of *kōan*."[27] On the subject of raising children, there are also titles like *Zen in the Art of Child Maintenance* (1993)[28] and *Zen and the Art of Fatherhood* (1997).[29]

---

22. Charles C. Lee, *Zen and the Art of Foosball: A Beginner's Guide to Table Soccer* (Lincoln, NE: Writers Club Press, 2002).

23. Jay Sankey, *Zen and the Art of Stand-Up Comedy* (New York: Routledge, 1998).

24. Jay Sankey, *Zen and the Art of the Monologue* (New York: Routledge, 2000).

25. Paul David Pursglove, ed., *Zen in the Art of Close Encounters: Crazy Wisdom and UFOs* (Berkeley, CA: The New Being Project, 1995).

26. Sarah Arsone, *Zen and the Art of Changing Diapers* (Los Angeles: Sarah Arsone, 1993).

27. A *kōan* is a puzzling, sometimes paradoxical statement or story given by Zen masters to pupils as an aid to meditation and attaining spiritual awakening.

28. Michael Pastore, *Zen in the Art of Child Maintenance* (Dayville, CT: Zorba Press, 1993).

29. Steven Lewis, *Zen and the Art of Fatherhood: Lessons from a Master Dad* (New York: Plume, 1997).

There are many, many more books like this. Some intriguing titles are *Zen in the Art of Rhetoric* (1996),[30] *Zen and the Art of Anything* (1999),[31] *Zen and the Art of Postmodern Philosophy* (2000),[32] *Zen and the Art of Knitting* (2002),[33] *Zen and the Art of Diabetes Maintenance* (2002),[34] *Zen and the Art of Falling in Love* (2003),[35] *Zen in the Art of the SAT* (2005),[36] *Zen and the Art of Happiness* (2006),[37] *Zen and the Art of Dodgeball* (2006),[38] *Zen and the Art of Faking It* (2007),[39] and *Zen and the Art of Housekeeping* (2008).[40] Even this list with all of these titles does not include all of the *Zen in/and the Art of . . .* books that have been published.

Zen in/and the Art of . . . can be found not only in the world of literature, but also in articles in serious professional journals. The contents of these articles are highly specialized, so I will just list the titles and the names of the journals in which they appeared. Of course, this does not exhaust all of the *Zen in/and the Art of . . .* articles that exist:

"Zen and the Psychology of Education," *The Journal of Psychology* (1971)[41]
"Zen and the Art of Management," *Harvard Business Review* (1978)[42]

30. Mark Lawrence McPhail, *Zen in the Art of Rhetoric* (New York: State University of New York Press, 1996).

31. Hal French, *Zen and the Art of Anything* (New York: Broadway Books, 1999).

32. Carl Olson, *Zen and the Art of Postmodern Philosophy* (New York: State University of New York Press, 2000).

33. Bernadette Murphy, *Zen and the Art of Knitting* (Avon, MA: Adams Media, 2002).

34. Charles Creekmore, *Zen and the Art of Diabetes Maintenance* (Alexandria, VA: American Diabetes Association, 2002).

35. Brenda Shoshanna, *Zen and Art of Falling in Love* (New York: Simon & Schuster, 2003).

36. Matt Bardin and Susan Fine, *Zen in the Art of the SAT : How to Think, Focus, and Achieve Your Highest Score* (Boston: Houghton Mifflin, 2005).

37. Chris Prentiss, *Zen and the Art of Happiness* (Los Angeles: Power Press, 2006).

38. Alex Karasz, *Zen and the Art of Dodgeball* (Charleston, SC: BookSurge, 2006).

39. Jordan Sonnenblick, *Zen and the Art of Faking It* (New York: Scholastic Press, 2007).

40. Lauren Cassel Brownell, *Zen and the Art of Housekeeping: The Path to Finding Meaning in Your Cleaning* (Avon, MA: Adams Media, 2008).

41. Alonzo M. Valentine Jr., "Zen and the Psychology of Education," *Journal of Psychology* 79 (1971): 103–10.

42. Richard Tanner Pascale, "Zen and the Art of Management," *Harvard Business Review* 56:2 (1978): 153–62.

"Zen and the Art of Supervision," *The Family Journal: Counseling and Therapy for Couples and Families* (1998)[43]

"Zen and the Art of Higher Education Maintenance," *Journal of Higher Education Policy and Management* (1999)[44]

"Zen and the Art of Policy Analysis," *The Journal of Politics* (2001)[45]

"Zen and the Art of Medical Image Registration," *NeuroImage* (2003)[46]

What do Japanese people think about this phenomenon of "Zen" being used in such a seemingly indiscriminate manner? I would like to emphasize that I am not ridiculing these books and articles. Most of these authors are quite serious and you can sense the enthusiasm they have for their subject matter. However, the majority of these books and articles do not say a single thing about Zen even though they use "Zen" in their titles. Apparently in English, "Zen" does not just refer to a sect of Buddhism; it also appears to be used to refer to introductory or basic knowledge. I have also heard that in the West the word "Zen" is used to mean "cool."

At the risk of repeating myself, I want to state again that most of these books are serious books. Then why, when I line up the titles, do they seem kitschy to me? Is it perhaps because Japanese have a self-image of what they want to be—in this case it is the Japanese image of "Zen"—and these books do not reflect the image Japanese have of themselves? Let us consider this point in depth. Japanese have a reputation for being especially sensitive to, and appreciative of, the opinions of foreigners. This kitschy world of *Zen in/and the Art of . . .* must also be an "image of Japan as seen through the eyes of foreigners." Why then do the Japanese ignore the world of *Zen in/and the Art of . . .* and brush it off as phony "Zen"?

It seems as though there is a hidden mechanism concerning the creation of Japanese culture in this particular area. Japanese people do not simply swallow whole foreign images of Japan just as they receive them. Rather,

43. Marina Oppenheimer, "Zen and the Art of Supervision," *Family Journal: Counseling and Therapy for Couples and Families* 6:1 (1998): 61–63.

44. Patricia M. Shields, "Zen and the Art of Higher Education Maintenance: Bridging Classic and Romantic Notions of Quality," *Journal of Higher Education Policy and Management* 21:2 (1999): 165–72.

45. Kenneth J. Meier et al., "Zen and the Art of Policy Analysis: A Response to Nielsen and Wolf," *Journal of Politics* 63:2 (2001): 616–29.

46. W. R. Crum et al., "Zen and the Art of Medical Image Registration: Correspondence, Homology, and Quality," *NeuroImage* 20 (2003): 1425–37.

from among myriad possibilities for Japanese culture presented by foreigners, the Japanese select specific things as they fashion their self-image.

THE ROCK GARDEN IN NEW YORK

In addition to the *Zen in/and the Art of. . . .* books, there are other things that make one think about the dividing line between the real and the fake when it comes to Zen. I would like to consider Ryōanji-style rock gardens in foreign countries as an example of this.

On the northern edge of Wall Street, New York City's famous center of finance, one can find the Chase Manhattan Bank building. Below street level, as seen looking down from the plaza in front of the building, there is a modern garden patterned after the rock garden at Ryōanji. This circular garden, which was designed to be seen from above, has stones from the Uji River in Kyoto arranged amidst a design made from stone tiles placed so as to imitate a pattern of flowing water created by raking sand with a bamboo rake. In the summer, water flows into the garden so that the stones float like islands, and in the winter the garden is dry. A wall of glass surrounds the garden, which is on the first underground level of the building, and it can be viewed from the adjacent aisle. The garden creates a weird spatial distortion in the inorganic landscape of Manhattan. It is one of the famous works of the avant-garde artist Isamu Noguchi (1904–1988) and was created in 1964.

I wonder what Japanese people think when they see this garden. It is easy to imagine reactions like "A rock garden in New York! How interesting! And to have been created by a mixed-race Japanese!" or "I guess it is an example of how Japanese traditions have influenced modern art." Looking at it from the opposite perspective, there are probably few people who get from this garden a sense of "genuine Japanese culture" or the "Zen thought" contained within it.

Having said that, however, I have no confidence that I can say for sure that Noguchi's rock garden is a fake dressed up as Japanese culture. After all, it is a well-known work by a famous artist who was active all over the world. In the sense that it is a work by Noguchi, it is the genuine article. However, everyone would probably agree that it is not representative of traditional Japanese culture. It seems that Noguchi's garden may hold a key for finding our self-image as it relates to Japanese culture. I will discuss Noguchi in detail later, so let us leave him for the moment.

In the 1960s when Noguchi created the rock garden at the Chase Man-hattan Bank, copies of Ryōanji were being made in other parts of the United States as well. At the Japanese Embassy in Washington, D.C., for example, there is a scaled-down copy of the rock garden at Ryōanji. The Japanese ambassador at the time, Asagai Kōichirō (1906–1995), and a member of the lower house of the Japanese Diet, Takasaki Tatsunosuke (1885–1964), proposed the idea for this garden to commemorate the one hundredth anniversary of the friendship between Japan and the United States, and it was constructed in 1960 with the support of the Japanese financial community. The rock garden is located in front of a teahouse called Ippakutei, which is built in the style of the Katsura Detached Villa in Kyoto.

A pamphlet printed by the Japanese Embassy describes the garden as follows:

> One element recalls the sand garden and masonry wall of the Ryoanji [sic] in Kyoto. The very austerity of the garden, barren of all vegetation and con-structed entirely of fine gravel and stone, is calculated to induce meditation. It is not meant to evoke a particular image, though the impression most often imparted is one of solitude—a desert, perhaps, or bleak islands in a vast sea.[47]

In the year this garden was made, the head priest of Ryōanji at the time, Matsukura Shōei (1908–1983) visited the Japanese Embassy. In an ar-ticle published in the journal Zen bunka (Zen culture), he divulged his feel-ings as follows: "The garden itself is exquisite, but I was disappointed that the surrounding atmosphere did not match it, even though I know that it could not be helped."[48]

I have not seen this garden. When I called the Japanese Embassy, I was told that they still use it to explain the atmosphere of Japanese gardens to visitors, but that since there is no gardener it is not cared for as well as it should be, and it probably is not in the same condition as when it was first made. In the photograph of this garden published in Zen bunka, the white sand is already rank with weeds.

There was also a rock garden from the 1960s until the 1980s at the

47. *Ippakutei: The Ceremonial Tea House & Garden* (Washington, DC: The Embassy of Japan, n.d.).

48. Matsukura Shōei, "Tōzenkō, "*Zen bunka* 22 (1961): 61.

Brooklyn Botanical Gardens, one of the places where New Yorkers go to relax. This rock garden was different from the one at the Japanese Embassy in Washington, D.C., being a full-sized replica of the actual rock garden at Ryōanji. The garden was made by Tono Takuma (1891–1985), who taught landscape architecture at the Tokyo University of Agriculture as well as at other colleges in Japan and the United States. I sent an inquiry to the Brooklyn Botanical Gardens for information about the history of this garden from its original construction until it was dismantled, but never received a response.

In Portland, Oregon, there is a garden called the Japanese Garden of Portland. With the local Japanese Garden Society spearheading the effort, work was begun around 1962 on a large site that was originally a zoo. Tono Takuma was in charge of the landscaping, just as he was for the garden at the Brooklyn Botanical Gardens. This is an honest-to-goodness Japanese garden with a tea house, a reading room, a pond, a waterfall, a brook, an arched bridge, and many moss-covered garden lanterns, where visitors can enjoy a variety of blooming flowers throughout all four seasons as well as the beautiful fall foliage. It is a place of rest and relaxation for the Japanese community where people dance the *Bon Odori* (Bon Festival dance) in honor of deceased ancestors and send lanterns floating down the brook.

Within the Japanese Garden of Portland there is a rock garden modeled after the rock garden at Ryōanji. The number of rocks and their placement are different, so it is not exactly like Ryōanji. However, the design concept, with the rectangular site enclosed by an earthen wall, not a single tree or a blade of grass to be seen, and a pattern of flowing water in white sand, specifically recalls Ryōanji. I was told that they used Shirakawa sand,[49] just like at Ryōanji. Brimming with confidence, the descriptive pamphlet for the Japanese Garden of Portland describes the rock garden as follows:

> Portland's Sand and Stone Garden, unlike the Ryoan-ji [*sic*], is not overwhelmed with thousands of visitors, disgorged from dozens of filled tour buses, led by guides using bull horns to squire their charges through an overly visited sanctuary, the Ryoan-ji is often a most un-Zen-like place. Portland's Zen garden, on the other hand, has the advantage of relative quiet.[50]

49. White sand from Shirakawa in the eastern part of Kyoto.

50. Bruce Taylor Hamilton, *Human Nature, the Japanese Garden of Portland, Oregon* (Portland, OR: Japanese Garden Society of Oregon, 1996), 68.

Would Japanese people consider the Oregon rock garden to be the real thing? It is inside a well-crafted Japanese garden, so the atmosphere is rather nice. Since a professional Japanese landscape architect supervised the construction, it makes a favorable impression. However, since it is not on the grounds of a temple, there is no religious aspect, and so the question of whether anyone would feel any Zen from it is difficult to answer.

The rock garden at Ryōanji has even made its way into the world of toys. Bookstores in North America and England sell the Mini Zen Gardening Kit, a toy which comes in a small box and sells for about $7.00. It is a set consisting of a box about three inches wide by four inches long, some white sand, three small rocks, and a little rake. You can play at making your own little rock garden by putting the sand in the box, arranging the stones, and raking the sand.

The kit was conceived as a way to relax while traveling. The following blurb is written on the container:

> Does travel leave you frazzled? Carry along The Mini Zen Gardening Kit and you'll have tranquility wherever you go. Based upon a centuries-old tradition, the kit includes a base, sand, rocks, and miniature wooden rake, plus a 36-page introduction to the beauty of Zen gardening.

However, there cannot be many people who would experience Japanese culture or Zen from making this miniature rock garden. Regardless of whether one is Japanese or not, most people would regard this as a fake. The people who sell this kit also seem to be selling it as a gag item. The publishing company which makes this kit also sells things like the Mini Bonsai Kit and the Mini Water Gardening Kit. It appears that the Mini Zen Gardening Kit is selling well compared to the other kits.

The pamphlet included in the kit has a description of the Zen garden. An excerpt follows:

> This is the Zen rock garden, called *kare-sansui* [sic] (withered landscapes) in Japanese. These gardens cannot be entered in the usual sense, but are meant to be viewed. Embodying the Zen Buddhist desire to turn away from the life of this world in order to find our true and essential natures, Zen rock gardens both disarm and empower us. . . . Emptied of the usual garden elements such as plants and trees, Zen rock gardens serve as perfect back-

drops to empty ourselves of our own frivolous clutter and to see the world in a new way.[51]

This kind of stereotypical description of rock gardens is very common. Reading this, most Japanese would probably nod in agreement and accept it without thinking it strange. The description has a feeling of "genuineness." One could say that the humor in this kit comes from the combination of the "fakeness" of the kit itself and the "genuineness" of the description.

But there is a question we have to ask here. This question is: why do we get a feeling of "genuineness" from reading this kind of description? Is it only because we frequently hear Zen gardens described like this? People usually do not believe something just because they hear it a lot. When people believe something without verifying it, it is because they want it to be true.

There is one theory that holds that the basis for determining if something is Zen or not is whether it has an air of simplicity and solitude. If we base our judgments on this, then Noguchi's rock garden and the Mini Zen Gardening Kit are not Zen, and the rock gardens at the Japanese Embassy in Washington, D.C., and Portland are on the borderline. Neither of them can be considered "real" rock gardens.

However, the inference that rock gardens = an air of solitude = Zen is itself nothing more than a stereotype. For example, the gaudy Kinkaku (the Golden Pavilion) is located at the temple of Rokuonji in Kyoto, a bona fide Zen temple that belongs to the same Rinzai Zen sect as Ryōanji. A rock garden and the Kinkaku are just about polar opposites, and there is probably no one who sees Zen in the Kinkaku. However, a dazzling multistoried building like the Kinkaku is also one concrete example of a Zen temple. In spite of that, the Kinkaku is ignored in discussions of Zen. Why is that?

THE MOVING BORDERLINE

The dividing line between the real and the fake is not fixed and immovable. Depending on the situation, that which was considered "real" can

51. Abd al-Hayy Moore, *Zen Rock Gardening* (Philadelphia and London: Running Press, 2000), 22–24.

Figure 1. Photograph of an archer by Baron Raimund von Stillfried. Collection of the
International Research Center for Japanese Studies, Kyoto.

become "fake" and vice versa. Moreover, the same thing can be seen as
either real or fake depending on the knowledge and experience of the person viewing it.

Let us look at some concrete examples through photographs. Figure 1
was taken in the Meiji period (1868–1912) by the photographer Baron
Raimund von Stillfried (1839–1911) and was sold as a souvenir for foreign

Figure 2. Photograph of kneeling archer by Nakajima Matsuchi.
Collection of Yokohama Archives of History.

tourists. From the picture, one gets a feeling that one is looking at a master of archery. A book that featured this photograph describes it as follows: "Removing his arm from one of his kimono sleeves, the archer draws the bow to its fullest. From his serious expression one can feel the tension where even a single instant of mental weakness cannot be allowed."[52]

At first glance, this photograph seems to be genuine. However, anyone who is experienced in *kyūdō* can see immediately that it is a fake. For purposes of comparison, let us look at another photograph of what appears to be a genuine archer that was taken at roughly the same time (figure 2). How do these photographs differ? When shooting a bow, the archer must remove the kimono sleeve from his bow arm. If he does not do so, the string will slap the sleeve when the arrow is released, causing it to fly

---

52. *Ikokujin no mita bakumatsu Meiji Japan* (Tokyo: Shin Jinbutsu Ōraisha, 2003), 69.

off course. The archer in figure 1 has removed the wrong arm from his kimono sleeve. In addition, the way he is gripping the bow is totally wrong,
and the way he holds the string in his right hand is unnatural. I can say
unequivocally that the model in this photograph has absolutely no *kyūdō*
experience whatsoever and was posed so he would look just enough like
an archer to satisfy the photographer.

Now let us look at figure 2. No matter which detail one examines, everything is completely natural: how the archer holds the bow, where on the
floor he has placed his arrows, the position of his right hand, and where he
has fixed his gaze. More than anything else, his bulging shoulder muscles,
out of place on a man his age, attest to his rigorous daily training. Since
this photograph was printed in a book it is hard to see, but it looks as
though he has what is called a *bōshi kazari*, or decoration, on the thumb
of his shooting glove, which in past years only a high-ranking archer was
permitted to wear.

Now that we have trained our eyes, let us look at figure 3. This is a page
from the book *Martial Arts* (1987)[53] written by Peter Payne (1945–), a
martial artist and student of psychology. A picture of the rock garden at
Ryōanji appears next to a picture of a karate practitioner knocking down
an arrow in midflight with his bare hand. The commentary accompanying
this picture of *kyūdō* and a rock garden, which perfectly matches the theme
of my book, is as follows:

> The Zen garden, with its rock mountains and sand waves, embodies the har-
> mony and controlled spontaneity which characterizes the masterly perfor-
> mance of the martial arts .... In this picture sequence a Karate master splits
> an arrow fired at him from point-blank range. Such a feat, which is used as a
> training exercise in several martial arts schools, clearly demands a controlled
> spontaneity of the highest order.[54]

This description embraces martial arts and rock gardens as bona fide Zen.
However, readers who have been educated by the two photographs discussed above should realize that figure 3 is also a fake. Since the archer
has removed his sleeve from the incorrect arm, it is obvious that he knows
nothing about *kyūdō*. I do not think the author planned this, but the lay-

53. Peter Payne, *Martial Arts: The Spiritual Dimension* (London: Thames & Hudson,
1981).
54. Ibid., 92.

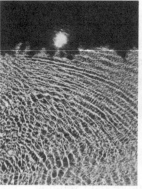

Spontaneity

The profoundly disciplined martial arts master responds to attack without conscious thought or deliberation. But his reaction is no thoughtless reflex or formless jerk; it is a precise and fully appropriate action in accord with the principles of natural movement.

The ripples in water emerge without artifice or plan, yet they are perfect and harmonious manifestations of the laws of wave and flow. The Zen garden, with its rock mountains and sand waves, embodies the harmony and controlled spontaneity which characterizes the masterly performance of the martial arts. Having 'returned to the pre-birth body', uncovering through long discipline the natural energy and movement of the unified body/mind, the master's action is as perfect and spontaneous as that of the wind and waves. (Zen garden, Ryoanji Temple, Kyoto, Japan.)

In this picture sequence a Karate master splits an arrow fired at him from point-blank range. Such a feat, which is used as a training exercise in several martial arts schools, clearly demands a controlled spontaneity of the highest order.

92

Figure 3. Page from *Martial Arts: The Spiritual Dimension* (1981) by Peter Payne. Courtesy of Thames & Hudson, London and New York.

out of this page covers up the suspect nature of the martial arts photograph by juxtaposing it with a genuine rock garden and Zen.

The reason I can distinguish the real from the fake is because I know a little bit about *kyūdō*. If I did not, I would probably assume that the photographs represented the real thing. Stereotypes of Japanese culture are created through the accumulation of these seemingly real images.

It is not easy to tear down a stereotype. When people believe this stereotype and traditional culture to be one and the same thing, it often happens that national ideology stubbornly hardens it into an ossified mass. A lot of things we consider to be traditional culture unique to Japan are in reality social systems created quite recently. When Japan was inundated by the post-Meiji wave of modernization, people became conscious of things like martial arts, landscape architecture, and Zen, and reorganized them. Actually, the great wave of this reorganization started in the decades after World War II and still continues. This point is the heart of the issue presented in this book.

If we look at the social system called traditional culture with this sensibility, we can free ourselves from a simple "either/or" dichotomy when we consider the issue of the real versus the fake in Japanese culture. Being able to take apart things we thought were real, and, conversely, seeing real Japanese culture in things that were thrust aside as fake—this kind of flexible thinking is important.

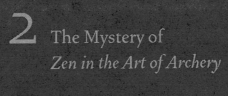

2 The Mystery of
Zen in the Art of Archery

THE BEGINNING OF THE STORY

Now, let us finally make our way into the story of *Zen in the Art of Archery* and the mystery hidden within it.

In May 1924, a German scholar of philosophy, accompanied by his wife, came to Sendai, Japan. His name was Eugen Herrigel. Exactly forty years of age with the piercing gaze of a philosopher, he cut a conspicuous figure. Herrigel's heart was full of expectations. He was going to be in close proximity with living examples of the mysticism he had been pursuing for so long—this is the thought that first came to his mind when some former students of his at Heidelberg University invited him to teach at Tōhoku Imperial University. He wanted above all to study Zen. But the Japanese people Herrigel consulted did not encourage him to leap right away into the world of Zen. Instead, they named several of the "Japanese arts associated with Zen" and suggested that he study one of those as an introduction to Zen.

Herrigel was proud of his skill in pistol shooting, so he chose *kyūjutsu*. Through the introduction of a colleague at Tōhoku Imperial University, Komachiya Sōzō (1893–1976), Herrigel became a student of Awa Kenzō, who had once been Komachiya's *kyūjutsu* teacher. It is here that the story of *Zen in the Art of Archery* begins.

What did Herrigel learn through his study of Japanese *kyūjutsu*? He talks about this in two publications. One is "Die Ritterliche Kunst des Bogenschiessens" (The chivalrous art of archery; 1936),[1] a short transcript of his Berlin lecture, and the other is *Zen in the Art of Archery* (1948).[2] Compact and easy to read, "Die Ritterliche Kunst des Bogenschiessens" gives one a good general picture of Herrigel's experiences, but it is lacking in detail. To really understand Herrigel, we must focus our attention on the definitive version, *Zen in the Art of Archery*.

Zen in the Art of Archery has gone through multiple printings in English, and it can be easily purchased at any large bookstore in major cities or via the Internet. I would like to recommend that people buy the book and read it. But since this is not a very kind thing to say to readers of this book, I will summarize the gist of Herrigel's archery experience as it is presented in *Zen in the Art of Archery*. In order to facilitate the flow of the story, I have deleted some things and changed the phrasing except in the case of actual quotations.

SPIRITUAL ARCHERY AND HERRIGEL'S MEETING WITH ITS TEACHER

> At first sight it must seem intolerably degrading for Zen ... to be associated with anything so mundane as archery. ... Nothing could be more mistaken than this expectation. ... The "Great Doctrine"[3] of archery tells us some-

1. Eugen Herrigel, "Die Ritterliche Kunst des Bogenschiessens" [The chivalrous art of archery], *Nippon, Zeitschrift für Japanologie* 2:4 (1936): 193–212.

2. Eugen Herrigel, *Zen in der Kunst des Bogenschiessens* (Muenchen-Planegg: Otto Wilhelm Barth-Verlag, 1948; trans. Richard F. C. Hull as *Zen in the Art of Archery* [1953; New York: Vintage Books, 1999]). Unless otherwise indicated, all citations are to the 1999 edition.

3. As I will discuss later, Awa had founded a religious sect called Daishadōkyō before Herrigel met him. While Daishadōkyō can be most accurately translated as the "Doctrine of the Great Way of Shooting," Herrigel rendered it as the "Great Doctrine" instead. However, I have decided to use "Great Doctrine," as it is found in the English-language version of *Zen in the Art of Archery*, since this will be more familiar to readers who have already read Herrigel. Thus, when Herrigel discusses the "Great Doctrine" in *Zen in the Art of Archery* (5, 11ff.) the actual referent is Awa's Daishadōkyō, not Zen. "Doctrine" implies Awa's personal belief; however, Herrigel avoided mentioning that fact and used "Doctrine" as a general

thing very different. According to it, archery is still a matter of life and death to the extent that it is a contest of the archer with himself.[4]

For masters of archery, Herrigel says, "the contest consists in the archer aiming at himself—and yet not at himself, in hitting himself—and yet not himself, and thus becoming simultaneously the aimer and the aim, the hitter and the hit."

According to Herrigel, this strange mode of expression is exceedingly clear to Easterners but bewildering to Westerners. He also says that judging from their internal form, the various arts of Japan hark back to a common origin, namely Buddhism, and, in particular, Zen. He stresses that it is impossible to overlook the fact that those who have been reborn through Zen, that is, those who have been purified by the "fire of truth" (9) live lives of unshakable conviction. However, there is practically nothing in the writings of Zen adepts that describes the process or the stages of the journey to reach that goal. Herrigel's goal was to illuminate the true nature of Zen as it functioned in, and was expressed through, the various arts to which it had given form.

Herrigel believed that his intention could be most effectively achieved by describing the training process a *kyūdō* trainee must undergo. Therefore, Herrigel wrote *Zen in the Art of Archery* as a report on the almost six years of training that he received from one of the most accomplished instructors in the art during his stay in Japan.

BECOMING A DISCIPLE

Herrigel had been preoccupied with mysticism from the time he was a student, as though driven by a secret urge. When asked whether he was interested in teaching the history of philosophy at Tōhoku Imperial University, he was ecstatic that he would have the chance to get to know firsthand the people and the country of Japan. This was because he had heard that in Japan there were "teachers of Zen astonishingly well versed in the art of spiritual guidance" (15).

---

term. In the Japanese edition of *Zen in the Art of Archery*, "Doctrine" is translated as *ōgi* (secret, or inner, teachings).

4. Herrigel, *Zen in the Art of Archery*, 3–5. Further citations to pages from this work will be given parenthetically in the text.

His Japanese acquaintances told him that "it was quite hopeless for a European to attempt to penetrate into this realm of spiritual life—perhaps the strangest which the Far East has to offer—unless he began by learning one of the Japanese arts associated with Zen" (15). For this purpose, they named a number of such arts. Without much hesitation, Herrigel's wife decided upon *ikebana* (flower arranging) and *sumie* (ink painting). Herrigel thought that *kyūdō* would be most suitable for him. This was based on the completely mistaken assumption that his experience in rifle and pistol shooting would be helpful.

Herrigel asked one of his colleagues, Komachiya Sōzō of the Law Department, to ask Komachiya's teacher, the famous Master Awa Kenzō, to accept him as a student. Komachiya had twenty years of *kyūdō* experience and was acknowledged to be the most knowledgeable person about *kyūdō* at the university. Master Awa refused the request at first, his reason being that he had once taught a foreigner and found it to be an unpleasant experience. Herrigel swore that he did not want to practice *kyūdō* as a pastime but to understand the "Great Doctrine," and so he and his wife were accepted as students on the condition that Komachiya serve as interpreter.

BREATHING

The day for the first practice session arrived. The Master demonstrated how to shoot the bow and said the following: "Now you do the same, but remember that archery is not meant to strengthen the muscles. When drawing the string you should not exert the full strength of your body, but must learn to let only your two hands do the work, while your arm and shoulder muscles remain relaxed, as though they looked on impassively. Only when you can do this will you have fulfilled one of the conditions that make the drawing and the shooting 'spiritual'" (18).

Herrigel drew the bow, but he had to exert strength in order to hold it and as a result, in a few seconds his hands started to shake and his breathing became labored. No matter what he did, it did not appear that his shooting would become "spiritual."

"You cannot do it," explained the Master, "because you do not breathe right" (19–20). Saying that if Herrigel breathed properly the shooting would become easier day by day, he drew a strong bow and told Herrigel to stand behind him and feel his muscles. They were completely relaxed.

When the Master told Herrigel to relax his shoulders and chest muscles when drawing the bow, Herrigel's leg muscles stiffened violently without his being aware of it. The Master pounced on him like lightning and without saying anything, pressed painfully on Herrigel's leg muscles in a particularly sensitive spot. To excuse himself, Herrigel remarked that he was conscientiously making an effort to keep relaxed. The Master replied: "That's just the trouble, you make an effort to think about it. Concentrate entirely on your breathing, as if you had nothing else to do!" (21–22).

It took a long time before Herrigel could breathe as the Master demanded. However, he was finally able to do it successfully. He learned how to become absorbed in the breathing without worrying about it, and there were times when he even felt that he was not breathing but that he was being breathed. Herrigel finally thought that he understood what it must mean to draw the bow "spiritually."

THE RELEASE

After a year, Herrigel at last was satisfied that he could draw the bow "spiritually," that is, with a kind of effortless strength. The next item to attend to was the release. At this point, Herrigel was shooting at a *makiwara* (practice target made of straw) that was no more than two meters away, so hitting it was not difficult. In such a situation, Herrigel had been just pulling and releasing the string without much thought.

One day, the Master found nothing more to object to in Herrigel's relaxed manner of drawing the bow and said, "All that you have learned hitherto . . . was only a preparation for loosing the shot. We are now faced with a new and particularly difficult task, which brings us to a new stage in the art of archery" (27).

The Japanese bow is drawn using a version of what is called the "Mongolian draw," where the thumb of the right hand holds the string just under the arrow and the arrow is held in place against the right-hand side of the bow by placing the first two or three fingers over the thumb. Herrigel found that when attempting to release the arrow, he could not open the three fingers which pressed down on the thumb without effort. The result of this was that at the moment of release, a jerk would occur which caused the shot to wobble.

The Master exclaimed to Herrigel, "Don't think of what you have to do, don't consider how to carry it out! You mustn't open the right hand on purpose," to which Herrigel replied, "I understand well enough that the hand mustn't be opened with a jerk if the shot is not to be spoiled. But however I set about it, it always goes wrong."

"You must hold the drawn bowstring like a little child holding the proffered finger. It grips it so firmly that one marvels at the strength of the tiny fist. And when it lets the finger go, there is not the slightest jerk. Do you know why? Because a child doesn't think."

"When I have drawn the bow, the moment comes when I feel: unless the shot comes at once I shan't be able to endure the tension. And what happens then? Merely that I get out of breath."

"Do you know why you cannot wait for the shot and why you get out of breath before it has come? The right shot at the right moment does not come because you do not let go of yourself. You do not wait for fulfillment, but brace yourself for failure."

Herrigel explained, "For ultimately, I draw the bow and loose the shot in order to hit the target. The drawing is thus a means to an end, and I cannot lose sight of this connection."

In a loud voice the Master cried: "The right art is purposeless, aimless! The more obstinately you try to learn how to shoot the arrow for the sake of hitting the goal, the less you will succeed in the one and the further the other will recede. What stands in your way is that you have a much too willful will. You think that what you do not do yourself does not happen."

"But you yourself have told me often enough that archery is not a pastime, not a purposeless game, but a matter of life and death!"

"I stand by that. We master archers say: one shot—one life! What this means, you cannot yet understand. But perhaps another image will help you, which expresses the same experience. We master archers say: with the upper end of the bow the archer pierces the sky; on the lower end, as though attached by a thread, hangs the earth. If the shot is loosed with a jerk there is a danger of the thread snapping. For purposeful and violent people the rift becomes final, and they are left in the awful center between heaven and earth."

"What must I do, then?" Herrigel asked thoughtfully.

"You must learn to wait properly."

"And how does one learn that?"

"By letting go of yourself, leaving yourself and everything yours behind you so decisively that nothing more is left of you but a purposeless tension."

"So I must become purposeless—on purpose?" The question escaped Herrigel's lips before he was aware of saying it.

"No pupil has ever asked me that, so I don't know the right answer."

"And when do we begin these new exercises?"

"Wait until it is time" (29–32).

PURPOSEFULNESS AND PURPOSELESSNESS

No matter what he did, Herrigel was unable to prevent his effortless concentration from flagging precisely at the moment when the shot should be loosed. Not only did he simply get tired while waiting at full draw for the release to come, he could not bear the tension.

"Stop thinking about the shot!" the Master called out. "That way it is bound to fail."

"I can't help it," Herrigel answered, "the tension gets too painful."

"You only feel it because you haven't really let go of yourself" (47).

No matter what he did, Herrigel was simply unable to wait without worrying about it until the shot "fell" of its own accord. He kept releasing the arrow on purpose, just as he had always done. In this state, three years had already passed since he had begun practicing.

During his summer vacation, Herrigel and his wife went to the seashore and Herrigel practiced day in and day out, concentrating single-mindedly on the release. Finally, he hit upon a simple and obvious solution. After drawing the bow, if he cautiously and gradually eased the pressure of the three fingers on the thumb, a moment would come when the thumb would be torn out of place as if spontaneously. By doing it in this way the shot was released like lightning. Herrigel was convinced that he was on the right track. Using this method, almost all of his shots went well, smoothly and spontaneously.

When practice resumed, Herrigel's first shot was a brilliant success in his opinion. The release was smooth and spontaneous. The Master looked at Herrigel for a while and then said hesitantly, like someone who could scarcely believe his eyes, "Once again, please!" (50). To Herrigel, his second shot seemed even better than the first. At that point, the Master stepped up to Herrigel without a word, took the bow away from him and sat down on a cushion with his back facing him. Understanding what this meant, Herrigel left.

The next day, Komachiya told Herrigel that the Master refused to teach him any further because Herrigel had tried to deceive him. Through Komachiya's intercession, the Master finally agreed to reconsider, but made continued training conditional on Herrigel's promise to never again go against the spirit of the "Great Doctrine."

Herrigel's training had already entered its fourth year. One day, Herrigel asked the Master: "How can the shot be loosed if 'I' do not do it?"

"'It' shoots," the Master replied.

"I have heard you say that several times before, so let me put it another way: How can I wait self-obliviously for the shot if 'I' am no longer there?"

"'It' waits at the highest tension."

"And who or what is this 'It'?"

"Once you have understood that, you will have no further need of me. And if I tried to give you a clue at the cost of your own experience, I would be the worst of teachers and would deserve to be sacked! So let's stop talking about it and go on practicing" (51–52)

Several weeks passed.

One day, after Herrigel released a shot, the Master bowed courteously and broke off the practice. As Herrigel stared at him bewildered, the Master cried, "Just then 'It' shot!" When Herrigel finally understood what the Master meant, he could not suppress the joy which suddenly came welling up inside him.

"What I have said," the Master told Herrigel severely, "was not praise, only a statement that ought not to touch you. Nor was my bow meant for you, for you are entirely innocent of this shot. You remained this time absolutely self-oblivious and without purpose in the highest tension, so that the shot fell from you like a ripe fruit. Now go on practicing as if nothing had happened" (52–53).

After considerable time had passed, Herrigel finally was able to perform a correct shot occasionally. The Master recognized these shots by a silent, polite bow.

THE TARGET IN THE DARK

Herrigel's archery training now entered a new phase. Up to that point, he had been shooting at a *makiwara* on a wooden stand, which served as both a target and a means to stop the arrow. In contrast to that, the actual target was placed on a sandbank fifty feet away.[5]

The slender bamboo arrows flew off in the right direction, but failed to hit even the sandbank, much less the target, and buried themselves in the ground just in front of it.

"Your arrows do not carry," observed the Master, "because they do not reach far enough spiritually" (54).

Herrigel supposed that there must be a relationship between the arrow tip and the target and therefore an approved method of sighting which made hitting the target possible.

"Of course there is," answered the Master, "and you can easily find the required aim yourself. But if you hit the target with nearly every shot you are nothing more than a trick archer who likes to show off. For the professional who counts his hits, the target is only a miserable piece of paper which he shoots to bits. The 'Great Doctrine' holds this to be sheer devilry" (55).

Herrigel obediently kept practicing and shooting without aiming. In the beginning, he remained completely unmoved no matter where his arrows flew. Even his occasional hits did not affect him since he knew that they were only flukes. However, as he continued practicing, he got to the point where he could no longer stand this kind of haphazard shooting.

"You worry yourself unnecessarily," the Master comforted him. "Put the thought of hitting right out of your mind!" (56).

Herrigel asked: "Is it not at least conceivable that after all your years of practice you involuntarily raise the bow and arrow with the certainty of a sleepwalker, so that, although you do not consciously take aim when drawing it, you must hit the target—simply cannot fail to hit it?" Then he blurted out, "Then you ought to be able to hit it blindfolded."

"Come to see me this evening," the Master said (57–58).

The training hall was brightly lit. The master instructed Herrigel to place a long thin stick of incense in the ground front of the target but to not turn on the light in the target stand. The Master's first arrow flew from brilliant light into pitch blackness. Herrigel could tell from the explosive sound that it was a hit. The second arrow also hit the target.

---

5. This is an error on Herrigel's part; the actual distance is twenty-eight meters, or, almost 92 feet.

When Herrigel switched on the light in the target stand, he was dumb-founded to see that the first arrow was in the center of the black and that the second arrow had splintered the nock of the first arrow, plowed through the shaft, and was embedded in the black right next to it. Not daring to remove the arrows separately, he took the arrows and the target back to the Master.

The Master surveyed the arrows critically and then said, "The first shot was no great feat, you will think, because after all these years I am so famil-iar with my target-stand that I must know even in pitch darkness where the target is. That may be, and I won't try to pretend otherwise. But the second arrow which hit the first—what do you make of that? I at any rate know that it is not 'I' who must be given credit for this shot. 'It' shot and 'It' made the hit. Let us bow to the goal as before the Buddha!" (59).

The Master's two shots had also pierced Herrigel.

One day, at the moment that one of Herrigel's shots "fell" of its own ac-cord, the Master cried "It is there! Bow down to the goal!" After bowing, Herrigel looked at the target and saw that the arrow had only grazed the target frame. "That was a right shot," said the Master decisively, "and so it must begin. But enough for today, otherwise you will take special pains with the next shot and spoil the good beginning" (60).

Another day, after a particularly good shot, the Master asked Herrigel, "Do you now understand what I mean by '*It* shoots,' '*It* hits'?" (61).

Herrigel replied, "I'm afraid I don't understand anything more at all. Even the simplest things have got in a muddle. Is it 'I' who draws the bow, or is it the bow that draws me into the state of highest tension? Do 'I' hit the goal, or does the goal hit me? Is "It" spiritual when seen by the eyes of the body, and corporeal when seen by the eyes of the spirit—or both or neither? Bow, arrow, goal and ego, all melt into one another, so that I can no longer separate them. And even the need to separate has gone. For as soon as I take the bow and shoot, everything becomes so clear and straightforward and so ridiculously simple."

"Now at least," the Master broke in, "the bowstring has cut right through you" (61).

In this way, Herrigel was awarded a fifth degree ranking,[6] and he re-turned to Germany.

---

6. The ranking is presumed to be that of Awa's original system.

THE RIDDLE OF "IT"

The above is a general outline of what Herrigel's archery training was like. As I said before, I have abbreviated it considerably, so for a more complete picture, please read Herrigel's book in its entirety.

Herrigel's book gives an account of the process of *kyūjutsu* training unknown even to Japanese. One cannot help but think in admiration, "is this really what Japanese *kyūjutsu* is like?" Yet one is also chagrined to think that a German who spent only six years in Japan could be more knowledgeable about an aspect of Japanese culture than the Japanese themselves.

However, there are parts of this account that at first glance are somewhat bewildering. For example, this teacher explained that the arrows did not reach the target because they were not "spiritual" enough. This is ridiculous. An arrow is not propelled by spiritual power. The reason the arrows did not reach the target is not because they were not shot spiritually enough, it is because the angle of elevation was insufficient compared the arrow's initial velocity.

As befits a bestseller that caused a sensation in intellectual circles, I have heard that even today there are many people who start practicing *kyūdō* after reading *Zen in the Art of Archery*, especially in Germany. A *kyūdō* teacher in Germany told me that he tells people who start practicing *kyūdō* after reading Herrigel to forget everything that they have read in *Zen in the Art of Archery*. While it may be an excellent thesis on Japanese culture, it can be an obstacle when teaching *kyūdō* to beginners, apparently.

In considering *Zen in the Art of Archery*, particular attention must be paid to the concept of "It," which lies at the heart of the story. This is the teaching that says that the archer does not shoot the bow but that "It" does the shooting; the idea that an entity beyond human understanding called "It" acts upon the archer and brings forth a good shot.

In the original German, "It" is expressed by the term "Es." "Es" is a familiar word in psychoanalysis and refers to the unconscious. Psychoanalysis teaches that a person's spiritual growth comes from establishing the Self (the Ego) on the foundation of "It" (the Id). To put it another way, when a person experiences a crisis of the Ego, the power of the Id becomes too dominant. Psychoanalysts treat this by analyzing the unconscious and bringing the Id to the person's consciousness so that the person can integrate it into the Ego. The "It" that Herrigel wrote about fits quite neatly into this Freudian way of thinking.

However, for historians of Japanese *kyūjutsu*, there is a big problem here: in the six hundred years that have passed since the founding of organized school of *kyūjyutsu*, evidence of the teaching of "'It' shoots" is nowhere to be found. And as far as I have been able to determine, there is no record even that Awa Kenzō, Herrigel's own teacher, taught "'It' shoots" to any of his disciples other than Herrigel.

I find it strange that even though "'It' shoots" is a teaching that cannot be found anywhere except in *Zen in the Art of Archery*, it has spread all over the world as if it were a central teaching in Japanese *kyūjutsu*. Up to the present, the Japanese intelligentsia and those involved with *kyūdō* have not made an issue of this. To me, this suggests that I am watching someone gazing into a magic mirror.

For readers who are not familiar with *kyūdō*, this may seem to be of no significance. However, paying close and scrupulous attention to little doubts like this is what allows us to see the various forms in which Japanese culture is understood in foreign countries and how it is reimported back into Japan.

3   Dissecting the Myth

THE SPREAD OF *ZEN IN THE ART OF ARCHERY*

What kind of associations are conjured up by the word *kyūdō*? Reading Herrigel's book, a person will instantly think of words like silence, ceremonial etiquette, spiritual training, and Zen. Many people also say *"kyūdō leads to spiritual focus"* or *"kyūdō resembles Zen."* However, looking back over the history of *kyūdō*, one can say that it was only after the end of World War II that *kyūdō* became strongly associated with Zen. To be even more specific, this is a unique phenomenon that occurred after 1956 when *Zen in the Art of Archery* was translated and published in Japanese.

What was *kyūdō* like prior to that time? From the Meiji period (1868–1912), after the era of the samurai had ended, most people practiced *kyūdō* for physical training or as a pastime. During this time, an archer named Ōhira Zenzō (1874–1952) established an organization called the Dai Nippon Shagakuin (the Great Japan Institute for Awakened Archery), took the name Shabutsu (the Shooting Buddha), and preached the doctrine of *shazen kenshō* (seeing true nature through the Zen of shooting).[1] During

1. Ōhira and Awa were "brother" disciples under Honda Toshizane. Ōhira's Dai Nippon Shagakuin and Awa's Daishadōkyō were established at almost the same time. It is natural to think that they were mutually influenced by each other.

the Zen boom from the Taishō period (1912–1926) through the beginning of the Shōwa period (1926–1988) there was a movement to explain archery using Zen terminology. Herrigel's experience is inseparably linked to the atmosphere of this era.

With the exception of those written by Ōhira, prewar *kyūjutsu* texts which note a deep relationship between Zen and archery are rare. Even today it is very unusual for a person in Japan to practice *kyūdō* as a form of Zen training. This suggests that the emphasis on the relationship between the bow and Zen is due to the influence of *Zen in the Art of Archery*.

The Kyūdō Chair at the University of Tsukuba conducted a survey in 1983, asking 131 West German *kyūdō* practitioners what motivated them to begin their study of *kyūdō* (table 1). A full 84 percent responded "for spiritual training," a further 61 percent cited their interest in Zen, and 49 percent said they began *kyūdō* because they had read *Zen in the Art of Archery*. No similar polls have been conducted in Japan, but I believe that most Japanese practice *kyūdō* for physical training or for pleasure and that Zen has little to do with it. I am sure that Herrigel's book accounts for the divergence of motivation between Japanese and German *kyūdō* practitioners.

This may seem surprising, but while Awa was famous, he was also an exceedingly eccentric instructor. What I mean by this is that he was not in step with *kyūjutsu* as it had been practiced up to that point in time. The core of Awa's teaching was radically different in nature from the teachings of the traditional schools of *kyūjutsu*.

Awa's eccentricity was fairly common knowledge among *kyūdō* professionals. Most commentators who are ignorant of *kyūdō*, however, accept what Herrigel presented as being an accurate description of *kyūdō*. Of course, if Herrigel's account is considered not as a treatise on *kyūdō* but as a discussion of Japanese culture or as just a report of his experiences, it is of great interest. However, when one compares real *kyūdō* and the *kyūdō* that Herrigel described, one cannot help but wonder about the discrepancy between them. Is it because Awa was on a supremely high level and the *kyūdō* that most people practiced was inferior? I do not think it is that simple. In any case, it is dangerous to unquestioningly accept Herrigel's account at face value.

It should be possible to understand the reason for the gap between real *kyūdō* and what Herrigel described by carefully rereading Herrigel's books and related documents and reconstructing his experiences. By doing this, we should also be able to clarify how the myth of *Zen in the Art of Archery* came to be born.

Table 1. The reasons 131 West German *kyūdō* practitioners began *kyūdō*.

For spiritual training	84.0%
Interest in Japanese culture	66.4%
Interest in Zen	61.1%
To acquire a beautiful posture	54.2%
Read Herrigel's *Zen in the Art of Archery*	48.9%

Note: Multiple answers OK, conducted by *Kyūdō* Chair at the University of Tsukuba, 1983.

THE MOMENT THE MYTH WAS BORN

Both "Die Ritterliche Kunst des Bogenschiessens" (The chivalrous art of archery) and *Zen in the Art of Archery* relate two mystical and inspiring things. The first of these is the teaching of "'It' shoots" and the second is the "Target in the Dark" episode. These two things are what elevate Herrigel's story to the level of myth and, at the same time, make it a wellspring that pumps out a mystical image of Japan. To begin with I would like to reexamine these two issues.

Let us look at the first issue—the teaching of "'It' shoots." Before investigating this issue, however, I would first like to clarify the language barrier that existed between Herrigel and Awa. The conversations between Awa and Herrigel took place through the mediation provided by Komachiya Sōzō in his role of interpreter.

Awa used many cryptic words when talking to Herrigel. Regarding how difficult it was to interpret Awa's words, Komachiya offers the following reminiscence:

> At every lesson Awa would explain that *kyūdō* is not a matter of technique but is a means of religious training and a method of attaining awakening. Indeed, like an improvisational poet, he would freely employ Zen-like adages at every turn. When he grew impatient, in an effort to get Herrigel to understand what he was saying he would immediately draw various diagrams on the chalkboard that was hanging on the wall of the practice hall. One day, for instance, he drew a figure of a person standing on top of a circle in the act of drawing a bow and drew a line connecting the lower abdomen of the figure to the center of the circle. He explained that this figure, which represented

Herrigel, must put his strength into the lower abdomen, enter the realm of no-self, and become one with the universe.[2]

Sakurai Yasunosuke, who was a disciple of Awa, says that "At first I struggled to understand due to the abstruse nature of Awa's instructions. I was able to grasp an outline of Awa's teachings and persevere at practice only because I relied on senior students to interpret his meaning for me." He also criticizes Awa's writings by saying that "their logic is not rigorous, and long sentences, in particular, exhibit a lack of coherence."[3]

It is hard to imagine the difficulty of interpreting Awa's unintelligible lectures. Even leaving that aside, however, there is one instance where it appears that Komachiya's interpreting was less than exact. Herrigel wrote the following in "Die Ritterliche Kunst des Bogenschiessens":

Thus, the foundation that actually supports archery is so infinitely deep that it could be called bottomless. To use an expression that is well understood among Japanese masters, when shooting a bow everything depends on the archer becoming an "unmoved center."[4]

This is what Herrigel says, but my guess is that there are a lot of archery teachers who would not clearly understand what is meant by an "unmoved center." Shibata Jisaburō, who translated "Die Ritterliche Kunst des Bogenschiessens," says that an "unmoved center" probably refers to the kyūdō term kai.[5] Even a kyūjutsu teacher who does not clearly understand the concept of an "unmoved center" would probably instantly understand if it was explained to him in those terms. Kai refers to the condition where the archer, having drawn the bow to its fullest, tries to bring the opportunity for the release to fruition by continuing to stretch even further to the left and right. The term kai (meeting) originally comes from the Buddhist saying eshajōri (those who meet are destined to part). The term an "un-

2. Komachiya Sōzō, "Herigeru-kun to yumi" (1940; repr. in Eugen Herrigel, Nihon no kyūjutsu [Tokyo: Iwanami Bunko, 1982]), 86–87. Citations are to the 1982 edition.

3. Sakurai Yasunosuke, Awa Kenzō: Ōi naru sha no michi no oshie (Sendai: Awa Kenzō Sensei Seitan Hyakunensai Jikkō Iinkai, 1981), 6–7.

4. Eugen Herrigel, "Die Ritterliche Kunst des Bogenschiessens" [The chivalrous art of archery], Nippon, Zeitschrift für Japanologie 2:4 (1936): 194.

5. Shibata Jisaburō, "Kyūhan e no yakusha kōki kara" (1941; repr. in Herrigel, Nihon no kyūjutsu [1982]), 102. Citations are to the 1982 edition.

moved center" probably suggested itself to Komachiya as a translation for *kai* because of the nature of the activity taking place during *kai*.

Komachiya explicitly acknowledged that his interpreting frequently distorted the meaning of Awa's abstruse language:

> For that matter, in those days, there were many occasions when Awa would say something that seemed to contradict what he had taught previously. At such times, I did not interpret for Herrigel but remained silent. When I did that, Herrigel would think it strange. He would insistently ask me about what Awa had just said, which left me feeling completely flummoxed. Even though I felt bad for doing so, I would say, "Oh, Awa is just extremely intent on his explanation and he is repeating what he always says about putting an entire lifetime of exertion into each shot (*issha zetsumei*) and that all shots are holy (*hyappatsu seisha*)," and put a brave front on the situation. In effect, as Awa expounded on the spirit of archery he would become spontaneously excited, and, wanting desperately to express his feelings he would use various Zen terms. Even today I think that both Awa and Herrigel knowingly let me get away with my translation strategy of "sitting on and smothering" [difficult sentences].[6]

This is an astonishingly straightforward confession. These words were written as the afterword to *Nihon no kyūjutsu* (Japanese archery). Komachiya is confessing that, acting partially as a knowing accomplice, he deliberately covered up Awa's contradictory words and attempted to convey what he understood to be Awa's meaning instead. I am amazed that the editors at Iwanami Shoten allowed these words to appear in the book at all, seeing as how they seem to invalidate Herrigel's reverential text.

This is a significant issue that bears on the credibility of what Herrigel experienced. Komachiya probably read "Die Ritterliche Kunst des Bogenschiessens" and, realizing that his free translation had taken on a life of its own, felt he had no choice but to explain what had really happened. To be sure, it is unjust to criticize Komachiya. Just imagine, for a moment, how difficult it must have been to interpret cryptic Awa-esque sentences like the following:

> If the target and I become one, this means that the Buddha and I become one. Then, if the Buddha and I become one, this means that the arrow is in

6. Komachiya, "Herigeru-kun to yumi," 87–88.

the unmoved center of both existence and non-existence, and thus in the center of the target. The arrow is in the center. If we interpret this with our awakened consciousness, then we see that the arrow issues from the center and enters the center. For this reason, you must not aim at the target but aim at yourself. If you do this, you will hit yourself, the Buddha, and the target all at once.[7]

This passage has undergone a double translation from Japanese to English through German, compounding the problem: we simply have no idea what Awa actually said.

Komachiya's freestyle translation was not the result of any malicious intent. Komachiya later became a professor of maritime and international law at Tohoku University and was active in an international capacity, so I think it is more proper to regard Komachiya as a man who had a diplomatic sensibility and consideration even from a young age.

This should suffice as an introduction. We can now analyze the main issue of "'It' shoots." There are two big problems with the teaching of "'It' shoots." The first problem, as I mentioned previously, is that there is no record of Awa ever having taught "'It' shoots" to any of his disciples other than Herrigel. The second problem is that the phrase "'It' shoots" is only mentioned in the briefest way in "Die Ritterliche Kunst des Bogenschiessens," which can be considered the first draft of *Zen in the Art of Archery*.

There is a voluminous work on Awa's life called *Awa Kenzō: Ōi naru sha no michi no oshie*,[8] written by Sakurai Yasunosuke and published in commemoration of the one hundredth anniversary of Awa's birth. Due to the circumstances of its publication one cannot say that it is free of bias, but as a study of Awa, it has no equal.

A thorough reading of Sakurai's research on Awa reveals that the teaching of "'It' shoots" appears only in the section concerning Herrigel. Even books and memoirs written by Awa's disciples contain no record that he taught "'It' shoots" to any of them. These facts back up my first contention.

The second issue is illustrated by the fact that while "It" appears in the "Target in the Dark" episode in *Zen in the Art of Archery*, it does not appear in the same episode as related in "Die Ritterliche Kunst des Bogenschiessens." In this version of the "Target in the Dark," when Awa struck the nock of the first arrow with his second arrow, he says the following:

7. Herrigel, "Die Ritterliche Kunst des Bogenschiessens," 204.
8. Sakurai, *Awa Kenzō*.

But what do you make of the second shot? Since it did not come from "me," it was not "me" who made the hit. Here, you must carefully consider: Is it possible even to aim in such darkness? Can you still maintain that you cannot hit the target without aiming? Well, let us stand in front of the target with the same attitude as when we bow before the Buddha![9]

In *Zen in the Art of Archery*, however, the exact same scene has been changed to the following:

But the second arrow which hit the first—what do you make of that? I at any rate know that it is not "I" who must be given credit for this shot. "It" shot and "It" made the hit. Let us bow to the goal as before the Buddha![10]

Without carefully comparing "Die Ritterliche Kunst des Bogenschiessens" and *Zen in the Art of Archery*, there is a danger of missing this point. There definitely is no mention of "It" in this section in the first essay. In the German original as well, "Es," which corresponds to "It," is not used. In *Zen in the Art of Archery*, however, Herrigel has Awa saying, "'It' shot" when referring to the second shot which struck the target in exactly the same place as the first shot.

What is the reason for this inconsistency? In response to these reservations, I propose the following two hypotheses.

Hypothesis #1:
Herrigel fabricated the doctrine of "'It' shoots" when he wrote *Zen in the Art of Archery*.

Hypothesis #2:
Miscommunication occurred between Awa and Herrigel concerning "'It' shoots."

Let us examine the first hypothesis. "Die Ritterliche Kunst des Bogenschiessens" was first delivered as a lecture, so it is possible that Herrigel did not go into any great depth or detail. It is also possible that at the time he gave the lecture in 1936, Herrigel himself had not been able to solidify his understanding of "'It' shoots."

9. Herrigel, "Die Ritterliche Kunst des Bogenschiessens," 206.
10. Eugen Herrigel, *Zen in the Art of Archery*, trans. Richard F. C. Hull (1953; New York: Vintage Books, 1999), 59. Unless otherwise indicated, citations are to the 1999 edition.

It is true that "It" does not appear in the "Target in the Dark" episode in "Die Ritterliche Kunst des Bogenschiessens." On the other hand, "It" is used in two other places in this book in connection to shooting. However, there is no explanation whatsoever as to what "It" might mean in the context in which it is used. The term "It" just suddenly appears.

In the first Japanese translation of "Die Ritterliche Kunst des Bogenschiessens," which appeared in 1936 in the magazine *Bunka*, the translator Shibata rendered these two instances of "It" as follows:

"that now is the very time to shoot 'It'"
"It was now that I really knew what is meant by '"It" shoots.'"[11]

However, in the first revised translation published by Iwanami Shoten in 1941, Shibata rewrote the same two passages as follows:

"already being time to loose the arrow"
"It was now that I truly knew what it meant to loose the arrow."[12]

Briefly, this is what happened. At first Shibata translated the German "Es" directly as "It"; but it did not make sense in Japanese. Thus, in the version published by Iwanami Shoten, he deleted the impersonal pronoun "Es" from the translation and translated it as "to loose [the arrow]."

The confusion surrounding "It" can be palpably felt from this instance. As can be seen in the version of *Nihon no kyūjutsu* in circulation today, which was published by Iwanami Bunko based on the 1941 translation, Herrigel did not touch upon "It" in "Die Ritterliche Kunst des Bogenschiessens" (so far as the Japanese-language version is concerned).

How did the translator himself feel about this revised translation? In the translator's afterword in the Iwanami Shoten version, Shibata wrote:

Subsequently, I saw that there were not a few places where my understanding was deficient, and ever since then I have earnestly hoped that I could discharge my obligations as a translator by publishing this revised version.[13]

11. Eugen Herrigel, "Kyūjutsu ni tsuite," trans. Shibata Jisaburō, *Bunka* 3:9 (1936): 1020, 1027.

12. Eugen Herrigel, *Nihon no kyūjutsu*, trans. Shibata Jisaburō (Tokyo: Iwanami Shoten, 1941), 26, 40.

13. Shibata, "Kyūhan e no yakusha kōki kara," 101.

I do not know whether or not "places where my understanding was deficient" refers to "It," but I think it is reasonable to assume that Shibata felt that the Iwanami version, where he deleted "It," was a more accurate translation than the version in *Bunka*, where he used "It."

Twelve years passed between the publication of "Die Ritterliche Kunst des Bogenschiessens" and *Zen in the Art of Archery*. Whether he revised his thinking or whether he fabricated something new, what is clear is that Herrigel took a great deal of time finalizing *Zen in the Art of Archery*.

In the preface to *Zen in the Art of Archery*, Herrigel declares, "And so I can well say that there is no word in this exposition which the Master would not have spoken, no image or comparison which he would not have used."[14] If this declaration is to be believed, the first hypothesis starts to look weak. However, as I have already stated, Komachiya stood between Awa and Herrigel in his capacity as interpreter, and he was somewhat cavalier about translating Awa's words precisely. The result is that what Herrigel wrote is probably not what Awa actually said. However, that is not Herrigel's fault.

Next, let us consider the feasibility of the second hypothesis. Concerning "'It' shoots" ("'Es' schießt") and "Just now, 'It' shot!" ("Soeben hat 'Es' geschossen"), the cultural critic Nishio Kanji (1935–) points out that "We really do not know whether Awa actually said the Japanese word 'It' or whether Herrigel merely inserted the German-language third-person pronoun for some Japanese words that were spoken to him. The German-language third-person pronoun 'Es,' which corresponds to 'It,' is an impersonal pronoun that expresses something which transcends the self."[15]

In German, the word "Es" is used in a unique way. For example, to ask "How are you feeling?" in German, one would say, "How well does it make you?" ("Wie geht es Ihnen?"); and when one wants to say, "I cannot bear it," one says in German "It confuses me" ("Es wird mir zu bunt"). To say, "excuse me," one can say "It makes me feel sorry" ("Es tut mir Leid"). Like the English "It," the German "Es" refers to a power surpassing human understanding and expresses the concept that a person's action is the result of that person being moved by that power. The Japanese language does not have these kinds of expressions, and so there is a strong possibility that Komachiya translated some words of Awa's using the impersonal pronoun "Es" as the subject.

At the first International Kyūdō Symposium held in 1994 in Hamburg,

14. Herrigel, *Zen in the Art of Archery* (1953), 12.
15. Nishio Kanji, *Kōi suru shisaku* (Tokyo: Chūō Kōronsha, 1982), 32.

Germany, Feliks Hoff (1945–), the past president of the German Kyūdō Federation, presented a paper that argued that the cause of the confusion was that the Japanese phrases "that's it" and "that was it," were translated so that "Es" was used as the subject. This paper generated a lot of discussion. The phrases "that's it" and "that was it" are very natural expressions of praise used when a student performs well. Hoff is saying that since these phrases were related to Herrigel as "'It' shoots" and "Just then 'It' shot," Herrigel understood them to mean something like "an entity called 'It,' which transcends the self, shoots."

Hoff's thesis is very convincing. I also think that the real identity of "It" must be something like this. When Herrigel made a good shot, Awa cried, "That's it!" Komachiya then mistakenly translated this as "'It' shot!"[16]

Judging from context, Awa first said "'It' shot" when Herrigel was still practicing at the straw practice target and had not yet been permitted to shoot at a regulation target. It is utterly inconceivable that Herrigel could have realized the advanced level of spirituality suggested by the term "It" when he was still very much a raw beginner. It is far more natural to conclude that Awa simply praised Herrigel by saying "That's it," meaning "That was a good shot." In *Zen in the Art of Archery*, however, Herrigel reached the following conclusion about the true identity of "It":

> and just as we say in archery that "It" takes aim and hits, so here "It" takes the place of the ego, availing itself of a facility and a dexterity which the ego only acquires by conscious effort. And here too "It" is only a name for something which can neither be understood nor laid hold of, and which only reveals itself to those who have experienced it.[17]

"That's it" was mistakenly translated to Herrigel as "'It' shoots," and Herrigel understood "It" to mean "something which transcends the self." If that is what happened, then the teaching of "'It' shoots" was born when an incorrect meaning filled the void created by a single instant of misunderstanding.

Now let us dissect the second myth of *Zen in the Art of Archery*, the "Target in the Dark" episode. At a practice hall in the dark of night, a master archer demonstrates before a solitary disciple. Facing a target that is prac-

16. According to the memory of a student of Awa, "sore desu" (That's it!) was one of his master's favorite phrases.

17. Herrigel, *Zen in the Art of Archery*, 76.

tically invisible, the master shoots an arrow and hits the mark. Then, the master's second shot strikes the nock of the arrow that is in the center of the target and splits it. Anyone would be moved by this story.

A person who has actually practiced kyūdō will understand the frequency with which this happens. In kyūdō, an arrow striking the nock of an arrow that has already been shot so that the two arrows look like they are joined together is called tsugiya (connected arrows). Cases of tsugiya are fairly rare, but they do happen occasionally.[18] Even if tsugiya does not occur, it often happens that an archer will break the nock of an arrow by hitting it with a succeeding arrow.

Some people might think "No, the 'Target in the Dark' episode occurred when it was so dark that the target was invisible, so it must be something special after all." However, if one looks closely at the "Target in the Dark" episode, Herrigel says that while the target stand was dark, "the practice hall was brightly lit."[19] If that is the case, then it may have been possible to see the target faintly by the light reflected from the practice hall, and even if Awa could not see the target, he would know right away where he had to stand by looking at the floorboards of the practice hall, with which he was intimately familiar. Moreover, a stick of burning incense indicated where the target was located.

It has been shown by experiments in sports psychology that the smaller the target is, the more the archer concentrates and the more accurate his shooting becomes. In this case, the light of the burning incense served as the target, and so Awa was in a psychological state where he was aiming at a target that was infinitesimally small. Therefore, it is conceivable that the likelihood of a "Target in the Dark"—like event occurring in such a situation would be higher than during a normal practice session. Even given that, however, the incident described in "The Target in the Dark" was certainly a rare thing.

Let us look at it from a different angle. Among archers who practice traditional schools of kyūjutsu, an archer breaking the nock of his own arrow is considered a shameful thing, since the archer thereby damages his own equipment. It would not be strange for Awa, who had mastered a traditional school of kyūjutsu, to hold the same view. This event was by no means something about which an archer would boast. Herrigel wrote, "The Master surveyed them [the two arrows] critically." Perhaps Awa was secretly thinking: "Blast! I have ruined one of my favorite arrows!" In fact,

18. Herrigel did not clearly mention that tsugiya occurred.
19. Herrigel, Zen in the Art of Archery, 58.

Awa did not speak of this episode to anyone except Anzawa Heijirō (1887–
1970), one of his senior disciples. Awa probably did not want to divulge
that he had broken the nock of his arrow because he was ashamed of it. In
any event, that is what I think.

In an interview in the magazine *Kyūdō*, Anzawa related that Awa described this incident in the following fashion:

> Master Awa told me: "On that occasion I performed a ceremonial shot.
> The first arrow hit the target, and the second arrow made a 'crack' sound as
> though it had struck something. Herrigel went to retrieve the arrows, but no
> matter how long I waited he didn't come back. I called 'Eugen! Oh, Eugen!'"
> Master Awa said, "What's wrong? Why don't you answer?"
>
> Then, well, there was Herrigel sitting up straight right in front of the tar-
> get. Master Awa went up to him like this [Anzawa imitated someone walking
> nonchalantly] and asked, "What's the matter?" Herrigel was speechless, sit-
> ting rooted to the spot. Then without pulling the arrows from the target he
> brought them back....
>
> Master Awa said, "No, that was just a coincidence! I had no special inten-
> tion of demonstrating such a thing."[20]

These are the words that Awa reportedly related to Anzawa. In short,
it was a coincidence. Awa's words are very easy to understand and do not
have even the slightest whiff of mysticism about them. However, the words
that Awa supposedly said to Herrigel have a different ambience altogether.
Let us review the passage in *Zen in the Art of Archery*:

> "The first shot," he then said, "was no great feat, you will think, because after
> all these years I am so familiar with my target-stand that I must know even
> in pitch darkness where the target is. That may be, and I won't try to pretend
> otherwise. But the second arrow which hit the first—what do you make of
> that? I at any rate know that it is not "I" who must be given credit for this shot.
> "It" shot and "It" made the hit. Let us bow to the goal as before the Buddha!"[21]

These words are radically different, enigmatic, and extremely difficult
to understand. What accounts for the discrepancy between the words that

---

20. "Zadankai: Awa Kenzō-hakase to sono deshi Oigen Herigeru-hakase no koto o
Komachiya-hakase ni kiku: Sono san," *Kyūdō* 183 (August 1965): 4–7.

21. Herrigel, *Zen in the Art of Archery*, 59.

Awa is supposed to have said to Anzawa and those he is supposed to have said to Herrigel? Here one's suspicions must rest on the interpreting, after all. During regular practice, Komachiya translated Awa's instructions for Herrigel. However, during this particular episode, Awa and Herrigel were alone. Komachiya offers the following testimony:

> Herrigel's 1936 essay describes an incident when, in pitch darkness, Awa lit a stick of incense, put it in front of the target and shot two arrows, hitting the nock of the first arrow with the second. It also recounts what Awa said at that time. Since I was not there to interpret that evening, I think that Herrigel, relying on his own ability to understand Japanese, understood all of that by means of mind-to-mind transmission, as truly amazing as that is. This essay is probably the first place where he spoke publicly about what happened on that day. He never told me about it. After I read his essay, I asked Master Awa about this incident one day. He laughed and said, "You know, sometimes really strange things happen. That was a coincidence." While I am impressed at Herrigel's restraint in not telling me of this strange incident during the time he was in Japan, it is truly admirable that Master Awa did not mention this even once until Mr. Shibata's translation was published.[22]

This should finally clarify what actually happened. Komachiya knew Herrigel's Japanese language ability. He read "Die Ritterliche Kunst des Bogenschiessens" and judged that it was "truly amazing" that Herrigel understood what Awa said during the "Target in the Dark" incident. It seems to me that Komachiya intended this to be sarcastic.

Komachiya, astonished by what Herrigel wrote, went so far as to write him a letter in which he asked: "Did you really see that? Did you just think it up, or did you write your essay to make it appear that is what master Awa actually said?" It seems that Komachiya thought that Herrigel's words must be a fabrication. Komachiya says that Herrigel answered his letter saying, "I assure you that I actually experienced it."[23]

There is no way for us to know now what sort of conversation took place between Awa and Herrigel. However, it is easy to imagine that Awa, speaking a language Herrigel did not understand, experienced tremendous difficulty in trying to explain this coincidental occurrence. The co-

---

22. Komachiya, "Herigeru-kun to yumi," 98–99.

23. "Zadankai: Awa Kenzō-hakase to sono deshi Oigen Herigeru-hakase no koto o Komachiya-hakase ni kiku: Sono san," 6.

incidence of the second arrow hitting the first produced a void that had to be filled with some kind of meaning. One can imagine Herrigel striving to find some kind of mystical significance in this coincidence. However, for this Westerner who ceaselessly searched for Zen, introducing the Buddha into his explanation only served to amplify the mystical nature of the event to no purpose.

I believe that Herrigel anguished greatly over how to interpret both "'It' shoots" and the "Target in the Dark." This is illustrated by the fact that it took twelve long years, even granting that a war intervened, from "Die Ritterliche Kunst des Bogenschiessens", which does not touch on "It" at all, to the publication of *Zen in the Art of Archery*, which has "It" as its centerpiece. In the foreword to *Zen in the Art of Archery*, Herrigel wrote:

> But, in the conviction of having made further spiritual progress during the past ten years—and this means ten years of continual practice—and of being able to say rather better than before, with greater understanding and realization, what this "mystical" art is about, I have resolved to set down my experiences in new form.[24]

It is impossible to know exactly what Herrigel means by "further spiritual progress." However, this phrase certainly contains the feeling that he was now able to understand "'It' shoots" and the "Target in the Dark" to his satisfaction so that he could discuss them with somewhat more confidence.

Thus, Herrigel not only made up the question asking "what is this 'mystical' art about," but he also provided his own answer. He then presented his creation to the world, where it eventually found its way back to Japan.

WHAT IS JAPANESE ARCHERY?

What was Japanese archery like before Awa came upon the scene? I would like to give a brief historical overview of the course it followed. Without understanding the position Awa occupied in the history of Japanese archery, a number of things cannot be clearly understood.

Bows have been used since ancient times as hunting implements. Wooden bows and countless stone arrowheads have been excavated from

24. Herrigel, *Zen in the Art of Archery* (1953), 12.

ruins dated to the Jōmon period (ca. 12,000 BC–400 BC), such as the San'nai Maruyama site in Aomori prefecture.

The Japanese bow has two distinguishing characteristics: it is a long-bow, over two meters in length, and to shoot it the archer grips it at a point below the center of the bow stave. The below-center grip is unique to the Japanese bow and is something which is not found in foreign archery.

On a bronze bell-shaped object (*dōtaku*) datable to the Yayoi period (ca. 400 BC–AD 400) that was reportedly excavated from Kagawa prefecture and which has been designated as a National Treasure, there is a scene depicting an archer aiming at a deer. It appears that the archer is gripping the bow below the center of the bow stave. In addition, the well-known Chinese chronicle *Weishu* (written before AD 297) relates that "Japanese soldiers use a wooden bow that is short below and long above."[25] From this we can see that since the Yayoi period the Japanese have used bows that have a below-center grip.

Historians believe that bows and arrows came to be used as weapons from the Yayoi period onward. They base this conclusion on the fact that Yayoi-period excavations have yielded arrowheads that are visibly larger than those from the preceding Jōmon period, as well as skeletons that show evidence of arrow wounds. As time went on, literary works began to celebrate the exploits of famous archers, such as Minamoto no Yorimasa (1104–1180), who killed a mythical beast known as a *nue*,[26] and Minamoto no Tametomo (1139–1170), who drew an exceptionally powerful bow. During the Genpei War (1180–1185), bows and arrows came into full flower as military weapons.

The organized schools of archery that have survived to the present day have their roots in the period of the Ōnin War (1467–1477). During this time there lived a legendary archer named Heki Danjō Masatsugu, who refined his skills in the battles in Kyoto and afterward purportedly toured other provinces teaching archery. There is also a theory that Heki Danjō was a fictional character. Scholars have not come to an agreement as to whether such a person actually existed.

In any case, Heki Danjō Masatsugu supposedly taught his exquisite archery techniques to Yoshida Shigekata (1463–1543) and Yoshida Shigemasa (1485–1569), who were father and son. From the time of the Yoshidas the transmission of this archery lineage can be traced through his-

---

25. *Shintei gishi wajin den hoka san pen* (Tokyo: Iwanami Bunko, 1951), 109.
26. A Japanese chimera; see the *Heike monogatari* and the *noh* drama *Nue*.

torical sources. The school they transmitted is known as the Heki-ryū (Heki school or lineage). It eventually split into various branch schools (*ha*), such as the Insai-ha, the Sekka-ha, the Dōsetsu-ha, the Sakon'emon-ha, the Ōkura-ha, and so forth. Even today a few of these schools still exist in various parts of Japan. In addition, a Shingon Buddhist priest named Chikurin'bō Josei, who officiated at a temple sponsored by the Yoshida family and who was also a skillful archer, founded a school known as the Heki-ryū Chikurin-ha. Although the name of this school starts with the appellation "Heki-ryū," the general consensus is that it has no direct connection to Heki Danjō Masatsugu.

In addition to the various branches of the Heki-ryū there also exists another celebrated archery school known as the Ogasawara-ryū. Founded at the beginning of the Kamakura period (1185–1333) by Ogasawara Nagakiyo, this school taught horsemanship, archery, and etiquette. It specialized in the ceremonial use of the bow and arrow and in equestrian archery such as *yabusame*.[27] The early Ogasawara teachings, however, were lost during the Muromachi period (1336–1573). During that time the Ogasawara family split into a number of collateral groups so that by the Edo period (1603–1868) there were at least five clans among regional lords (*daimyō*) alone using the Ogasawara surname. Tokugawa Yoshimune (1684–1751), the eighth Tokugawa shōgun, collected *kyūjutsu* texts from throughout Japan and ordered Ogasawara Heibei Tsuneharu (1666–1747), one of his middle-level retainers (*hatamoto*), to study their contents so as to revive the lost Ogasawara teachings of equestrian archery and ceremonial precedents. In this way, Ogasawara Heibei Tsuneharu became the direct founder of the Ogasawara-ryū that now exists in Tokyo.

From a technical standpoint, Japanese archery can be divided into two categories: ceremonial archery (*reisha*) and military archery (*busha*). Ceremonial archery is concerned with the ritual and thaumaturgic aspects of *kyūjutsu*, and one can safely say that this is the exclusive domain of the Ogasawara-ryū. Military archery can be further divided into three categories: foot archery (*hosha*), equestrian archery (*kisha*), and what is called hall archery (*dōsha*).

Foot archery refers to the archery used by foot soldiers on the battlefield. In foot archery, the archers must be able to accurately hit their targets with sufficient force to penetrate traditional Japanese armor at a dis-

27. Archers on horseback ride down a straight course and shoot at three stationary targets placed along the length of the course.

tance of about thirty meters, the optimum killing range, even in the heat of battle while their lives hang in the balance. Training in foot archery aims to develop an extremely accurate, subtle technique and to cultivate a death-defying spiritual fortitude. The Heki-ryū Insai-ha is one of the schools that specialize in foot archery.

Equestrian archery refers to the technique of shooting a bow from horseback. Equestrian archery dominated the battlefield only from the Heian period (794–1185) through the Kamakura period. Since this was so long ago, it is impossible to know what equestrian archery on the battlefield was actually like. In the past there was a sport called *inuōmono* (dog chasing), where archers on horseback chased dogs around a circular enclosure while shooting blunted arrows at them. Records indicate that this sport was practiced up until the beginning of the Meiji period, but today it is completely extinct. Since the line of transmission has been broken, just as with battlefield equestrian archery, it is nearly impossible to tell what *inuōmono* was like.

However, judging from texts regarding *inuōmono* and from the characteristics of modern-day *yabusame*, it appears that the technique of equestrian archery consisted of skillfully managing a horse so that the archer could approach close enough to the target to shoot from a distance where it would not be too difficult to hit it. Consequently, equestrian archery training focuses on how to ride a horse while carrying and shooting a bow. Even though they are both forms of *kyūjutsu*, it is obvious that equestrian archery has a different feeling than foot archery.

Finally there is hall archery, which concentrated exclusively on a contest called the *tōshiya*. In *tōshiya* contests the archers competed to see who could shoot the most arrows (*ya*) down the entire length (*tōsu*) of the outside veranda of Sanjūsangendō (Hall of Thirty-three Bays) of the Rengeōin temple in Kyoto, using only the space between the bottom of the overhanging eaves of the temple's roof and the veranda itself, which measures one hundred and twenty meters in length by five meters in height. It is hard for a modern person to imagine, but during the Edo period, the *tōshiya* was furiously contested and various feudal domains, staking their prestige on the outcome, sent their archers to compete. There were different classes of competition: the *ōyakazu* competition, where archers would shoot for twenty-four hours straight to see who could shoot the most arrows down the length of the veranda, and the *hyakusha-gake*, where archers would shoot one hundred arrows, the victor being the archer who successfully shot the most arrows the entire length of the veranda. The record for the *ōyakazu* was set in 1686 by an archer from the Kishū domain (present-day Wakayama prefecture) named Wasa Daihachirō, who, out of a total of 13,053 arrows shot, succeeded in shooting 8,133 the full length of the veranda.

Hall archery requires mastery of a technique that allows the archer, with minimum fatigue, to shoot light arrows with a low trajectory. Insofar as the arrows are not required to penetrate armor, the technique differs considerably from that of foot archery and equestrian archery. Moreover, hall archery entailed aspects of sport or spectacle. From a spiritual perspective, too, it differs from foot archery and equestrian archery, which were based on the experience of facing death in battle. Some domains forbade the practice of hall archery, saying it was nothing but a warrior's game. However, both the Heki-ryū Chikurin-ha and the Heki-ryū Sekka-ha participated extensively in this type of archery contest.

The length of the modern-day *kyūdō* range is twenty-eight meters from firing line to target. This distance is based on the optimum range for battlefield foot archery, so foot archery solidly survives in the form of modern *kyūdō*. Equestrian archery survives in the form of *yabusame*. Hall archery, however, declined when competition at Sanjūsangendō ceased with the end of the Tokugawa shogunate. With the loss of this traditional shooting area, the archery schools that specialized in hall archery must have been in a confused and desperate situation.

Awa studied *kyūjutsu* under two teachers, both of whom came from schools that specialized in hall archery: Kimura Tatsugorō of the Heki-ryū Sekka-ha and Honda Toshizane (1836–1917) of the Bishū (present-day Aichi prefecture) Chikurin-ha. Familiarity with the characteristics of hall archery and the situation faced by its practitioners at that time may help us to better understand Awa. Also, the fact that the founder of the Chikurin-ha, Chikurin'bō Josei, had been a Shingon priest and the teachings of the school were influenced by Buddhism must also have had an effect on Awa's way of thinking.

THE GREAT DOCTRINE OF THE WAY OF SHOOTING

Let us bring the discussion of the history of *kyūdō* closer to Herrigel. First, I will give a brief description of the life and career of Awa Kenzō, the man who taught *kyūjutsu* to Herrigel. There are no primary sources regarding Awa that are publicly available, so I have no choice but to rely on the book by Sakurai that I mentioned earlier.[28] Sakurai's narrative style is a bit melo-dramatic: he describes Awa's personality by referring to the geography and native fauna of the region around Ishinomaki Bay where Awa was born and grew up, and intimates that that Awa was born of the oceanic energy generated by the meeting of the southern-flowing Kurile (a.k.a. Okhotsk) Current and the northern-flowing Black (a.k.a. Japan) Current. Still, because Sakurai cites a wealth of sources, he provides ample material for understanding Awa.

Awa was born in 1880 in the village of Kawakitamachi in Miyagi prefecture, the eldest son of the Satō family, which operated a *kōjiya* (a factory for producing malted rice used in the manufacturing of *sake* and *miso*). Awa's formal education consisted of only primary school, but at the age of seventeen he opened a private school for teaching the Chinese classics. It is not clear, however, exactly what curriculum was taught at this school. At the age of nineteen, he married into the Awa family, which was also in the malted rice business in the city of Ishinomaki, and thereby acquired the Awa family name.

At the age of twenty, Awa began training in Heki-ryū Sekka-ha *kyūjutsu* in Ishinomaki under the tutelage of Kimura Tatsugorō, a former vassal of the Sendai domain. Awa's progress was rapid, and after only two years Kimura awarded him his diploma of complete transmission (*menkyo kaiden*), the highest rank possible. Thus, when Awa was only twenty-two he established his own *kyūjutsu* training hall near his house.

In 1909, when Awa was twenty-nine, he moved to the city of Sendai, where he opened a new *kyūjutsu* training hall and began studying Heki-ryū Chikurin-ha *kyūjutsu* under Honda Toshizane, who was the *kyūjutsu* master at Tokyo Imperial University. At about the same time, Awa became the *kyūjutsu* master at the Number Two College in Sendai. It appears that at this juncture, Awa was an expert archer, capable of hitting the mark nearly one hundred times for every one hundred shots (*hyappatsu hyakuchū*). His instruction to students also emphasized accuracy in shooting. Sometime around the beginning of the Taishō period, however, Awa began having doubts about *kyūjutsu*. He began to call it "a kind of hereditary disease that prizes technical training" and began to preach the doctrine of *shadō* (the Way of Shooting), which he characterized as being "austere training in which one masters the study of humanity." As a result, the *kyūjutsu* community treated him like a lunatic, and on occasion people even threw

28. Sakurai, *Awa Kenzō*.

rocks at him when he went to places where traditional *kyūjutsu* was firmly entrenched. Honda Toshitoki (1901–1945), the grandson of Honda Toshizane and later the headmaster of the Honda-ryū, harshly criticized Awa's shooting style, saying that Awa shot merely as his whims and moods moved him. Ōhira Zenzō, who was a fellow disciple of Awa's under Honda Toshizane, was equally scathing. In reference to the doctrine of "putting a lifetime of exertion into each shot" (*issha zetsumei*; sometimes translated as "one shot, one life") that Awa later expounded, Ōhira said that it was "idiotic to tell people just to persevere until they dropped dead."[29] From this we can see that the members of the Honda-ryū were merciless in their criticism of Awa.

It appears that Kanō Jigorō's (1860–1938) success with his Kōdōkan *jūdō* was behind Awa's advocacy that people convert "from *kyūjutsu* to *shadō*." Kanō had synthesized a new school of *jūjutsu* from elements of various traditional *jūjutsu* schools and named his new art *jūdō* (the Way of Flexibility). According to Sakurai, in one of the manuscripts he left behind Awa wrote: "To give the closest example, the reason why Kanō Jigorō's Kōdōkan school of *jūdō* is praised not only in Japan but in foreign countries as well is because, first of all, it is taught as a Way [*dō*], and, rather than restricting its techniques to just one lineage or style alone, it blends the strong points of all schools."[30] In short, Kanō's successful conversion of *jūjutsu* into *jūdō* prompted Awa to come up with the idea of transforming *kyūjutsu* into *shadō*.

In 1920, when Awa was forty years old, he had an experience that proved to be decisive. To borrow Sakurai's words, Awa experienced a "great explosion." Using some short compositions and drawings left by Awa as clues, Sakurai describes this experience as follows:

> Late one evening, the family was fast asleep, all was wrapped in silence, and all that could be seen was the moon peacefully illuminating the evening darkness. Alone, Kenzō went to the shooting hall and with his beloved bow and arrows quietly faced the target.
>
> He was determined.
>
> Would his flesh perish first? Would his spirit live on?
>
> No release. Total focus.

29. Ibid., 162.
30. Ibid., 145.

He was determined that with this shot there would be no retreat, not even so much as a single step.

The bitter struggle continued. His body had already passed its limit. His life would end here.

Finally: "I have perished."

Just as this thought passed through his mind, a marvelous sound reverberated from the heavens.

He thought it must be from heaven since never before had he heard such a clear, high, strong sound from the twanging of the bowstring and from the arrow piercing the target. At the very instant that he thought he heard it, his self flew apart into infinite grains of dust, and, with his eyes dazzled by a myriad of colors, a great thunderous wave filled heaven and earth.[31]

This is just what Sakurai imagined to have happened, so there is no proof that Awa actually experienced this. However, judging from the changes in Awa's words and actions beginning in 1920, and from the writings he left behind, it appears that there was some change in his state of mind.

If Awa actually experienced this kind of "great explosion," then this mystical experience may well have formed the foundation of his thought. This type of experience very often becomes the starting point for the founding of religions. For example, the story of the morning star flying into the mouth of Kūkai (774–835), the founder of Shingon Buddhism, during his religious austerities in Muroto-misaki in Kochi prefecture, resembles Awa's experience.[32]

After his "great explosion," Awa began to vigorously preach that one "must put an entire lifetime of exertion into each shot" (*issha zestumei*) and that "one can see true nature in the shot" (*shari kenshō*). Sakurai explains the essence of these teachings as follows:

Even though we are speaking of the power of nature, one must train one's mental energy and generate spiritual energy (in order to unite with this power). In this way, one enters the Absolute Way that eliminates all relativity. Space is destroyed as one passes through it. Then for the first time one becomes wrapped in the radiance of the Buddha and can perceive the self

31. Ibid., 159–60.

32. According to legend, when Kūkai was meditating in a cave at Muroto-misaki, the morning star came into his mouth and he was enlightened.

which reflects the radiance of the Buddha. At this moment the self is both the self yet not the self.[33]

In 1927, when Awa was forty-seven, he overruled the bitter objections of his students at the Number Two College and founded an organization called Daishadōkyō (Great Doctrine of the Way of Shooting). His students at the Number Two College subsequent to that time testified that Daishadōkyō consisted of "archery as a religion," that "the founder of this religion is Master Awa Kenzō," and that "the Master described his teaching trips to various regions not as just practice or as teaching, but as missionary work."[34] Thus, it is clear that Awa's Daishadōkyō possessed religious characteristics.

The phrase the "Great Doctrine" of kyūdō appears in *Zen in the Art of Archery*. In the Japanese-language version, this is translated as ōgi, a word that means the "secret principles" or "inner mysteries" of an art. To give one example, in the Japanese version, ōgi is used like this: "The ōgi holds this to be sheer devilry"[35] (in the English version, "Great Doctrine" is used instead of ōgi). However, the term "Great Doctrine" does not mean the ōgi of kyūdō but rather refers to Awa's Daishadōkyō. Herrigel offered no explanation of what the "Great Doctrine" might be, so it is impossible for readers of *Zen in the Art of Archery* to know that this was simply Awa's personal philosophy.

The year after Awa established Daishadōkyō he fell ill. Although at one point he appeared to recover, from that time on he remained in a partially incapacitated condition until his death of an illness in 1939, at the age of fifty-nine. Today there are many practitioners of kyūdō who are grand-disciples or great grand-disciples of Awa and who practice kyūdō in the style of Awa's Daishadōkyō. Nonetheless, as a religious organization, Daishadōkyō died with Awa.

WHAT HERRIGEL STUDIED

The kenshō (to see true nature, that is, attain awakening) of shari kenshō, one of the doctrines that Awa preached, is a Zen term, but there is not that

33. Sakurai, *Awa Kenzō*, 164.
34. Ibid., 210–11.
35. Herrigel, *Zen in the Art of Archery*, 55.

much of a Zen feeling in Awa's teaching itself. Surprisingly, it appears that Awa himself never spent any time at a Zen temple or received proper instruction from a Zen master. Sakurai, who has conscientiously researched Awa's life, wrote that "no evidence can be found that Kenzō ever trained with a Zen priest"[36] and that "while Kenzō used the phrase 'the bow and Zen are one' and used the philosophical language of Mahayana Buddhism in particular to describe *shadō*, he did not approve of Zen unconditionally."[37] If that is the case, then a straightforward question presents itself: why did Herrigel connect Awa's teaching with Zen?

Herrigel wrote that from his student days he had "as though driven by some secret urge, been preoccupied with mysticism."[38] The mysticism to which Herrigel referred was that of the German mystic Meister Eckhart (ca. 1260–1327). As a result of his interest in mysticism, Herrigel became interested in Zen, which he regarded as the most mystical of religions, and through Zen he developed an interest in Japanese culture. In *Zen in the Art of Archery*, Herrigel explained how his interest in Zen was behind his decision to go to Japan:

> For some considerable time it has been no secret, even to us Europeans, that the Japanese arts go back for their inner form to a common root, namely Buddhism.... I do not mean Buddhism in the ordinary sense, nor am I concerned here with the decidedly speculative form of Buddhism, which, because of its allegedly accessible literature, is the only one we know in Europe and even claim to understand. I mean Dhyana Buddhism, which is known in Japan as "Zen."[39]

No matter how one looks at it, the statement that "all Japanese arts can be traced back to Zen" is an exaggeration. For example, *ukiyoe* (Japanese woodblock prints) is a famous example of a Japanese art tradition, but it cannot be connected to Zen. *Kabuki* and *buyō* (forms of Japanese drama and dance), with their flamboyant styles, are a far cry from Zen. When Herrigel says that Zen is the root of all Japanese arts, he is simply parroting the ideas of Daisetsu T. Suzuki (1870–1966). In *Zen in the Art of Archery*, Herrigel says:

36. Sakurai, *Awa Kenzō*, 223.
37. Ibid., 266.
38. Herrigel, *Zen in the Art of Archery*, 13.
39. Ibid., 6.

In his *Essays in Zen-Buddhism*, D.T. Suzuki has succeeded in showing that Japanese culture and Zen are intimately connected and that Japanese art, the spiritual attitude of the Samurai, the Japanese way of life, the moral, aesthetic, and to a certain extent even the intellectual life of the Japanese owe their peculiarities to this background of Zen and cannot be properly understood by anybody not acquainted with it.[40]

We can divine from the above passages that Herrigel, influenced by D. T. Suzuki and driven by his own preoccupation with mysticism, tried as hard as he could to detect Zen elements within Japanese culture. Regarding his purpose in visiting Japan, Herrigel wrote:

Why I set out to learn the art of archery and not something else requires some explanation. Already from the time I was a student, I had assiduously researched mystical doctrine, that of Germany in particular. However, in doing so I realized that I lacked something that would allow me to fully understand it. This was something of an ultimate nature, which seemed as though it would never come to appear to me, something which I felt I would never be able to resolve. I felt as though I was standing before the final gate and yet had no key with which to open it. Thus, when I was asked whether I wanted to work for several years at Tōhoku Imperial University I accepted with joy the opportunity to know Japan and its admirable people. By doing so I had the hope and welcomed the idea of making contact with "living" Buddhism, and that thereby I might come to understand in somewhat more detail the essence of so-called "detachment," which Meister Eckhart had so praised but yet had not shown the way to reach.[41]

I imagine that most Japanese, reading this, would feel quite pleased. To think that Japanese culture possesses such wonderful aspects must conjure up feelings of happiness and pride. However, while Herrigel did not undergo any actual Zen training during his stay in Japan, he wrote a lot about Zen, and his writings were collected and published posthumously in 1958 under the title *Der Zen-Weg* (*The Method of Zen*).[42] From these essays it is clear that Herrigel read extensively about Zen.

40. Ibid., 7.
41. Herrigel, "Die Ritterliche Kunst des Bogenschiessens," 197–98.
42. Eugen Herrigel, *Der Zen-Weg*, comp. Hermann Tausend (Munich: Otto Wilhelm Barth-Verlag, 1958).

In *The Method of Zen*, Herrigel relates an episode that led him to passionately seek out Zen after he arrived in Japan. Early during his stay in Japan, when he was meeting with a Japanese colleague at a hotel, an earthquake occurred and many guests stampeded to the stairs and elevators:

> An earthquake—and a terrible earthquake a few years before was still fresh in everyone's memory. I too had jumped up in order to get out in the open. I wanted to tell the colleague with whom I had been talking to hurry up, when I noticed to my astonishment that he was sitting there unmoved, hands folded, eyes nearly closed, as though none of it concerned him. Not like someone who hangs back irresolutely, or who has not made up his mind, but like someone who, without fuss, was doing something—or not-doing something—perfectly naturally . . . .
>
> A few days later I learned that this colleague was a Zen Buddhist and I gathered that he must have put himself into a state of extreme concentration and thus become "unassailable."
>
> Although I had read about Zen before, and had heard a few things about it, I had only the vaguest idea of the subject. The hope of penetrating into Zen—which had made my decision to go to Japan very much easier—changed, as a result of this dramatic experience, into the decision to start without further delay.[43]

The "terrible earthquake a few years before" probably refers to the Great Kantō Earthquake in 1923. Amid the panic of everyone around him, a single Zen practitioner sits unperturbed. This, indeed, was how the "admirable people" of Japan whom Herrigel was seeking were supposed to act. "Yes," Herrigel must have assured himself, "Zen practitioners who have mastered Zen and achieved the Immovable Mind must be everywhere here!" At the same time, Herrigel was completely oblivious to the fact that the vast majority of the Japanese people at the hotel were thrown into a panic by the earthquake. For Herrigel, the Japanese had to be special.

After this experience, Herrigel relayed his request to become Awa's disciple through his colleague at Tōhoku Imperial University, Komachiya Sōzō. In 1924, Herrigel and Komachiya were both invited to teach in the Department of Law and Letters that had been established at Tōhoku Imperial University the previous year and they took up their posts at the same time.

43. Herrigel, *Der Zen-Weg*, 126–27.

Komachiya, who was fluent in German, must have been a good friend for Herrigel.

As a favor to Herrigel, Komachiya made the arrangements for him to become Awa's disciple. Looking back on the situation at that time, Komachiya wrote:

> I think it was in the spring of 1926. Herrigel came to me and said, "I want to study the bow. Please introduce me to master Awa." The bow is difficult to approach, even for Japanese. I wondered what caused him to want to try his hand at it. When I asked him the reason he replied: "It has been three years since I came to Japan. I have finally realized that there are many things in Japanese culture that must be studied. In particular, it appears to me that Buddhism, especially Zen, has exerted a very strong influence on Japanese thought. I think that the most expedient way for me to get to know Zen is to study *kyūdō*."[44]

Awa was reluctant to accept a foreigner as a student, but Komachiya subsequently prevailed upon him and Awa agreed to teach Herrigel on the condition that Komachiya accept the responsibility of interpreting. Thus, Herrigel began taking lessons from Awa once a week.

Here again, a question arises. When exactly did Herrigel become Awa's disciple? The true duration of Herrigel's actual *kyūjutsu* training hinges on the answer to this question. This should be a very fundamental issue of fact, but when the various accounts are compared, there are discrepancies.

In his own writings Herrigel states that he became Awa's student immediately after arriving in Japan and spent nearly six full years training in *kyūjutsu* until he returned to Germany. He writes as though he was Awa's student throughout the whole six years he was in Japan, saying things like "To be more precise, I shall try to summarize the six-year course of instruction I received from one of the greatest Masters of this art during my stay in Japan"[45] and "More than five years went by, and then the Master proposed that we pass a test."[46] However, the figure of six years is sus-

44. Komachiya, "Herigeru-kun to yumi," 69–70. The person who suggested to Herrigel that he study *kyūdō* is assumed to be Takeda Bokuyō (Tsunejirō), the *ikebana* teacher of Herrigel's wife who was associated with Awa.

45. Herrigel, *Zen in the Art of Archery*, 11.

46. Ibid., 63.

picious. First of all, Herrigel lived in Japan from May 1924 until August 1929, so the length of his stay in Japan was five years and three months. Therefore, there is no possibility that he studied *kyūjutsu* "for almost six years" as he states.

In Komachiya's reminiscence quoted above, he says, "I think it was spring of 1926" when Herrigel asked to be introduced to Awa. The spring of 1926 was nearly two full years after Herrigel had arrived in Japan. Not only that, Komachiya relates that Herrigel told him that "It has been three years since I came to Japan." "Three years since I came to Japan" probably means "the third year since I came to Japan." No matter how vague Komachiya's recollection might be, he would certainly not make a mistake about whether he introduced his workplace colleague to his mentor just after he met him or after a few years had passed.

There is another inconsistency regarding the length of time Herrigel practiced *kyūjutsu* in Japan. This is brought forth in the section in *The Method of Zen* where Herrigel describes the episode of the Zen practitioner being unperturbed by the earthquake. He says that this happened "shortly after I arrived in Japan" while also saying how the "terrible earthquake a few years before was still fresh in everyone's memory." The Great Kantō Earthquake of 1923 occurred the year before Herrigel arrived in Japan, so if the earthquake occurred "a few years before" Herrigel started training in *kyūjutsu*, Komachiya's memory of Herrigel becoming Awa's student in the spring of 1926 best matches the facts.

It seems most reasonable to conclude, then, that Herrigel trained in *kyūjutsu* for a total of three years from around the spring of 1926, the third year after he came to Japan, until just before leaving Japan in August of 1929. If that is the case, then we are forced to conclude that Herrigel is telling a bald-faced lie about the most fundamental of issues—the duration of his training.

A person who is familiar not only with *kyūjutsu* but with Japanese arts in general will easily be able to imagine what level a man past the age of forty would be able to attain practicing once a week for only three years. In spite of that, *Zen in the Art of Archery*, boosted by the widespread popularity of D. T. Suzuki at that time, became an international bestseller, and so the myth began its march around the world. In 1953, the eighty-three-year-old Suzuki, impressed with *Zen in the Art of Archery*, went all the way to Germany to visit Herrigel. Herrigel related to Inatomi Eijirō (1897–1975), one of the people who worked on the Japanese translation of *Zen in the Art of Archery*, that "just the other day Professor Suzuki came to visit and we spent the entire day deep in conversation. It was most enjoyable."[47]

Zen in the Art of Archery continues to be reprinted. *Nihon no kyūjutsu* ("Die Ritterliche Kunst des Bogenschiessens"), however, has not been widely published outside of Japan, even in Germany. Although the afterwords by Komachiya and the other Japanese people involved in this story that appear in the Japanese-language versions of *Zen in the Art of Archery* and *Nihon no kyūjyutsu* have been partially translated into German, most people outside of Japan are unaware of their existence. Thus, Herrigel's foreign devotees remain ignorant while what actually happened is obvious to anyone who reads Komachiya's text.

Consider the characteristics of the two protagonists. On one side was Awa, who was trying to make *kyūjutsu* into a religion, while on the other side was Herrigel, who had no way of knowing about Awa's idiosyncratic nature. There was Herrigel, who was avidly seeking Zen, and Awa, who by no means affirmed Zen. I believe that on the whole, we now have been able to verify what the conversations between these two men were actually like.

If I were to venture an interpretation of the two mystical episodes that lie at the heart of Herrigel's *Zen in the Art of Archery*, I would say this: they constitute empty signs or symbols that emerged in the voids created by the misunderstanding resulting from the faulty translation of "'It' shoots" and by the coincidental occurrence in the "Target in the Dark" episode. The French critic Roland Barthes (1915–1980) explained that this emptiness is the wellspring for the mythic function. The intentionality of individuals and the ideology of societies breathe meaning into these voids and through this process we generate our myths. In *Zen in the Art of Archery*, the personal aims of Herrigel, who searched for Zen-like elements in *kyūjutsu*, gave birth to a modern myth. This is how Herrigel created his version of "Japaneseness."

The Japanese-language version of *Zen in the Art of Archery*, *Yumi to zen* (Zen and the bow), is the culmination of a circular translation process whereby Awa's original words were translated from Japanese to German and then back to Japanese, thus altering them to such an extent that it is impossible to know what he originally said. As a result of reading this

47. Inatomi Eijirō, "Herigeru sensei no omoide," in Eugen Herrigel, *Yumi to zen* (Tokyo: Kyōdō Shuppan, 1956), 15.

book, even Japanese themselves have come to have a somewhat skewed view of Japanese archery. Even Sakurai, himself a disciple of Awa, clearly saw the main problem:

> Awa did use the expression "bow and Zen are one." Nonetheless, he did not expound archery or his *shadō* as a way leading to Zen. Regardless of how Herrigel acquired that impression, today when many Japanese have the same misunderstanding we should not place the blame on Herrigel. Rather the responsibility must be placed squarely on our own Japanese scholars who have failed to clarify the difference between the arts of Japan and Zen.[48]

How did this come to happen? It was because the image of Japan reflected in the mirror of Herrigel's book was so ideal that almost no one in Japan wanted to criticize it.

---

48. Sakurai, *Awa Kenzō*, 238.

4 The Erased History

THE BLANK SLATE

Until now, the life story of the person named Eugen Herrigel has not been well known. Why did he become interested in Zen even though he lived in Germany? How did he acquire his knowledge of Zen? What did he study and what sort of a life did he lead after returning to Germany? All of these important questions have been shrouded in mystery.

Based on his history as introduced in his various writings, this is the outline of Herrigel's life:

- Born in 1884 in Lichtenau near Heidelberg
- Studied theology at Heidelberg University; later studied philosophy under Wilhelm Windelbandt (1848–1915), Emil Lask (1875–1915), and Heinrich Rickert (1863–1936)
- Served in the army during World War I from 1914 to 1918.
- Returned to Heidelberg University after the war as a private lecturer of philosophy
- Invited to Tōhoku Imperial University as a lecturer and arrived in Japan with his wife Auguste (1887–1974; often called "Gusty") in May

1924; lectured on philosophy while learning *kyūjutsu* from Master Awa Kenzō

- Returned to Germany in August 1929 and became a tenured professor at the University of Erlangen
- Left Erlangen after the end of World War II lived a secluded life in Garmisch-Partenkirchen
- Died of lung cancer in the spring of 1955

Even though Herrigel has had a profound influence on the discourse on Japanese culture, only the scantiest details are known about him. In particular, there is practically no information about his early years or the period of his life that shaped his determination to travel to Japan. If we look even more closely, we see that his career during one of the most important periods in modern German history is completely missing. This gap is nothing other than the period of Nazi rule.

This seems very strange. For German scholars who lived through the Nazi era, how they conducted themselves during that time is an extremely delicate issue. There are even some scholars such as Martin Heidegger (1889–1976) who were continuously censured for their participation in the Nazi effort. The question of how scholars behaved during this time is similar to the situation of a devoutly religious person who finds him or herself being forced to choose between death or apostasy. How one responds in a situation where a life-and-death choice must be made reveals where one truly stands.

Some members of the post–World War II European intelligentsia publicized the fact that Herrigel had been a Nazi party member and censured him severely for the opportunistic way he lived his life. For example, the famous authority on Jewish mysticism, Gershom Scholem (1897–1982), claimed that Herrigel was "a convinced Nazi" (this he had heard from an old friend of Herrigel's). He wrote that "This was not mentioned in some biographical notes on Herrigel published by his widow, who built up his image as one concerned with the higher spiritual sphere only."[1]

Rodney Needham (1923–) argued that "the actual consequence, a few years after he had assumed the position of professor of philosophy at the University of Erlangen, was that Herrigel voluntarily joined the Nazis," and, presumably in reference to Herrigel's denazification hearing, that "the

---

1. Gershom Scholem, "Zen-Nazism?" *Encounter* 16:2 (1961): 96.

tribunal concluded, to its regret, that, since his resistance to the Nazis did not satisfy the requirements of the law, it was unable to accede to Herrigel's petition for exoneration."[2]

Furthermore, the Jewish scholar Zwi Werblowsky (1924–) stated in an interview that Herrigel was "a convinced Nazi" and a "follower of Hitler."[3] Werblowsky was probably relying on what Scholem had written. However, neither Scholem nor Needham produced any conclusive proof to back up their claims. This gave some the impression that Herrigel's connection with the Nazis was just speculation.

In Japan there has been no discussion whatsoever about Herrigel's Nazi past. Even people who are thoroughly conversant with Herrigel's writings would be shocked to hear that he had been a Nazi. The writings of Scholem and Needham are not easily accessible to the average Japanese, so what they wrote would have no way of becoming known in Japan.

However, among German researchers who are familiar with the Nazi period, the rough outlines of Herrigel's Nazi connection are discussed as semi-common knowledge. When I asked a scholar whose field was research into the history of the University of Erlangen about Herrigel, the first words out his mouth were "Oh, yes, he was a Nazi." I remember being rather shocked at the bluntness of his opinion of Herrigel.

The facts are these: Herrigel joined the Nazi party on December 5, 1937, and from 1938 to 1944, when the Nazi party controlled the German educational system, he served as vice rector of the University of Erlangen and then as rector from 1944 to 1945. These facts do not entirely match the image of Herrigel as the person who introduced the West to the lofty spirituality of Zen. That is probably why all evidence of Herrigel's connection with Nazism has been excluded from the biographical information included in his books, thus rendering the overall image of his life ambiguous. Here, flitting in and out of hiding, can be seen the unspoken intention of a certain group of people to make sure that the image of Herrigel the Nazi was not reflected in the mirror of Japanese culture.

Why has there been practically no research into Herrigel's life, even though nearly fifty years have elapsed since his death? The reason is because there is so little information about him. Another factor that blunted the desire of researchers to investigate his life is the statement that, on the

2. Rodney Needham, *Exemplars* (Berkeley: University of California Press, 1985), 13.

3. "An Interview with R. J. Zwi Werblowsky: ZEN," *The Center Magazine* 3:2 (March/April 1975): 61–70.

verge of death, "knowing that he had not long to live, Herrigel ignored his wife's attempts to restrain him and burned voluminous quantities of his manuscripts to ashes."[4]

It is probably true that Herrigel burned his manuscripts. However, I never abandoned a faint hope that some information about Herrigel might still be left in the files of the organizations to which he had belonged. When I had the opportunity to go to Germany in the winter of 2000, I visited the University of Erlangen and I was able to examine a great deal of material on Herrigel. I next visited the archives at Heidelberg University where Herrigel had studied, and it was there that I stumbled upon a veritable treasure trove of information. I could hardly believe my eyes when a pile of material concerning Herrigel's entire family, including a large quantity of Herrigel's unpublished materials, was produced from the stacks of the library and arrayed in neat rows on a desk in the reading room.[5] These materials had been preserved and organized by Herrigel's nephew, who donated them to the university in 1993 (hereafter, these materials will be referred to as the Heidelberg documents). This nephew was the oldest son of Herrigel's younger sister. Herrigel was his godfather, and it appears that a portion of Herrigel's unpublished materials passed to him because he and Herrigel had been especially close. Using the material in the Heidelberg documents as clues, I would like to recover Herrigel's "erased" history and reveal the true form and identity of the mirror which reflected *Zen in the Art of Archery*.

HERRIGEL'S EARLY YEARS

What follows is Herrigel's personal history according to the Heidelberg documents.

Herrigel was born on March 20, 1884, in Lichtenau, near Heidelberg. His father's name was Gottlob (1850–1926) and his mother's name was Johann[6] (1850–1915). There were seven siblings in all: Oskar (1874–1934), Hermann (1876–1932), Emma (1878–1946), Friedrich (1880–1886),

---

4. Shibata Jisaburō, "Shinpan e no yakusha kōki," repr. in Herrigel, *Nihon no kyūjutsu* (Tokyo: Iwanami Bunko, 1982), 117. Unless otherwise indicated, citations are to the 1982 edition.

5. I thank both Professor Wolfgang Schamoni of Heidelberg University and Ms. Mieko Akisawa-Schamoni, who gave me suggestions and provided help with this research.

6. Johann is a male name; however, I have followed the spelling given in the original document.

Eugen (1884–1955), Else (1887–1977), and Hedwig (1894–1963) (since Friedrich died young, they grew up as a family of six siblings.)

Gottlob Herrigel was an educator and an organist. When Eugen was born, Gottlob was vice principal at the school in Lichtenau, but soon after, he was transferred and the family moved to Number 6 Philosophenweg in Heidelberg. The two-story house in which they lived was located on a small rise surrounded by greenery, and had a nice view of the old city of Heidelberg across the Neckar River.

Mutai Risaku (1890–1974), a philosopher and a professor at Keio University, was a boarder at the Herrigel home from April to September of 1926 while Herrigel was in Japan. The philosopher Takahashi Satomi (1886–1964), who later became the rector of Tohoku University, was an exchange student in Heidelberg at the time and arranged for Mutai to board with the Herrigel family. Mutai remembers the area around Herrigel's home: "The freesias, the chestnuts, and the cherries in the orchard are all blooming and the clusters of wisteria are giving off their sweet scent— it is the most beautiful time of the year, just when all of the most beautiful flowers bloom at once. The grey thrushes are singing with their harmonious voices in the luxuriant hedges that still remain in the town, country capital though it is."[7] From the time he was a child until he came to Japan, Herrigel lived in this beautiful house.

Gottlob was highly regarded as an organist and occasionally gave concerts at the Heiliggeistkirche in the center of Heidelberg. It appears that when any important guest came to the church, Gottlob was asked to perform. He also published collections of stories. After Gottlob retired at the age of sixty-five, he accommodated Japanese, French, and English overseas students at the Herrigel home and tutored them. Mutai was probably among them. Eugen's younger sister Else writes in her memoirs that "some Japanese named Ōe came to the house often to visit Eugen."[8] Mutai, who came to stay at the Herrigel home just as Herrigel was leaving for Japan, left Heidelberg in September 1926 and went to study with Edmund Husserl (1859–1938) of Freiburg. Gottlob died the same year on August 31, so it is probable that Mutai left Heidelberg after attending the funeral.

---

7. Mutai Risaku, "Ryūgaku jidai no Takahashi Satomi-san," in *Shisaku to kansatsu: Wakai hitobito no tame ni* (Tokyo: Keisōshobō, 1968), 170–79.

8. Dietrich Eugen Schopfer, "Meine Mutter Else Schopfer-Herrigel erzählt von ihrem Elternhaus," typescript, Herrigel and Schopfer family history papers, Universität Archiv Heidelberg.

After Gottlob's death, the house in Heidelberg was sold to a university professor and was later destroyed during World War II. The area where Herrigel's house once stood is now occupied by a parking lot belonging to the Physics Research Center at Heidelberg University. Only a few piles of bricks remain in what appears to be the area that was once the old garden.

Oskar, the oldest of the Herrigel sons, was a minister. He was fluent in Eastern languages in addition to Esperanto, and published a series of newspaper articles on the life of Johannes Kepler (1571–1630). In his capacity as a minister, he also taught religion, as well as German, French, and history at the Karlsruhe Gymnasium (a traditional German middle school). The second Herrigel son, Hermann, also chose to become a minister. The eldest daughter, Emma, was a French teacher and published a book for the study of the language. The emphasis in the Herrigel home on education and religion must have had a profound effect on the path Eugen chose to follow and on his way of thinking.

Eugen, the third son, studied at the national elementary school and then at the gymnasium, receiving his diploma in 1903. He continued on to Heidelberg University and studied theology from 1907 to 1908 and neo-Kantian philosophy from 1908 to 1913. He received his doctorate studying under Wilhelm Windelbandt in 1913 and established a relationship with Emil Lask. During World War I, he worked as a medic (1914–1916), and from 1917 to 1918 he was a delegate of Imperial Commissioners and Military Speculators. In 1923, he received his certification as a university professor under Heinrich Rickert. At this time, he helped to proofread the anthology *Zen: der lebendige Buddihismus in Japan* (Zen—the living Buddhism of Japan; 1925)[9] authored by Ōhazama Shūei (1883–1946; an educator and later the principal of Seikei College) and edited by the philosopher August Faust (1895–1945).

In 1929, after returning to Germany from Japan, Herrigel became a tenured professor of philosophy at the University of Erlangen. From 1936 to 1938, he was the head of the Philosophy Department. He officially joined the Nazi party on May 1, 1937. His party membership number was 5499332. After becoming a party member, Herrigel rapidly rose through the ranks at the university. He was vice rector from 1938 to1944, became an official member of the Bayern Science Academy in 1941, and was rector of the University of Erlangen from 1944 to 1945. After the war, he was

---

9. Schuej Ohasama [Ōhazama Shūei], *Zen: der lebendige Buddihismus in Japan*, ed. August Faust (Gotha: Verlag Friedlich Andreas Perthes, 1925).

demoted to vice rector on May 31, 1945, and then to tenured professor on
January 14, 1946. Herrigel retired in 1948.

Herrigel wrote the following essays, which are virtually unknown:

"Die Aufgabe der Philosophie im neuen Reich" (The question of philosophy
in the new empire; 1934)[10]
Nationalsozialismus und Philosophie (National socialism and philosophy;
1935)[11]
"Die Tradition im japanischen Volks = und Kulturleben" (The traditions
and cultural life of the Japanese people; 1941)[12]
"Das Ethos des Samurai" (The ethos of the samurai; 1944)[13]

Concerning his Japanese language ability, which was an issue in the
"Target in the Dark" episode, Herrigel plainly stated in the documents he
submitted to the district chief of the Nuremburg Provincial Education
Ministry on September 15, 1943, that "my Japanese language ability is very
limited. I don't have knowledge of the reading and the writing."[14] These
documents substantiate the strong likelihood that a language barrier existed between Awa and Herrigel, as discussed in the previous chapter.

Now let us turn to Herrigel's wife. It has been thought that Herrigel's
wife Auguste accompanied him to Japan. She studied *ikebana* (flower arranging) in addition to *kyūjutsu* and is known as the author of the book
The Way of Flowers (1958).[15] However, according to the Heidelberg documents, Auguste was Herrigel's second wife. Up until now this fact has been
completely unknown.

Herrigel's first wife was a baroness, Paula von Beulwitz (1893–1924),

10. Eugen Herrigel, "Die Aufgabe der Philosophie im neuen Reich," *Pfälzische Gesellschaft zur Förderung der Wissenschaften* (1934): 26–32. (The author has not seen the text.)

11. Eugen Herrigel, Nationalsozialismus und Philosophie (1935), unpublished manuscript, Collection of Universitätsbibliothek Erlangen-Nürnberg.

12. Eugen Herrigel, "Die Tradition im japanischen Volks = und Kulturleben," in *Kulturmacht Japan*, ed. Richard Foester (Vienna: Die Pause, 1942), 14–15.

13. Eugen Herrigel, "Das Ethos des Samurai," *Feldpostbriefe der Philosophischen Fakultät*
3 (1944): 2–14.

14. Letter from Eugen Herrigel to An den Herrn Bereichsleiter, des Gauschulungsamtes,
Nürnberg-O, September 15, 1943. Eugen Herrigel Correspondence/Papers, Collection of
Bundesarchiv, Berlin.

15. Gusty L. Herrigel, *Der Blumenweg* [The way of flowers] (Munich: Otto Wilhelm
Barth, 1958).

and it was she who accompanied Herrigel to Sendai. It appears that she was pregnant when they arrived in Japan, for on August 8, 1924, less than three months after their arrival, Paula gave birth to a daughter. Sadly, the child was stillborn. She was given the name Ulla. Perhaps it was due to the strain of the long voyage to Japan in addition to the stillbirth, but five days after giving birth, Paula herself passed away on August 13.

Herrigel never spoke about his first wife or the daughter he lost in Japan. He must have kept it hidden away deep in his heart. The Heidelberg documents contain a photograph of Eugen together with Paula and Ishihara Ken (1882–1976), a scholar of the history of Christianity who later became the president of Tokyo Women's Christian University. Ishihara certainly knew about Paula and Ulla. Since the deaths of Herrigel's wife and daughter occurred shortly after their arrival in Japan, it is likely that very few people realized what had happened. Perhaps Komachiya was one of those who was informed.

Herrigel married Auguste L. Seefried on September 16, 1925, one year and four months after he came to Japan. The Heidelberg documents contain a copy of the marriage certificate bearing that date, which was issued by the mayor of Sendai. This means that the part of Herrigel's personal history that states that "Herrigel was invited to be an instructor at Tōhoku Imperial University and came to Japan with his wife Gusty"[16] is mistaken.

In *Zen in the Art of Archery*, Herrigel writes that he and his wife became Awa's students at the same time. Bearing this statement in mind, and considering the fact that Gusty married Herrigel in 1925, the Heidelberg documents bear out my thesis that Herrigel became Awa's student in 1926, two years after coming to Japan, and that he trained in *kyūjutsu* for a total of three years.

THE JAPANESE IN HEIDELBERG

The foregoing gives us a good overall picture of Herrigel's personal history before and after he went to Japan. Next, I would like to clarify why Herrigel attempted to study Zen in Japan.[17]

16. Shibata Jisaburō, "Shinpan e no yakusha kōki," repr. in Herrigel, *Nihon no kyūjutsu*, 114.

17. I referred to citations in the following articles by Niels Gülberg: "Eugen Herrigels Wirken als philosophischer Lehrer in Japan (1)," *Waseda-Blätter* 4 (1997): 41–66,

In addition to Mutai and Takahashi, Herrigel had close and friendly relations with a number of Japanese overseas students in Heidelberg, among them Amano Teiyū (1884–1980), a philosopher and later the president of Dokkyo University; Ishihara Ken; Kita Reikichi (1885–1961), a philosopher and later a member of the lower house of the Japanese Diet who was also the younger brother of Kita Ikki (1883–1937; a famous Japanese ultranationalist); and Miki Kiyoshi (1897–1945), a philosopher, cultural critic, and later a professor at Hosei University. Contrary to the commonly accepted story that Herrigel came to Japan and studied Zen, it was during the Heidelberg period that Herrigel acquired considerable knowledge of Zen through his association with these overseas students.

Miki was an overseas student in Germany from 1922 to 1925. Inflation was rampant in Germany at that time, and this enabled Japanese overseas students to live lives of luxury. They could buy all the books they wanted and could hire instructors at Heidelberg University as private tutors. One could even say that a kind of system developed whereby the Japanese overseas students supported the teachers in Heidelberg economically. In his memoirs, Miki offers the following reminiscence:

> Luckily—this word has a somewhat strange meaning here—I was able to buy all of the books I wanted during this time. Thanks to the unprecedented inflation in Germany, we were unexpectedly able to live like millionaires for a time.... I translated an essay by Professor Hoffman and published it in the magazine *Shisō* [Thought]. Because of the inflation, the German intelligentsia were having economic difficulties at that time and so, thinking that they would be happy with any amount of money for their work, I asked the professor to write an essay. Because of the situation, all the young professors gladly gave private lessons to the Japanese students.[18]

It appears that Herrigel gave lectures to Miki on Lask's philosophy. In addition to Herrigel, Miki received private lessons from the scholars Hermann Glockner (1896–1979) and Karl Mannheim (1893–1947).

The following people were among the Japanese whom Miki knew in Heidelberg. All of these men, either singly or in groups, hired the professors and young lecturers of Heidelberg as private tutors.

---

and "Eugen Herrigels Wirken als philosophischer Lehrer in Japan (2)," *Waseda-Blätter* 5 (1998): 44–60.

18. Miki Kiyoshi, *Miki Kiyoshi zenshū*, Vol. 1 (Tokyo: Iwanami Shoten, 1966), 412–18.

- Abe Jirō (1883–1959; philosopher, aesthetician, professor of Tōhoku Imperial University)
- Amano Teiyū
- Ishihara Ken
- Ōuchi Hyōei (1888–1980; economist, professor of Tokyo Imperial University, president of Hosei University)
- Ōhazama Shūei
- Obi Hanji (social education theorist, birth and death dates unknown)
- Kita Reikichi
- Kuki Shūzō (1888–1941; philosopher)
- Kuruma Samezō (1893–1982; economist, professor at Hosei University, researcher at the Ōhara Institute for Social Research)
- Kokushō Iwao (1895–1949; historian of economics, professor at Kyoto Imperial University, rector of the Osaka University of Economics, president of Okayama University)
- Suzuki Munetada (1881–1963; theologian, philosopher, professor at Tōhoku Imperial University)
- Naruse Mukyoku (1884–1958; scholar of German literature, essayist, dramatist, professor at Kyoto Imperial University)
- Hani Gorō (1901–1983; historian)
- Fujita Keizō (1894–1985; small business administration theorist, president of the Osaka University of Economics)

According to Miki, Herrigel was of central importance for the Japanese overseas students who had come to Heidelberg to study philosophy during this period, leading reading groups that met at the lodgings of Ōhazama and Kita.[19]

According to Glockner's memoir, *Heidelberger Bilderbuch* (A picture book of Heidelberg; 1969),[20] in addition to the aforementioned people, Herrigel was also close with Akamatsu Kaname, Ōe Seiichi and his younger brother Ōe Seizō, and Iwasaki Tsutomu.[21] The Akamatsu Kaname mentioned by Glockner is probably the economist and professor at Hitotsubashi University of same name (1896–1974), and Iwasaki Tsutomu is probably the philosopher and professor at Waseda University (1900–1975). The Ōe brothers are most likely the "Japanese named Ōe" mentioned in Herri-

---

19. Ibid.
20. Hermann Glockner, *Heidelberger Bilderbuch* (Bonn: H. Bouvier u. CO. Verlag, 1969).
21. Ibid., 231–32.

gel's younger sister Else's memoirs.[22] It is probably safe to assume that Ōe Seiichi refers to the philosopher (also known as Ōe Seishirō; 1897–?), and that Ōe Seizō refers to the scholar of the philosophy of science and professor at Nihon University (1905–?).

Herrigel formed his image of Japan and the Japanese through his association with these students. Ishihara, who was in Heidelberg from 1921 to around 1923 wrote, "When I was in Heidelberg, we would gather to conduct research into mysticism with Mannheim, who later became a professor in Frankfurt; Herrigel, who went to Japan; Faust; and a community minister."[23]

The mysticism referred to here is the German mysticism of Meister Eckhart. As Herrigel wrote in *Zen in the Art of Archery*, he had been absorbed in mysticism from his student days and had pursued academic research in this area. However, he realized that he himself lacked something that would enable him to understand it. It was with this state of mind that Herrigel met and became friendly with the Japanese overseas students. In particular, Herrigel believed that he had discovered the key to deepening his understanding of German mysticism in the "Zen" that the Japanese spoke about.

One of the Japanese students in Heidelberg was a man named Ōhazama Shūei, who wrote a Zen anthology together with August Faust.[24] As I mentioned previously, Herrigel helped with the proofreading. It is safe to assume that Ōhazama played a central role in Herrigel's Zen education. However, there are a lot of gaps in our knowledge of Ōhazama, and his life is something of a mystery. He was born in 1883 in Yamagata prefecture and graduated from the Number Two College in Sendai in 1904. After graduating from the Philosophy Department of the College of Humanities of Tokyo Imperial University in 1907, he worked variously as a teacher at the Ibaraki Prefectural Tsuchiura Middle School, a professor at the Niigata School of Medicine, and a professor at the Meiji Vocational School. The Japanese Ministry of Education subsequently sent him to Germany from 1921 to 1923 to study ethics and pedagogy. After returning to Japan, he held successive posts as a professor at the Taishō Academy for Eastern Culture and as the vice principal of Seikei College. Ōhazama was also a Buddhist layman who was affiliated with the Rinzai sect, and he had

---

22. Schopfer, "Meine Mutter Else Schopfer-Herrigel erzählt von ihrem Elternhaus."

23. Ishihara Ken, "Haideruberuku daigaku no omoide," *Risō* 87 (1938): 25–32.

24. Ohasama, *Zen*.

his own Zen training hall, called the Takuboku-ryō, in Tokyo near Nippori Station.[25]

Ōhazama was a student of Shaku Sōkatsu (1871–1954), who was a disciple of the chief abbot of Engakuji temple in Kamakura, Shaku Sōen (1860–1919). Shaku Sōen is well known as the teacher of D. T. Suzuki. The German theologian Ernst Benz (1907–1978) described Ōhazama as "the religious instructor of a Rinzai layman's group from 1942 until his death."[26] The Rinzai layman's group mentioned here refers to the Ryōbō-kai (later the Ryōbō Kyōkai) established at the beginning of the Meiji period by Imakita Kōsen (1816–1892), the teacher of Shaku Sōen. Many prominent people, such as the politician Katsu Kaishū (1823–1899), the politician and *kendō* master Yamaoka Tesshū (1836–1888), the philosopher Nakae Chōmin (1847–1901), D. T. Suzuki, and the novelist Natsume Sōseki (1867–1916) frequented the Ryōbō-kai. Benz also refers to Herrigel as Ōhazama's disciple.

In *Heidelberger Bilderbuch*, Glockner describes his first meeting with Ōhazama:

> A prominent religious figure, by no means young and with an old-fashioned and ceremonial deportment, came to Heidelberg from Japan with a few followers in tow and immediately set himself up as the central figure of a group composed of like-minded countrymen. These men all were interested in philosophy and studied very diligently, either asking to be admitted to Rickert's seminar, or if that was not possible, to at least be allowed to attend his lectures so they could listen to and follow his teachings.[27]

Robert Sharf (1953–), a scholar of Buddhism, identifies a trait common to most of the people who have been involved with spreading Zen in the West: they lack the training and qualifications required of legitimate teachers and existed on the periphery of Zen religious groups in Japan.[28] This is a very penetrating observation. Ōhazama was no exception.

25. Ōhazama Shūei, Rirekisho [curriculum vitae] (1931), unpublished handwritten manuscript, Collection of Seikei Gakuen Shiryōkan; *Nenkan jinbutsu jōhō jiten* (Tokyo: Nichigai Asociētsu, 1982), 398.

26. Ernst Benz, *Zen in westlicher Sicht* (Weilheim: O. W. Barth-Verlag, 1962), 66.

27. Glockner, *Heidelberger Bilderbuch*, 229.

28. Robert H. Sharf, "The Zen of Japanese Nationalism," *History of Religions* 33:1 (1993): 40.

Ōhazama's followers introduced him to Rickert as "a high ranking Zen priest who is the 79th generation in a direct line from the Buddha."[29] Faust also believed that at that time Ōhazama already had a prominent position in the Rinzai sect and that he had been "designated as the successor to the present abbot."[30] However, Ōhazama was a layman, not a priest, and as for being the successor to a Rinzai sect abbot, he was nothing of the sort.

Was Ōhazama a charlatan? I do not think that is necessarily so. A devout Buddhist would certainly want to count the generations from the Buddha so he could determine his place in the line of transmission. While Ōhazama was not the successor to any Rinzai sect abbot, he was regarded as the successor to Shaku Sōkatsu within the Ryōbō Kyōkai, a layman's group with a proud tradition. Unfortunately, Ōhazama died before his teacher and was not able to succeed him.

Nishiyama Matsunosuke (1912–), a well-known scholar of Edo-period culture, was a member of the Takuboku-ryō and received instruction from Ōhazama. Nishiyama offers the following reminiscence about his time in the Takuboku-ryō:

> The Zen that Master Sōkatsu transmitted to Senior Layman Chikudō [Ōhazama's Zen name] was a layman's Zen which had severed its relations with the temple and did not curry favor with power or wealth. It was truly filled with courage and with a clear and unpolluted purity.[31]

According to Glockner's recollection, "It was as though Herrigel's friendship with Ōhazama was predestined."[32] This was quite a contrast to Hoffman, who showed no interest in the Japanese. Glockner also says that "both of them got on famously and were friends almost from the first time they met. Not only did Ōhazama, who was more wealthy than normal, invite Herrigel on a grand tour of Germany he took on his vacation, he arranged for Herrigel to be a professor at Tōhoku Imperial University in 1924."[33] This is what Glockner says, but the only point of contact that

---

29. Glockner, *Heidelberger Bilderbuch*, 229.

30. August Faust, "Vorbemerkung des Herausgebers," in Ohasama, *Zen*, xii.

31. Nishiyama Matsunosuke, "Meguriai: Rōkoji no sei naru jissen ni odoroki: Ōhazama Shūei-sensei," *Mainichi shinbun*, July 29, 1981.

32. Glockner, *Heidelberger Bilderbuch*, 230.

33. Ibid.

Ōhazama had with Tōhoku Imperial University was the fact that he graduated from the Number Two College.[34] It is unlikely that Ōhazama was in
a position to arrange for a teaching post at Tōhoku Imperial University.

Glockner says that "it is true that Ōhazama was an eccentric, but he
was worthy of respect." Kita Reikichi also praised his character. Kita and
Ōhazama were teachers together at the Ibaraki Prefectural Tsuchiura
Middle School, and they were closer than brothers. According to Kita,
Ōhazama was so religious that the housewife at the home where he lodged
in Heidelberg called him "heaven sent," and ministers referred to him as
"a model Christian." He relates how Ōhazama, seeing as how the exchange
rate had made them rich, said that the Japanese overseas students should
be kind to the Germans and share life's bounty with them, and that "he
always had chocolate in his pocket for the neighborhood children, he
shared his meat with families in the community, and in response to the
children's requests he would let them ride on his bicycle, and, observing
how happy it made them, would be as delighted as if they were his own
flesh and blood."[35]

Once or twice a week Kita and Ōhazama would host evening get-
togethers for several university instructors and their wives. Herrigel was
a fixture at these events. In June of 1922, Kita gave a lecture on Zen in response to a request from Rickert, and he asked Herrigel to proofread the
text of the lecture. Kita remembers that "Herrigel himself, who proofread
the text, responded with great enthusiasm because of his natural affinity
to mysticism"; "I explained that the distinguishing characteristic of Zen is
its unique method of uniting contemplation and action," and "Professor
Herrigel, who was in attendance, said that there had never been a seminar
like it."[36] This testimony reveals that Herrigel learned about Zen from Kita
as well as Ōhazama.

There is also proof that Herrigel was directly influenced by Ōhazama
and his circle while he was forming his image of Zen. Herrigel referred to
Japanese Zen as "living Buddhism."[37] Herrigel probably got this expres-

34. Number Two College served as a preparatory school for Tōhoku Imperial University.

35. Kita Reikichi, *Tetsugaku angya* (Tokyo: Shinchōsha, 1926), 314–15.

36. Ibid., 70–74.

37. Herrigel, "Die Ritterliche Kunst des Bogenschiessens" [The chivalrous art of ar-
chery], *Nippon, Zeitschrift für Japanologie* 2:4 (1936): 198.

sion from the book written by Ōhazama and edited by Faust—*Zen: der lebendige Buddihismus in Japan* (which translates to Zen: the living Buddhism of Japan).[38]

Kita also discusses the details of how he used his influence to secure a position for Herrigel at Tōhoku Imperial University:

> There were various reasons for Herrigel's posting to Japan. With the outbreak of the Great War, Herrigel was sent to the French front as a paymaster attached to headquarters. Due to his length of service he contracted pneumonia which damaged his health, but luckily he was never wounded. After peace was concluded he continued for a long time with his military service due to the unfinished business of demobilization. As a result, he was away from the university for six years. He got his degree before the war, but it was during the time I was in Heidelberg that he became a private lecturer. His mentor Lask had been killed in the war, he had been unable to study for six years, and his life as a private lecturer was wretched. He had made many Japanese friends and to him Japan was becoming the country of his dreams, and he really hoped to be able to go there to quietly formulate his own system and to teach German philosophy. We brought this matter to the attention of Professor Sawayanagi who was visiting Germany at that time, and in a spirit of what could be called chivalry, he took Herrigel under his wing and mediated with Tōhoku Imperial University on Herrigel's behalf.[39]

Like Ōhazama, Kita too says that he used his influence to secure a teaching position for Herrigel. However, it is much more reasonable to think that the people who invited Herrigel to Japan were Abe and Takahashi of the Heidelberg Overseas Student Group, who were in the Tōhoku Imperial University Faculty of Law and Letters when Herrigel took up his post there.

Clearly, Herrigel was a person of some significance for the Japanese overseas students, and they thought highly enough of him to secure a post for him in Japan. However, while Herrigel was popular with the Japanese, he was not universally liked by everyone in his own circle. Faust, for example, had a low opinion of Herrigel and was critical of his character. This can be clearly seen from the following opinion he voiced to Glockner, which Glockner recorded in *Heidelberger Bilderbuch*.

38. Ohasama, *Zen.*

39. Kita, *Tetsugaku angya*, 320.

According to Faust, Herrigel won Ōhazama's complete confidence, even though Herrigel isn't worth even half that much. He says that this is because, essentially, Herrigel wheedled his way into the confidence of the Japanese students and is using them for his own purposes, just as he did with Professor and Mrs. Rickert. "Herrigel makes everything sensational. He tailors everything so that it makes a deep impression on that Ōhazama. But truth be told, that middle-aged man [Ōhazama] wants to do exactly the same thing. He's an instigator himself. When you come right down to it, they're two peas in a pod and they put on a show just like they do with Rickert. When Rickert and I are walking together, he will put on their little comic shows for me one after the other and he will get a great laugh out of it all over again. I'm sure he will do the same with you if he sees his chance! They're born actors, those three. But you saw yourself today with your own eyes that Ōhazama is just a harmless comedian. And Rickert, like a lot of people who are very talented, is just like a big child in some ways. But Herrigel is just the opposite of that. This may sound to you like nothing but mudslinging on my part, but there is nothing childlike about Herrigel, and he has no lack of guile. If you say he's putting on a show, the truth of it is that he is always putting on a show and he is always coolly calculating the effect it will have. That's what makes me so angry![40]

It appears from this that Glockner shared Faust's opinion of Herrigel. If not, why would he go to all the trouble of relating what Faust said? Glockner was one of Herrigel's acquaintances, so the fact that he was in agreement with such an extreme view of Herrigel is an important point. Faust was not alone in his views. Faust continued with his criticism of Herrigel:

When I think about how Herrigel told all those tales to Rickert for so many years, just like he is doing with that Zen high priest, I am reminded of the great impostor Cagliostro and his henchmen! Did Professor Rickert tell you about the story Herrigel made up about the surgery ward during the war? Has he told you about how Herrigel took a pistol and struck a tiny pebble with a bullet from a distance of ten meters in order to get a rival of his to call off dueling with him? It's like reading a novel by Alexandre Dumas! And now that big blowhard is trying to swagger around and do the same thing with philosophy![41]

40. Glockner, *Heidelberger Bilderbuch*, 234.
41. Ibid., 235.

What sort of a relationship did Glockner and Faust have that they could engage in this sort of conversation? Amano, who lived in Heidelberg from 1923 to 1924, writes that "while Herrigel went to work at Tōhoku Imperial University in 1924, Glockner and Faust lived at the Rickert home. Hoffman lived nearby and they went back and forth to see each other all the time and studied the classics together as well."[42] Since Glockner and Faust were fellow live-in disciples sharing a roof with their teacher, they probably had a close relationship where they openly discussed their deepest feelings with one another.

Regarding the plan to publish a book with Ōhazama, Faust told Glockner that "I am most assuredly not doing this to create anything sensational. I just want to clearly understand what 'Zen' is." Thus, Faust's motivation for editing *Zen: der lebendige Buddhismus in Japan* seems to have been a sincere desire to investigate Zen. Faust went even further, saying, "Herrigel would absolutely never take upon himself that kind of demanding and troublesome work. That's because it would be a problem for him if Zen were to be clearly explained. Zen must remain ambiguous. That's because Herrigel is trying to take advantage of that ambiguousness. Do you understand?"

Herrigel and Faust were rivals under Rickert, so it is important to recognize the fact that these are words spoken by someone who regarded Herrigel with hostility. Even given that, however, the fact that an associate of Herrigel had such a bitter opinion of him cannot be ignored. Seeing as how Glockner recorded Faust's words in his memoirs, we must also conclude that he endorsed what Faust said.

The fact of the matter is that Herrigel only helped with the proofreading of Faust and Ōhazama's book to a very minor degree, and the extent of his contribution is unclear. However, Herrigel and Ōhazama remained on good terms. This suggests that there was a struggle between Herrigel and Faust over who was in charge of publishing Ōhazama's book, and that Herrigel gave way.

Ōhazama stayed in Germany from September 1921 until around October 1923. Herrigel went to Japan in May 1924, and Ōhazama and Faust published their book on Zen in 1925. If we knew what transpired between Ōhazama and Herrigel during this time, we should be able to understand the interpersonal relationships surrounding the publication of this book.

The Heidelberg documents contain a copy of a letter that Herrigel

---

42. Amano Teiyū, "Haideruberuku gakuha no hitobito," *Risō* 87 (1938): 39.

sent on May 13, 1924, shortly after he arrived in Sendai. The opening line simply says, "My Dear Professor," so we do not know to whom it was addressed. There is a strong likelihood that it was sent to a professor at the University of Heidelberg, most likely to Rickert, Herrigel's mentor.

After relating how Ishihara had come to meet him when his ship arrived in Kobe and describing how he had seen Mount Fuji and the aftermath of the Great Kantō Earthquake on the train trip to Sendai, Herrigel discusses Faust and Ōhazama's book:

> First of all, I contacted Ōhazama from Kobe and told him that since his book is in the process of being printed he must send you the telegram he promised right away. He sent me a letter in which he sincerely apologized for having not yet sent the telegram. His teacher is of the opinion that he [Ōhazama] needs to train in Zen for another ten years before thinking about publishing such a book. I replied to Ōhazama right away and tried to put his mind at ease. I told him the book was already in the process of being printed and that it was too late to stop it. His teacher's words were in reference to a "bigger" book and were not directed at this "small" overview. I wrote him another letter and I hope that we will be able to get his agreement before long. He gave me the rights to publish his book, so he was obligated to inform me right away if he changed his mind. He did not do that—I wrote him and told him so—so it was too late to stop the printing. Therefore, I hope that the promised telegram which delegates the editorial rights to Faust will have arrived before this letter reaches you.

What is written here seems to be of great import, but since the context is not clear we can only surmise what is going on. It appears that before Herrigel went to Japan, the draft for *Zen: der lebendige Buddhismus in Japan* had been sent to Ōhazama, who had already returned to Japan. Herrigel was waiting for Ōhazama's response, but it never came, so Herrigel went ahead with the publication without Ōhazama's final approval. Ōhazama consulted with his Zen teacher—probably Shaku Sōkatsu—about publishing a book about Zen in German, but he did not receive a favorable response. Herrigel was prepared to try again to convince him, but perhaps he wanted the book to be published immediately with Faust as the editor. This can also be interpreted to mean that Herrigel thought that while he really should have been given credit as the editor, he wanted Faust alone to be identified as the editor, since it looked as though the publication of the book might be problematic.

This kind of behavior on Herrigel's part must not have sat well with Faust. Faust was suspicious of Herrigel's intentions, saying, "that's because it would be a problem for him if Zen were to be clearly explained. Zen must remain ambiguous." His criticism that Herrigel was trying to take advantage of that "ambiguousness" accurately hints at Herrigel's subsequent behavior. *Zen: der lebendige Buddihismus in Japan* is a serious anthology that would only appeal to dedicated scholars of Zen. The German text has not been translated into any other language.

In contradistinction to that, the Zen that Herrigel subsequently introduced after his visit to Japan created a sensation in intellectual circles. Just as Faust feared, Herrigel got the maximum benefit from the ambiguousness of Zen as seen from the West. In sum, Herrigel's book became known all over the world, while Faust's serious work faded into oblivion.

HOMECOMING AND THE NAZIS

Thus Herrigel went to Japan harboring the desire to be the one who would introduce Zen to the West. After completing his term of service at Tōhoku Imperial University, he returned to Germany in 1929; in September of the same year, he became a tenured professor of philosophy at the University of Erlangen.

Four years later, in 1933, Adolf Hitler (1889–1945) seized power in Germany. In July of the same year, it became a requirement to begin classes at the university with the Nazi salute. Herrigel also pledged that "I will be loyal and obedient to the leader of the German empire and people, Adolf Hitler." Herrigel's written oath containing this statement, dated August 20, 1934, is in the archives of the University of Erlangen. It is the day after Hitler assumed the post of führer, which combined the positions of prime minister and president.

On December 13, 1934, the Imperial Ministry of Education promulgated the Regulations for Awarding the Qualification of University Professor. These regulations stipulated that a candidate's Nazi worldview and loyalty to the empire had to be investigated before that person could be qualified as a university professor. Under the Imperial Ministry of Education's University Management Consolidation Directive of April 1, 1935, the right to fill all university posts was centralized under the Imperial Ministry of Education. In addition, the German Civil Servants Law of 1937 gave the governors of the states the right to dismiss any civil servant who did not swear loyalty to the empire. According to the research conducted by Yamamoto Yū (1930–), out of a total of 7,758 university instructors in all of Germany at the beginning of 1933, 3,120 of them left their posts between 1933 and 1938.[43]

As previously mentioned, as the Nazis progressively tightened their grip on the universities, Herrigel rose through the ranks, becoming head of the Department of Philosophy in 1936, vice rector in 1938, and rector in 1944. This fact is noteworthy. In a climate where right-minded scholars were leaving the universities in droves, only a person who had ingratiated himself with the Nazis could hope to climb as high as rector. This fact alone, however, does not justify immediately branding Herrigel a scoundrel. It is necessary to thoroughly investigate how Herrigel conducted himself as a member of the university in the midst of this great historical upheaval.

The Heidelberg documents contain a valuable source that is a great help in understanding Herrigel's relationship with the Nazis. This is a letter written after the war by Herrigel himself in which he explains his relationship to the Nazis in an attempt to clear his name (hereafter referred to as Herrigel's Defense). After the war, everyone who had held a public post under the Nazi regime was required to explain their relationship with the Nazis in order to clear themselves of any wrongdoing. Herrigel's Defense was probably written at that time. Judging from the date on some attached documents, Herrigel wrote it sometime between March and November of 1947.

The following is a summary of its contents. A full translation can be found in the appendix. Herrigel prefaces his self-defense with these words:

> The fact that during the last five months of the war I served as rector of the University of Erlangen suggests my inclusion in group II (activists, militarists, profiteers). I can present evidence that this legal assumption does not apply to me.

His letter consists of six typewritten pages, to which are appended signed testimonies from twenty-one witnesses who corroborate Herrigel's statement (the testimony of one witness is missing). The letter is divided into the following sections.

---

43. Yamamoto Yū, *Nachizumu to daigaku* (Tokyo: Chūkō Shinsho, 1985), 31.

I How I Became Rector

II How I Administered the Office of Rector

III My Attitude as Rector during the Last Months of the War Was Consistent with My General Attitude during the Years 1933–45

IV Cooperation with the Military Government

First of all, Herrigel describes the particulars of his appointment as rector as follows. He was surprised when he was appointed to succeed the previous rector, Hermann Wintz (1887–1947) at the time of Wintz's dismissal by the Imperial Minister of Education, Bernhardt Rust (1883–1945). This was because, he says, "I was still a provisional party member only (without membership book)" and also because the procedure for selecting rectors in the Bayern region at that time required taking into consideration the opinions of the head of the association of lecturers, the head of the district, and the head of the province. The outgoing rector appointed Herrigel to succeed him without following the usual protocol. This implies that Herrigel was thoroughly acquainted with conditions at the university and that the outgoing rector trusted him implicitly.

Herrigel also states that he did not join the Nazi party voluntarily, but that he had been required to do so in the fall of 1937. The reason he did not refuse is because he was worried that it "would have had an extremely unfavorable effect" on the university if he did not join. He decided to become rector because he thought that if he did not, someone who was "willing to dance to the tune" of the head of the association of lecturers and the head of the province would be given the post. He also emphasizes that he did not become rector "out of ambition or a craving for recognition."

During the war, Herrigel was asked three times to allow 2,500–3,000 refugees to reside at the University of Erlangen. Asking Herrigel to take in large numbers of refugees was tantamount to asking the university to close its doors. Rector Herrigel rebuffed these requests, which enabled him to protect the university, but he was criticized as an "'intellectual who acted heartlessly toward comrades (*Volkgenossen*) in bitter need.'"

Towards the end of the war, Herrigel conspired with an army lieutenant colonel to kill the head of the district who was advocating fighting to the end, but the plot failed and the colonel was arrested by the Gestapo. Herrigel states that if the occupation by the American army had come a few weeks later, he himself would have been in danger. He also claimed that he was an "'activist,' however, not for but against Hitlerism."

Concerning Nazi ideology and his attitude towards Jews, Herrigel explains himself as follows.

- His family doctor had been a Jew.
- He awarded a Jewish student a PhD with the highest possible grade.
- He permitted a mixed-race Jewish student to attend the university and supported him financially.
- He did not remove books by Jewish philosophers from the philosophy department library.
- He discussed the teachings of Jewish philosophers in his lectures and seminars.
- He did not test students on their Nazi worldview when he administered the state examinations.

Finally, Herrigel writes that "In my lectures and tutorials I took great pains to apply utmost objectivity and not to give any room to the Nazi ideology," and that he cooperated willingly with the Occupation forces and gained their trust.

This summary of Herrigel's Defense clearly illustrates the delicate position in which Herrigel found himself during the turbulent period after the war ended. However, there are some points in the defense that are at variance with the facts. Herrigel says that when he was appointed rector of the University of Erlangen he was "a provisional party member only (without membership book)." However, a copy of Herrigel's party membership book is among the documents from the old Berlin Document Center, which are now housed in the German National Archive. Just as Herrigel describes, it is dated December 5, 1937 (though Herrigel actually joined the party on May 1, 1937). An additional letter written in Herrigel's hand and signed by him informing the rector at that time that he had been issued a party membership book is in the collection of the University of Erlangen.

How should the discrepancies between Herrigel's Defense and these surviving documents be understood? Under the circumstances prevailing at that time, being a Nazi party member would certainly confer advantages in every aspect of life, including positions at the university. It is hard to believe that Herrigel would be ignorant of whether his party membership was provisional or not. Herrigel himself informed the rector of the university that he had a party membership book, and yet after the war was over, he reversed himself and wrote in his defense that he was "without membership book." There can be no doubt that Herrigel is lying here as well.

Herrigel insists repeatedly that his joining the Nazi party and becoming rector were not done for his own sake but for the sake of the university. However, it is an incontrovertible fact that his membership in the party aided his career advancement.

Herrigel's thrice-repeated refusal to take in large numbers of refugees is a problem as well. I cannot help but be disturbed by his refusal to help his fellow Germans displaced by the war. In modern parlance, this might perhaps be considered a "crime against humanity." It also goes against the Buddhist teachings which Herrigel professed to admire. Just how persuasive really is Herrigel's explanation that his refusal to allow the refugees into the university protected a place of learning?

Herrigel's rival Faust was also deeply involved with the Nazi party. Amano Teiyū writes that "the advent of the Nazis completely changed the situation in Germany, and it was inevitable that this wave would reach the students in their intimate and peaceful group. Harmony between the somewhat free-thinking Hoffman and the intensely nationalistic Faust was utterly impossible."[44]

Faust also joined the Nazi party in 1937, but he was much more extreme than Herrigel. According to a report about him written in the same year by the Guidance Division of Baden Province:

From the beginning of the National Socialist revolution, he immediately became actively involved in the movement. Faust was *Fachschaftsleiter* [the leader of a specialty division] of the teachers, and held the equivalent office for social questions for the Hitler Youth. His willing actions and his collaboration are recognized without exception by the acts of the party."[45]

Faust committed suicide in the closing days of the Nazi regime.

44. Amano Teiyū, "Haideruberuku gakuha no hitobito," 39.

45. Quoted from Victor Farias, *Heidegger and Nazism*, ed. Joseph Margolis and Tom Rockmore; trans. Paul Burrell, Dominic Di Bernardi, and Gabriel R. Ricci (Philadelphia, PA: Temple University Press, 1989), 259.

FROM THE END OF THE WAR TO RETIREMENT

Having received Herrigel's Defense in December 1947, the denazification court at Erlangen concluded that Herrigel had not been a committed Nazi. On the other hand, it found him to be a *Mitläufer* (passive fellow traveler) whose resistance to the Nazis had been insufficient to clear him of guilt. The fact that Herrigel had to write a letter to defend his actions would seem to substantiate his Nazi connections. The Occupation's denazification effort is considered to have formally ended in March 1948. Herrigel's trial took place towards the end of denazification activities. A record of his trial is included in the Heidelberg documents.

The severity of the punishment meted out to German war criminals differed from district to district depending on which army occupied that district. According to Yamamoto Yū, the percentage of "extremely guilty," "guilty," and "accessory" in American-occupied districts such as Erlangen was 13.7 percent, which was higher than in other districts. This resulted in the dismissal of a large number of university instructors, which in turn lowered the quality of education. Occupation authorities were forced to change their policy and to gradually allow the teachers who had been dismissed to be reinstated.[46] Herrigel was not reinstated, and he retired to the resort town of Garmische Partenkirchen in southern Germany where he spent the remainder of his life.

The Occupation forces confiscated the new home that Herrigel had built in Erlangen in August 1945, and the Herrigel family moved to 19 Schuhstrasse, Erlangen. Herrigel's old house is still there, in a prime area of Erlangen, and people are still living in it. Shibata Jisaburō, the translator of "Die Ritterliche Kunst des Bogenschiessens" (first in the article "Kyūjutsu ni tsuite" and later in the book *Nihon no kyūjutsu*), describes the circumstances surrounding the house:

> In the defeated Germany right after World War II, the naked power of the victors was rampant everywhere, just like it was in Japan. The American army suddenly requisitioned the new house that Herrigel had just built in Erlangen and looted much valuable property. Among this property were many irreplaceable keepsakes from Japan, including the bow that Herrigel had

---

46. Yamamoto, *Nachizumu to daigaku*, 177–78.

received from Master Awa. Herrigel, resigned to the looting of his property, left Erlangen in 1951 in a philosophical frame of mind.[47]

However, the facts revealed in surviving documents tell a somewhat different story from the one Shibata relates. At the University of Erlangen there is a document that shows that Herrigel received a substantial loan from the university when he built his house. Thus, one way to interpret what happened is that the Occupation forces viewed the house as the official residence of the rector of the university and requisitioned it on that basis. Moreover, the Heidelberg documents contain evidence that shows that in December 1955, subsequent to Herrigel's death, back rent was paid on the house dating all the way back to August 1945 when the house was requisitioned.

In addition, it can be seen from Herrigel's Defense that Herrigel had numerous discussions with the Occupation forces regarding his treatment. It is questionable whether Herrigel "left Erlangen in a philosophical frame of mind."

The bow that Herrigel received from Master Awa, which was reportedly stolen, is now housed at Engakuji temple in Kamakura. As to why Herrigel's bow is at Engakuji, Sakurai Yasunosuke wrote that it was stolen when the Occupation forces requisitioned the house, but that it was miraculously returned thanks to Mrs. Herrigel's efforts.[48] Der Zen-Weg (The Method of Zen) was created from manuscripts that Mrs. Herrigel retrieved from the storeroom of their old house, so it is probably true that Mrs. Herrigel put a lot of effort into recovering Herrigel's old possessions.

However, the Heidelberg documents contain a form which Herrigel submitted to the Erlangen police department on February 9, 1947, stating that he owned a Japanese short sword and bow. In short, Herrigel apparently remained in possession of his Japanese keepsakes when his house was requisitioned. If he took a Japanese bow with him at that time, it seems most natural to assume that it was the bow he received from Awa. Thus, it is possible that Herrigel himself had Awa's bow in his possession the entire time.

Why, then, were the manuscripts that were later published as Der Zen-Weg left at the house? The fact that Herrigel burned his papers when he

47. Shibata, "Shinpan e no yakusha kōki," 116–17.

48. Sakurai, Awa Kenzō: Ōi naru sha no michi no oshie (Sendai: Awa Kenzō Sensei Seitan Hyakunensai Jikkō Iinkai, 1981), 301.

realized he was dying suggests that he considered the manuscript to be of no importance. I do not know the quantity involved, but generally speaking, books and papers are heavy and bulky. Rather than being unable to take all of his manuscripts because the requisition was so sudden, it seems more likely that Herrigel discarded the manuscript because he had no use for it. In any case, a student of Herrigel entrusted the bow to Suhara Kōun (1917–), a priest of the Zokutōan at the temple of Engakuji and a Daishadōkyō-style archer, and so Awa's bow was brought back to Japan.

In the Heidelberg Folk Art Museum, there is a traditional Japanese costume with family crest and a bag for storing a short sword that Kinoshita Seitarō (1865–1942), a member of the lower house of the Japanese Diet, presented to Herrigel on the occasion of his return to Germany.[49] The following statement, written in classical Chinese with black ink, appears on the inner sword bag:

> The thirty-first of August, fourth year of Shōwa [1929]. The German professor of philosophy Mr. Herrigel has completed his term of service and is leaving Imperial Japan to return to his country. Even though great distances may lie between us, our mutual love and duty will ever remain unchanged as they were when he was here in the Empire. As a keepsake, we hereby present him with a famous Bizen sword, filled with the spirit of Japan, made by Kiyonori of Yoshii-zumi.

It is probable that the short sword that Herrigel had, along with the bow, was presented to him in this sword bag. The short sword was judged to be "useless" by a second lieutenant of the Occupation forces and so Herrigel was permitted to keep it. Unfortunately, the whereabouts of this sword by the smith Kiyonori are unknown. Herrigel owned two other Japanese swords, but these were requisitioned along with the house. I was unable to find any documents that supported the accepted story that the bow was confiscated and that Herrigel's widow recovered it after his death.

These facts seem to indicate that somewhat extended negotiations took place between Herrigel and the Occupation forces at the time the house was requisitioned. Shibata's description of the circumstances includes the phrase "Herrigel was resigned to the looting of his property," but this seems overly melodramatic, as though Shibata was attempting to make Herrigel into a tragic hero.

49. I thank Professor Inaga Shigemi for his suggestion to visit this museum.

In sum, when one carefully analyzes the surviving documents regarding Herrigel, one can glimpse the presence of a force that was attempting to erase Herrigel's Nazi connections and present him in a way that conformed to a certain image. Let me give one concrete example of how elements that would remind readers of Herrigel's Nazi connections have been expunged from his record. The first German edition of *Der Zen-Weg* opens with a reprint of Herrigel's obituary. The obituary states that Herrigel was the rector of the University of Erlangen and that his actions saved the town from destruction. Readers of this obituary would instantly realize that Herrigel had been rector—an important and powerful position at the university—under the Nazi regime.

For some reason, the obituary was omitted beginning with the publication of the second edition of *Der Zen-Weg* (1964). The English and Japanese translations were not based on the first edition and thus were read around the world without Herrigel's obituary.

As can be seen from this incident regarding Herrigel's obituary, Herrigel's translators and publishers hid every single piece of information related to him and the Nazis. Herrigel had supposedly penetrated into the heart of Zen with its lofty spirituality and had introduced it to the West. Without a doubt, they did not want anyone to know that he had been a Nazi.

The Zen scholar Brian Victoria (1939–) harshly criticizes prominent Japanese Zen priests for the way in which they enthusiastically embraced militarism and then covered up that fact after the war.[50] Zen and the war—this is a negative aspect of Japan's history that the Japanese have kept hidden. We have tried hard to keep the war from being reflected in the mirror of Zen and have done our best to not think about it. If others interpret this as suppressing the facts, we have no one to blame but ourselves. This is just as true in Herrigel's case.

However, no one ordered anyone to conceal anything. Scholem ascribes this phenomenon to the workings of a common, unspoken will to create an image of Herrigel as a spiritual man.[51] What gave birth to this unspoken, shared desire to create a particular image of Herrigel? It was the subconscious intention of those who were searching for the magic mirror.

---

50. Brian A. Victoria, *Zen at War* (New York and Tokyo: Weatherhill, 1997).
51. Scholem, "Zen-Nazism?" 96.

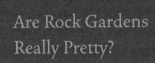

5   Are Rock Gardens
Really Pretty?

FROM THE "TIGER CUBS CROSSING THE RIVER" TO THE "HIGHER SELF"

The Daiunzan Ryōanji temple, located in northern Kyoto, is famous for its rock garden. As the literal embodiment of the Zen garden, it is thronged with visitors from near and far. Below is the introduction to the rock garden displayed on the wall of the resident abbot's quarters (hōjō) from where the garden can be viewed.

> Sit quietly and converse with the rock garden . . . it suggests fragrant peaceful islands dotting the vast expanse of the sea, or a series of mountain tops in cloud banks, all blending harmoniously with the facing earthen wall and expressing the "Higher Self" of the universe, heaven and earth. This garden directly expresses the ne plus ultra of Zen: as we meet the garden, our "Lower Selves" are smitten by the quiet, pure, and beautiful sincerity of the "Higher Self," which washes away the dust of the mundane world from our souls, bathing us in a pure, clean and heartfelt joy as our pre-garden selves receive the Buddha Nature. . . . This garden is without a doubt unequalled anywhere in the world. Rather than calling it a "rock garden" it should be called the

"Garden of the Void" or the "Empty Garden." In Zen, each tree and blade of grass is a representation of the divine and of the Buddha, and every inch of this garden teaches us the essence of Zen.

This presumably expresses the temple's official position on the garden. Reading this, however, I am forced to say that if the garden is a "Higher Self," understanding its essence is beyond the capabilities of a "Lower Self," such as myself.

The rock garden at Ryōanji is not a bad garden. It is a very intriguing garden, indeed, seeing as how something so simple has come to be so highly regarded. It is not in the least enjoyable when it is crowded, but on mornings during the off season, it is very pleasant to sit on the veranda of the abbot's quarters and view the garden while feeling the gentle breeze and listening to the chirping of birds. However, one can experience the same pleasant feeling sitting on one's own veranda at home. Even if I can put the sense of superiority that pervades this garden—that it alone deserves to be called a "world heritage garden"—out of my mind, I simply do not feel that it is anything special.

What did people in the Edo period (1603–1868) think about the rock garden at Ryōanji? The *Miyako rinsen meishō zue* (Illustrated guide to noted gardens of Kyoto), a typical guidebook to Kyoto gardens published in 1799 (figure 4), describes this rock garden as follows.

> Long ago, Hosokawa Katsumoto built a villa here as his residence. Since he went every day from his study to pray at the Otokoyama Hachimangū shrine, he planted some trees in the garden. The large irregularly shaped rocks create a beautiful scene. This garden was created by Sōami. It is called the garden of the Tiger Cubs Crossing the River [*tora no ko watashi*]. It is the finest garden among the famous gardens of northern Kyoto.[1]

What this means is that the arrangement of the stones in the garden looks like "tiger cubs crossing the river." This was a very typical way of describing gardens in the late eighteenth to nineteenth centuries. The phrase "tiger cubs crossing the river" alludes to the following ancient Chinese story: in a place called Hong Nong in the vicinity of the Hangu Pass,

1. Akisato Ritō, *Miyako rinsen meishō zue* (Kyoto: Ogawa Tazaemon, 1799).

the people were troubled by a rampaging tiger. A new governor named Liu
Kun was assigned to the area. As a result of Liu Kun's virtuous government, after a while the rampaging tiger left for parts unknown, crossing
the river carrying her cubs on her back. This story appears in the *Hou Han-
shu* (Records of the later Han; ca. 432).

The *Kōjien* dictionary[2] describes the "tiger cubs crossing the river"
as follows: a tiger gave birth to three cubs, but one was a panther. If the
mother tiger was not constantly on guard, the panther cub would eat the
other cubs. The tigress and cubs had to cross a river, but the mother tiger
could only carry one cub at a time. How was the mother tiger to carry the
three cubs across the river so that the panther cub would not eat the two
tiger cubs? First, the mother tiger carried the panther cub across the river.
She then carried one tiger cub across, and on the return trip she carried
the panther cub back with her. She left the panther cub there and then
carried the second tiger cub across the river. Finally she returned and carried the panther cub across the river again. This prevented the panther cub
from eating the tiger cubs.

Regardless of which story one prefers, describing the Ryōanji rock garden as "tiger cubs crossing the river" means that the arrangement of rocks
represents a mother tiger carrying her cubs across a river on her back.

The first recorded appearance of the phrase "tiger cubs crossing the
river" seems to be in a document called the *Shōhō ninen teikōchōki* (Public
government records of the second year of Shōhō [era]; 1645). Of course
the phrase "tiger cubs crossing the river," referring to the placement of
rocks in a rock garden, is still in use today.

Here one must stop and think. The impressions conveyed when the
rock garden is called "tiger cubs crossing the river" and when it is called
"the essence of Zen" or "the Higher Self" are completely different. This
makes one suspect that that how the rock garden at Ryōanji is viewed has
changed during the roughly two hundred years from the guidebook *Miyako rinsen meishō zue* to the present.

Mystery surrounds the rock garden at Ryōanji. First of all, it is not clear
who created it or when. Beyond that, why this garden is considered beautiful is a riddle in itself.

Simply put, this is what happened with the ideas surrounding the rock
garden at Ryōanji. Beginning in the 1920s, the discussion about who made

2. One of the most prestigious and comprehensive Japanese dictionaries.

Figure 4. Sketch of garden by Akisato (1799).

the garden and the discussion about its aesthetics began to reinforce one another, and after the war, ideas containing elements of Zen thought were added to the mix. This mixture of ideas spread widely in foreign countries and, riding the Zen boom, brought foreigners flocking to Ryōanji. As this trend developed, the opinion that the rock garden at Ryōanji expressed Zen enlightenment came to assume a position of dominance.

I am not particularly interested in clarifying who created the rock garden or why it is beautiful. Rather, what I want to know is this: what sort of controversy developed around the identity of the garden's creator and the issue of its beauty, and when and in what fashion was the Zen interpretation of the rock garden born?

Is this rock garden really beautiful? How have the reasons for its beauty been presented and explained? What I first want to do is look back on the relentless attempts of various people, some successful and some not, to unlock the secret of the beauty of this garden or to see Zen in it, as its beauty came to be accepted as "common knowledge" by the Japanese people.

第四〇圖　龍安寺の石庭

Figure 5. Photograph of garden by Tamura (1918).

THE NEGLECTED ROCK GARDEN

While Ryōanji today is known all over the world for its rock garden, up until around 1950, it was a poor, deserted temple standing in a bamboo grove, rarely visited by anyone. There was no road for tourists crossing in front of the gate, and the temple stood at the far end of an approach lane that passed through a thicket of trees.

During the seventeenth and through the nineteenth centuries, Ryōanji did not have a permanent chief priest, and it was managed by the temple of Myōshinji. When temple fields and forests were nationalized at the time of the Meiji Restoration (the second half of the nineteenth century), Ryōanji is said to have maintained itself by selling off some of the temple treasures and land within the temple precincts. In 1907, Ōsaki Ryōen became the twelfth chief priest of Ryōanji. The previous chief priest, Hakuho Eryō (1544–1628), had lived during the sixteenth and seventeenth centuries, and so Ōsaki became the first permanent chief priest that Ryōanji had had in approximately three hundred years. Ōsaki watched over the temple during its economic nadir, which lasted through the first half of the twentieth century.

Matsukura Shōei became the thirteenth chief priest in 1948. Looking back at the condition of the temple when he assumed his post, Matsukura says:

The temple was in such a wretched condition that it made me think of what it must have been like at the time of the Meiji Restoration. During the war, no one knew when the temple might be bombed, so none of the leaks in the roof were repaired, and the temple grounds, left to run wild with no one to care for them, were one vast expanse of weeds. Because of rationing, food was scarce, and there was barely enough for me alone to keep body and soul together. It was just miserable.[3]

Today, several thousand people visit Ryōanji on a busy day. In comparison, the temple back then must have been truly a pitiful sight. However, it was not only Ryōanji that had trouble supporting a single resident priest. The situation must have been much the same at any temple right after the war. From such humble beginnings, Ryōanji reached an astonishing level of popularity during Matsukura's tenure as chief priest, which lasted from 1948 to 1976.

How did people feel about the famous rock garden when Ryōanji was just a poor temple? If the rock garden was famous, Ryōanji should have been a popular temple, with visitors commensurate with the garden's fame. However, it appears that during the tenure of Ōsaki Ryōen, Ryōanji saw only sporadic visitors. It was by no means one of Kyoto's famous temples. Moreover, what did people think about the beauty of the rock garden? Does this mean that the prewar Ryōanji lacked the beauty to attract people?

There is a photograph (figure 5) that may help us answer these questions: it is a photograph of the rock garden at Ryōanji from before 1918. Half of the garden is buried in snow. Surprisingly, the white sand that appears from under the snow in the foreground of the picture shows no evidence of the familiar flowing water design raked into the sand. Not only that, if one looks closely, there appear to be some sort of tracks or marks on the sand. Since this picture was taken during the winter, perhaps these are not weeds, but footprints? It really is a photo that makes one want to doubt one's eyes.

This rare photograph was not taken by an eccentric with a mania for photography who intended to hide it away under lock and key. It was taken by Tamura Tsuyoshi (1890–1979), a professor of landscape architecture at Tokyo Imperial University. As a pioneer in the field of landscape architecture, he trained many students and had a great influence on the

3. Matsukura Shōei, "Ryōanji konjaku monogatari," *Zen bunka* 64 (1972): 44.

succeeding generations of landscape architects. Tamura is also considered the father of the national park in Japan. He included this photograph of the rock garden at Ryōanji in his textbook on landscape architecture, Zōengaku gairon (Introduction to landscape architecture; 1925).

Speaking of weeds, a large photograph of the rock garden at Ryōanji that shows weeds growing plentifully here and there amid the white sand appears in the book Kyōto bijutsu taikan: Teien (General survey of the art of Kyoto: gardens; 1933)[4] written by the landscape architect and leading authority on the history of Japanese gardens, Shigemori Mirei (1896–1975). Of course, there are numerous photographs from the early twentieth century showing elegant patterns in the white sand, so figure 5, which shows unraked sand, does not represent the rock garden's normal condition. However, the weeds that can be seen in Shigemori's photograph were probably always there.

Tamura praises the beauty of the rock garden as follows:

> The flat garden enclosed by an earthen wall is the height of simplicity and eloquently expresses the highest refinement of the craft of Japanese stone arranging. . . . One cannot but admire the power of the genius of Sōami's design, which penetrates to the hidden depths of the art of landscape architecture. The garden is named "Tiger Cubs Crossing the River." If one is not astonished at the beauty of the structuring of the space, uninfluenced by the garden's subject matter, one will never understand the true value of this garden.[5]

It is obvious that to Tamura, the beauty of this stone garden is not what we imagine it to be today—the pretty flowing water pattern and the balance of proportions which forbid the intrusion of anyone into it. (At least Tamura must have felt this way at the time he wrote Zōengaku gairon.) When Tamura was young, he visited gardens in Europe, the United States, India, and China as he solidified his position as an authority on landscape architecture. In this capacity, Tamura praised the rock garden at Ryōanji without reservation. There is no question that Tamura's assessment established the standard for Ryōanji in the field of Japanese garden history.

In the rock garden illustrated by Tamura's photograph, there are no

4. Amanuma Shun'ichi and Shigemori Mirei, Kyōto bijutsu taikan: Teien (Tokyo: Takayamadō Shoten, 1933).

5. Tamura Tsuyoshi, Zōengaku gairon (Tokyo: Seibidō Shoten, 1925), fig. 40.

raked patterns in the sand. For Tamura, this was also one of the ways the garden could look. While it is not clear what the marks here and there in figure 5 might be, what would it mean if they are footprints? Indeed, the illustration in figure 4 from the guidebook *Miyako rinsen meishō zue* shows priests walking in the garden. This suggests that it was once acceptable to go into the garden. What caused people to stop seeing the garden as an open space that one could enter and to start seeing it instead as a balanced space that could not be disturbed?

THE ROCK GARDEN IN TEXTBOOKS

Recently it has become very common for high schools to organize field trips to Ryōanji. This is probably exclusively due to the fact that the rock garden is featured in school textbooks. The teachers think that the students might be asked about the garden on their college entrance exams, so they want them to see the garden itself and commit it to memory. If they did not feel this way, it is hard to believe that they would go out of their way to organize trips to Ryōanji.

How did the rock garden come to be considered something that a properly educated Japanese should know about? One way to determine this is to research how the rock garden has been treated in school textbooks through the years. Table 2 shows the results of a study of how the rock garden at Ryōanji was treated in middle school history textbooks in the old prewar system compared with the new postwar system. Two hundred and eight pre-WWII textbooks published since the Meiji period (1868–1912) were examined, and of these, representative examples from the beginning of the Shōwa period (1926–1988) are shown. For postwar textbooks, representative examples from various publishers from 1945 to 1954 are listed.

After the war, a middle school education under the new system became compulsory. Therefore, it is reasonable to assume that the material that appears in middle school textbooks is considered the minimum that a Japanese citizen should know. A middle school education was not compulsory under the old system, so the material contained in those textbooks can be considered to represent what a somewhat well-educated Japanese was expected to know.

It is immediately obvious from looking at table 2 that there are only four textbooks from the old prewar middle school system that mention

Table 2. The rock garden at Ryōanji in middle school history textbooks.

Date	Author/editor	Title	Publisher	Information on Ryōanji	Remarks or notes
1927	Fujikake Shizuya	*Chūgaku kokushi* (History for middle school)	Tokyo Kaiseikan	none	
1928	Naganuma Kenkai	*Shinsetsu Nihon shi* (New Japanese history)	Kyōiku Kenkyūkai	none	
1929	Fuzanbō Henshūbu	*Jōkyūyō chūgaku kokushi* (History for middle school, advanced level)	Fuzanbō	none	
1931	Kurita Mototsugu	*Chūgaku sōgō Nihon shi jōkyūyō* (Comprehensive Japanese history for middle school, advanced level)	Chūbunkan Shoten	illustration explanation	Illustration from *Miyako rinsen meishō zue* (Illustrated guide to noted gardens of Kyoto) with the caption: "Muromachi-period garden, Ryōanji, Kyoto. Said to be by Sōami" (141).
1932	Kōda Shigetomo	*Shinsen Nihon rekishi shokyūyō* (Newly compiled Japanese history, beginning level)	Fuzanbō	none	
1932	Takayanagi Mitsutoshi	*Kaitei chūtō Nihon shi jōkyūyō* (Revised Japanese history for middle school, advanced level)	Shūbunkan	none	
1933	Ōmori Kingorō	*Shintai kokushi kyōkasho* (New style Japanese history textbook)	Sanseidō	none	

Year	Author	Title	Publisher	Notes
1933	Saitō Hishō	*Chūgaku kokushi san-go gakunenyō* (Japanese history for middle school, years 3–5)	Dainippon Tosho	none
1934	Shiba Kazumori	*Shinsei kokushi otsu junkyo* (New system Japanese history, conforming to lower level)	Meiji Shoin	none
1934	Miura Hiroyuki	*Chūgaku shin kokushi* (New Japanese history for middle school)	Kaiseikan	none
1935	Itazawa Takeo	*Shintai kōkokushi* (New imperial history)	Seirindō	none
1935	Nakamura Kōya	*Sōgō shinkokushi* (Comprehensive new Japanese history)	Teikoku Shoin	none
1935	Nishida Naojirō	*Chūgaku kokushi tsūki jōkyūyō* (Middle school national history basics, advanced level)	Sekizenkan	Photo caption: "Ryōanji is a Zen temple built by Hosokawa Katsumoto in 1450, located in Hanazono-cho in Kyoto . . . it is popularly called 'tiger cubs crossing the river' because its form resembles a mother tiger carrying its cubs across a river on its back" (60–61).
1937	Kimiya Yasuhiko	*Shin Nihon shi jōkyūyō* (New Japanese history, advanced level)	Fuzanbō	none

Table 2. continued

Date	Author/editor	Title	Publisher	Information on Ryōanji	Remarks or notes
1937	Oikawa Giemon	*Shinshū kokushi kōgakunenyō* (*chūgakkōyō*) (Newly compiled Japanese history for the upper grades [for middle school])	Hoshino Shoten	none	
1937	Uozumi Sōgorō	*Shinshū Nihon shi jōkyūyō* (Newly compiled Japanese history, advanced level)	Hoshino Shoten	photo and diagram	Photo caption: "The garden at the abbot's quarters at Ryōanji, Ukyō–ku, Kyoto. This garden is famous as a great garden. All it contains is fifteen stones scattered on a bed of white sand" (84–85).
1937	Watanabe Yosuke	*Shinsei chūgaku kokushi jōkyūyō* (New system Japanese history for middle school, advanced level)	Rokumeikan	none	
1937	Furuta Ryōichi	*Shinshū chūtō kokushi jōkyūyō* (Newly compiled secondary school Japanese history, advanced level)	Hōbunsha	none	
1937	Sanseidō Editorial Group	*Chūgaku kokushi kyōkasho daiyongakunenyō* (Japanese history textbook for fourth-year middle school)	Sanseidō	photo	Photo caption: "The garden at the abbot's quarters at Ryōanji. Said to be by Sōami"(140–41).

Year	Author	Title	Publisher	Illustration	Quote
1937	Matsumoto Hikojirō	*Shin chūgaku kokugoshi* (New Japanese history for middle school)	Sanseidō	none	
1938	Inobe Shigeo	*Shinshū kokoku shōkōkyūyō* (Newly compiled imperial history, advanced level)	Chūbunkan Shoten	none	
1938	Ryū Susumu	*Shin Nihon rekishi chūgakkō jōkyūyō* (New Japanese history for middle school, upper level)	Shibundō	none	
1939	Kiyohara Sadao	*Chūgaku kokushi yō jōkyūyō* (Middle school Japanese history basics, upper level)	Shūbunkan	none	
1945	Monbushō (Ministry of Education)	*Rekishi kōkoku hen* (Imperial history)	Secondary School Textbooks	none	
1951	Sakamoto Tarō, Ienaga Saburō	*Chūgaku Nihon shi* (Japanese history for middle school)	Gakkō Tosho	photo	"Like gardens in our homes, landscape gardens skillfully combine ponds, stones, and water to represent the quietness and profundity of nature. Zen temples originally began creating gardens in this fashion, and this style was adopted by the warrior class for the gardens in their own homes and has continued to the present day."

Table 2. continued

Date	Author/ editor	Title	Publisher	Information on Ryōanji	Remarks or notes
					Photo caption: "The garden at Ryōanji (Kyoto). This is famous as an example of the garden style of the Higashiyama period and is called *karesansui*, or 'withered landscape'" (95–96).
1951	Kodama Kōta	*Chūgakusei no rekishi* (History for middle school students)	Nihon Shoseki	photo	Photo caption: "Rock garden. There are many Japanese gardens which skillfully harmonize stones, trees, and water, but this garden at Ryōanji in Kyoto creates a beautiful effect using only stones" (101).
1951	Fujii Jintarō, Sugano Jirō	*Sodachiyuku Nihon* (Growing Japan, vol. 1)	Phoenix Shoin	photo	"Architecture was also heavily influenced by Zen, and the Zen style of building was adopted for residences. This style was called *shoin zukuri* and rooms were built with alcoves (*tokonoma*), and staggered shelves (*chigaidana*). People would sequester themselves in a secluded reading room and read books and compose poetry.

| 1951 | Tōkyō Bunrika Daigaku Rekishigaku Kenkyūkai | *Watashitachi no Nihon shi* (Our Japanese History) | Ai'ikusha | none | Outside the sliding doors would be a garden, not like the gardens in the homes of the ancient aristocracy, but a quiet garden imbued with a feeling of loneliness. It is said that since gardens like this were created under the influence of Zen, the meaning of the garden cannot be understood without an understanding of Zen." Photo caption: "Gardens in Ryōanji, Kyoto (left), Higashiyama Culture, Nijō Castle, Kyoto (upper right), Momoyama Culture, Tokyo, Rikugien (lower right), Edo period. What kind of feeling do you get from these gardens? Compare them while paying close attention to the text" (98–99). |

Table 2. continued

Date	Author/editor	Title	Publisher	Information on Ryōanji	Remarks or notes
1951	Tōkyō Daigaku Bungakubunai Shigakkai	*Nihon no ayumi* (Japan's journey)	Yamakawa Suppansha	text explanation	"At around this time many excellent gardens were created. The gardens at Tenryūji, Rokuonji, and Ryōanji are famous as great gardens" (80).
1951	Ozawa Eiichi, Sano Masanori	*Chūgaku Nihon shi* (Japanese history for middle school)	Shimizu Shoin	none	
1952	Wakamori Tarō	*Nihon no hatten* (The development of Japan)	Jitsugyō no Nihonsha	photo	"Unlike the gardens in the homes of the ancient aristocracy, gardens filled with a quiet and profound aspect and characterized by a sense of loneliness began to be created. With some of these gardens it seemed as though what the garden was expressing could not be understood without an understanding of Zen" (97).
1952	Hiroshima Shigaku Kenkyūkai	*Watashitachi no rekishi* (Our history)	Yanagihara Shoten	photo	
1952	Konishi Shirō, Ienaga Saburō	*Chūtō Nihon shi* (Secondary school Japanese history)	Sanseidō Shuppan	none	In *Social Studies, Middle School History* (approved in 1954) by the same

	Author	Title	Publisher	Illustration	
					authors, there is a diagram of the rock garden accompanied by the following caption: "The rock garden at Ryōanji. Compare it to a painting by Sesshū. You should feel some similarities" (121).
1953	Nishioka Toranosuke	*Atarashii Nihon shi* (New Japanese history)	Tokyo Shoseki	text explanation	"Gardens of this period were influenced by Zen, and there were many excellent gardens created which display a profound quietness. In addition to the garden at Rokuonji where the Kinkaku is located, the gardens at Saihōji and Ryōanji are famous as excellent gardens" (85–86).
1953	Toyota Takeshi	*Chūgakusei no shakaika: Nihon shi* (Social studies for middle school: Japanese history)	Chūkyō Shuppan	none	
1953	Morisue Yoshiaki, Matsuzaki Hisakazu	*Chūgakusei no Nihon shi* (Japanese history for middle school students)	Futaba	photo	"Under the influence of Zen, a new architectural style for the residences of the warrior class called *shoin zukuri* was born, and esoteric gardens which skillfully harmonized stones, trees, and water were constructed" (90).

Table 2. continued

Date	Author/editor	Title	Publisher	Information on Ryōanji	Remarks or notes
1953	Higo Kazuo	*Chūgaku no Nihon shi* (Japanese history for middle school)	Dainippon Yūbenkai/ Kōdansha	text explanation	"The garden at [Ashikaga] Yoshimasa's Higashiyama mountain retreat is representative of this entire period and is built in the *kaiyūshiki* or 'circular excursion' style; that is, it is built in a dynamic fashion so it presents a pleasing view from any angle. In comparison to this, rock gardens, like the rock garden at Ryōanji, attempt to express the form of nature in the simplest possible way, using only stones on a bed of white sand" (100).
1953	Kishiro Shūichi	*Chūgakusei no Nihon rekishi* (Japanese history for middle school students)	Shōryūdō	photo	Photo caption: "A rare rock garden. This is the garden at Ryōanji in Kyoto, which is constructed only of fifteen large and small rocks arranged on a bed of white sand without any trees or greenery" (100).
1954	Mutai Risaku	*Chūgaku shakai: rekishiteki naiyō o shu to suru mono* (Middle school social studies, history; vol. 1)	Kairyūdō	photo	Photo caption: "The rock garden at Ryōanji is very simple, consisting of nothing but fifteen stones arranged

| 1954 | Nakamura Ichirō | *Chūgaku shakai: kodai kara kindai e* (Middle school social studies: from the past to the present) | photo |

on a bed of white sand within a rectangular space, without any trees or greenery. However, the arrangement of the stones is done with such consummate skill that if even one of the fifteen stones were to be moved, the beauty of the garden would instantly disappear" (136–37).

"The Higashiyama culture was transmitted during the Warring States period by the Ōuchi clan, other powerful warlords, and Sakai merchants. One of the expressions of this culture was the creation here and there of gardens consisting of practically nothing but arrangements of stones, seemingly patterned after landscape paintings by Sesshū. In particular, the rock garden at Ryōanji, resembling an ink painting done in only a few strokes, is a good example of the distinctive characteristics of Higashiyama culture" (136–37).

Table 2. continued

Date	Author/editor	Title	Publisher	Information on Ryōanji	Remarks or notes
1954	Wakamori Tarō, Kimura Takeyasu, Matsuo Toshirō	*Shakai seikatsu no shinpo: rekishi-teki naiyō o shu to suru mono* (Advancements in social life: history)	Shūei Shuppan	photo	"Architecture for homes also adopted the Zen temple style, resulting in the *shoin zukuri* style, which forms the basis for the style of today's Japanese home. Along with this the attitude towards gardens also changed, and gardens imbued with a quietude and profundity began to be created. The gardens at Tenryūji and Ryōanji, among others, are famous as great gardens." Photo caption: "The rock garden at Ryōanji. This garden has no trees or shrubs and consists solely of an arrangement of a few stones" (136–37).
1954	Nihon Shakaika Kyōiku Renmei	*Rekishi no nagare* (The flow of history)	Kyōiku Shuppan	none	

| 1954 | Mori Katsumi, Takeuchi Rizō, Fujiki Kunihiko | *Chūgaku shakai: Nihon to sekai rekishi-teki naiyō o shu to suru mono* (Social studies for middle school: Japan and the world, history, vol. 1) | Teikoku Shoin | photo | "As the tea ceremony became more widely practiced, the aesthetics of the tea ceremony began to affect how gardens were made. The quiet and refined Zen spirit was grafted on to the gardens which were built to harmonize with the *shinden zukuri* [palace style] of architecture that had existed since the Heian period, resulting in gardens which were extremely symbolic. Representative gardens of this type are the gardens at Tenryūji and Saihōji [The Moss Temple] and the *karesansui* [withered landscape] garden at Ryōanji." Photo caption: "The garden at Ryōanji. This is popularly called a 'rock garden,' where a number of large stones are arranged on a bed of white gravel. It attempts to recreate the appearance of a vast sea" (136–37). |

Table 2. continued

Date	Author/ editor	Title	Publisher	Information on Ryōanji	Remarks or notes
1954	Kobayashi Fumio, Wakamori Tarō, Aono Hisao	*Shakai no shinpo* (The progress of society; vol. 1)	Kokon Shoin	photo	Photo caption: "The garden at Ryōanji. Fifteen rocks of varying sizes are scattered on a bed of white sand" (121).
1954	Kawahara Shunsaku, Tomita Yoshirō, Higo Kazuo	*Ningen to rekishiteki naiyō o shu to suru mono* (People and history)	Taishūkan	none	
1954	Kinoshita Kazuo, Matsumoto Hikojirō, Kitada Kōzō	*Nihon no seichō* (*rekishiteki naiyō o shu to suru mono*) (Japan's growth: history; vol. 1)	Nitchi Shuppan	photo	"In addition, gardens were built for *shoin zukuri* style homes making it possible for people to enjoy the magical charm of the natural landscape in their own homes. From this period onward gardens were built in great numbers. Warlords who spent their days concerned with struggles for political influence not only calmed their spirits through Zen meditation, they also sought spiritual comfort by

| 1954 | Rekishi Kyōiku Kenkyūkai | Sekai no ugoki to Nihon no ayumi (World trends and Japan's journey) | Nihon Shoin | photo | constructing their mansions in this fashion."

"Gardens were originally seen as accompaniments for architectural structures, but from this time onwards the garden became the center of attention and the buildings were secondary. Also, gardens came to be characterized by a clean, quiet, and elegant simplicity that harmonized with Zen aesthetics. Representative gardens of this type are the gardens at Tenryūji, Saihōji [The Moss Temple], and the garden at Ryōanji (143). |

Note: Representative textbooks from various publishers, 1926–1954. This list includes all of the pre–World War II textbooks mentioning Ryōanji that I was able to find.

the rock garden at Ryōanji: one each written by Kurita Mototsugu (1890–1955), Nishida Naojirō (1886–1964), and Uozumi Sōgorō (1889–1959), and one published by Sanseidō Henshūsho.

Kurita's book, *Chūgaku sōgō Nihon shi jōkyūyō* (Comprehensive Japanese history for middle school, advanced level; 1931), reproduces the illustration of the rock garden from the eighteenth-century *Miyako rinsen meishō zue*. Underneath the illustration is the following caption: "Muromachi-period garden, Ryōanji, Kyoto. Said to be by Sōami." There is no further explanation. This seems to be a rather offhand way to treat the garden.

The books by Nishida, Uozumi, and Sanseidō Henshūsho all include photographs of the rock garden. Among these, Nishida's book, *Chūgaku kokushi tsūki jōkyūyō* (Middle school national history basics, advanced level; 1935), sets aside a particularly large amount of space for the rock garden. He devotes an entire page to photographs of Tenryūji and Ryōanji, with the discussion of the photographs on the following page.

Usually, the discussion of Ryōanji is located in the section of the textbooks that discusses what is called the Higashiyama culture of the late fifteenth century. In prewar textbooks, the garden that was considered to represent Higashiyama culture was the garden at the Ginkaku (Silver Pavilion). If one were to look further, perhaps other prewar textbooks that discuss Ryōanji could be found. However, it can be said that old-style middle school Japanese history textbooks that include Ryōanji were not in the mainstream.

After the war was over, however, everything changed. Like bamboo shoots popping up after a rain, official textbooks for the new postwar middle school system prominently featuring the rock garden at Ryōanji, complete with photographs, started to appear en masse. The same is true of textbooks used in the new high school system. While not shown in table 2, this trend continued after 1955, and by a process of osmosis, the "knowledge" that the rock garden at Ryōanji was representative of Higashiyama culture became an unquestioned part of the "Japanese common understanding." This is probably the direct cause of Ryōanji becoming such a popular destination for school field trips.

The textbooks merely state the "fact" that the rock garden is representative of Higashiyama culture. Except for one or two of the textbooks, there is little or no mention of how beautiful the garden is, much less anything about how it expresses Zen thought. It is simply presented as part of a trio of related ideas for rote memorization: "Ryōanji, withered landscapes, Higashiyama culture." Therefore, the Japanese were by no means educated about the "beauty" of Ryōanji or shared its appreciation in common. In this sense, the theatrical forms of *kabuki*, *noh*, and *bunraku* are the same. Many Japanese have been educated to believe that things they have not seen themselves are "Japanese culture."

How did this "historical understanding" of Ryōanji come about in the first place? To discover this we should first consult that giant in the field of Japanese history, Kuroita Katsumi (1874–1946). Kuroita was a professor at Tokyo Imperial University who, leading the university's Historiographical Institute, completed the work that is a foundational text for the study of Japanese history—the sixty-four volume *Shintei zōho kokushi taikei* (New revised and expanded overview of Japanese history) published between 1929 and 1946. His primary work, *Kokushi no kenkyū* (Studies in Japanese history; 1908), served as a model for prewar comprehensive Japanese history texts.

Ryōanji is not mentioned in *Kokushi no kenkyū*. For Kuroita, Higashiyama culture was represented by the Ginkaku for architecture and gardens, the Shōren'in school for calligraphy, and the works of Sesshū (1420–1506) and Kanō Masanobu (1434–1530) for painting.[6] In addition, in *Shintei Nihon rekishi* (New revised Japanese history; 1906),[7] which Kuroita wrote as a textbook for use in the old middle school system, he presents the garden at Manpukuji temple in the city of Masuda in Shimane prefecture, said to have been designed by Sesshū, as a representative Higashiyama culture garden.

It was not until after the 1920s that the rock garden at Ryōanji began to attract attention, even among specialists in the history of Japanese gardens. Actually, it is more accurate to say that the field of Japanese garden history itself was not established until after the 1920s. So it is not so strange if Kuroita did not pay attention to Ryōanji during the Meiji period.

In the area of comprehensive history books for the general reader, for example, Ryōanji is not even mentioned in *Kokumin no Nihon shi* (Japanese history for the Japanese; 1923),[8] published under the editorial supervision of the novelist Tsubouchi Shōyō (1859–1935). Iwanami Shoten published a revised version of Kuroita's *Kokushi no kenkyū* in 1936, but Ryōanji re-

---

6. Kuroita Katsumi, *Kōtei kokushi no kenkyū kakusetsu ge* (Tokyo: Iwanami Shoten, 1936).

7. Kuroita Katsumi, *Shintei Nihon rekishi* (Tokyo: Yoshikawa Kōbunkan, 1906).

8. Usuta Zan'un, *Kokumin no Nihon shi dai 7 hen: Muromachi jidai* (Tokyo: Waseda Daigaku Shuppanbu, 1923).

mained unmentioned. It is quite conceivable that *Kokushi no kenkyū*, written by such an authority on Japanese history as Kuroita, continued to exercise an influence on Ryōanji's place in history. Broadly speaking, this is probably why Ryōanji is hardly ever mentioned in prewar Japanese history books.

While Kuroita ignored Ryōanji, there was another historian who looked upon Ryōanji differently: Nishida Naojirō of Kyoto Imperial University. Nishida specialized in Japanese history and had established his own "cultural history" approach, which placed history within the continuous flow of culture. He was a leading figure in the field of Japanese history with a stature equal to that of Kuroita.

Nishida featured the rock garden at Ryōanji prominently in his primary work, *Nihon bunkashi josetsu* (Introduction to Japanese cultural history; 1932), even including photographs. Continuing in this vein he devoted considerable space to the rock garden in textbooks for middle school. Nishida summed up the spiritual disposition of the Muromachi period (1336–1573) as an idealistic "World of the Lower Self." Nishida holds that during this period in history, a spiritualistic tendency developed and that a sort of self-centeredness was operating in the culture. The term "Lower Self" is identical to what is written in the commentary currently displayed on the wall of the abbot's quarters at Ryōanji. If we were to search for the origin of the phrase "the Lower Self," I think the trail would lead back to Nishida's book. Nishida explains the rock garden as follows:

> In this garden made only of stones, in order to perceive the spirit of all creation resting tranquilly behind an unnatural external form, the objective external appearance is not, in reality, the main issue, but, rather, a subjective attitude is of primary importance. It goes without saying that a great part of this lies in not depending on a feeling but rather on a spirit which transcends feeling, not on an objective value but on attempting to subjectively perceive the life of the garden.[9]

Nishida is saying that the garden must be viewed introspectively. Today, this is how the garden is understood in the popular imagination; it is my opinion that Nishida was the first historical scholar to say this. However, I

9. Nishida Naojirō, *Nihon bunkashi josetsu* (Tokyo: Kaizōsha, 1932), 472.

would like to point out that Nishida by no means referred to the rock garden as a Zen garden. He concluded by saying that the garden was an idealistic "World of the Lower Self."

Nishida's understanding of the rock garden influenced his disciple, the historical scholar Naramoto Tatsuya (1913–2001). Naramoto writes that when he was a student, "taking our cue from what our mentor Nishida Naojirō wrote in his well known book *Nihon bunkashi josetsu*, we felt that this garden should not be overlooked."[10]

Regarding what Nishida wrote about the rock garden, Naramoto says, "for me, who had been taught history up to that point from the perspectives of politics and economics, this made me deeply reconsider this approach. From that point on, I began to feel strongly that history was not just a matter of documents and records, but that we could learn about it from many different things."[11] This realization became the starting point for Naramoto's subsequent study of history.

On one side was the Kuroita/Tokyo Imperial University school of positivist history, which emphasized historical documents. On the other side was the Nishida/Kyoto Imperial University school of cultural history, which saw history in a multitude of different things. Ranging along this axis of opposition, some textbooks ignored the rock garden and others emphasized it.

One of the people who gave Ryōanji's rock garden a splashy debut in postwar textbooks was the historical scholar Ienaga Saburō (1913–2002). Ienaga prominently featured the rock garden at Ryōanji in *Chūgaku Nihon shi* (Japanese history for middle school; approved in 1951) which he coauthored for use in the new middle school system, and in his *Shin Nihon shi* (New Japanese history; approved in 1952) written for use in the new high school system.

Shin Nihon shi is conspicuous for the space it devotes to the rock garden. *Shin Nihon shi* is also notable in that it was not initially approved by the Ministry of Education. This was the first time in Ienaga's career that such a thing had happened, and he later successfully contested this decision in the so-called Textbook Trial. Beneath a photograph of the rock garden can be found the following explanation, which goes so far as to touch upon things like beauty and philosophy.

10. Naramoto Tatsuya, "Ryōanji zuisō," *Zen bunka* 64 (1972): 56.
11. Ibid., 57.

This garden, with nothing but stones arranged on white sand and expressing an air of elegant simplicity similar to an ink painting, succeeds brilliantly in symbolizing the vastness of heaven and earth in a limited area.[12]

Another book which has an article on the rock garden with accompanying photographs is *Nihon shi* (Japanese history), a textbook for the new high school system edited by the Historical Academy of the Faculty of Letters at the University of Tokyo. This textbook was approved in 1951. In it, the rock garden is still presented in an offhand manner: "The garden at Ryōanji is located in the city of Kyoto and is called the garden of the 'tiger cubs crossing the river.' The garden was reputedly created by Sōami."[13] Even after Kuroita was no longer there, the Historical Academy of the University of Tokyo simply referred to the rock garden as symbolizing "tiger cubs crossing the river." What accounts for the gap between this and Ienaga's "symbolizing the vastness of heaven and earth?"

It seems worth our while to look a little more closely at the historian Ienaga Saburō. Perhaps we can discover what was behind Ienaga's feelings about the rock garden at Ryōanji from his autobiography, *Ichi rekishi gakusha no ayumi* (One historian's journey; 1977).[14]

In 1931, Ienaga entered Tokyo College, which at that time operated under the old system, but due to his abhorrence of Marxism, the dominant philosophy in secondary education, he devoted himself to neo-Kantian philosophy. Neo-Kantian philosophy enjoyed a vogue in Japan around the mid 1920s, the same time that Herrigel was invited to Japan, so it seems that Ienaga was a little behind the times. In 1934, Ienaga entered the Japanese History Department of the Faculty of Letters of Tokyo Imperial University. At that time, Kuroita Katsumi was the presiding professor of the Japanese History Department. However, the classroom was really run by Hiraizumi Kiyoshi (1895–1984), who was known as a radical Japanese nationalist, and Ienaga remembers the classroom being permeated with Japanese nationalism.

Amid this atmosphere, in 1935, Ienaga visited temples and shrines in the Kansai region on a history department study tour. He was particularly impressed with the Buddhist art housed at the temple of Yakushiji and

---

12. Ienaga Saburō, *Shin Nihon shi* (Tokyo: Sanseidō, 1952), 105.

13. Tōkyō Daigaku Bungakubunai Shigakkai, ed., *Nihon shi* (Tokyo: Yamakawa Shuppan, 1951), 130.

14. Ienaga Saburō, *Ichi rekishi gakusha no ayumi* (Tokyo: Sanseidō, 1977).

from this point onward, he developed an increasing interest in Buddhism and became engrossed in religious questions. Even after starting to work for the Historiographical Institute, he devoted his energy to researching early Buddhism. If this switch from neo-Kantian philosophy to Buddhism seems familiar, that is not so surprising: Ienaga traveled a road very similar to Herrigel, who also started with neo-Kantian philosophy.

From the beginning, the road that Ienaga traveled as a scholar was not smooth. He faced an ordeal only three months into his job at the Historiographical Institute. Ienaga contributed a paper on the *Nihon Shoki* (The chronicles of Japan—an ancient work of Japanese history) to the magazine *Rekishi chiri* (Historical geography), which was edited by Ienaga's seniors in the Historiographical Institute. However, he was forced to withdraw it on the grounds that it could be interpreted as showing disrespect for the emperor. Disillusioned with the scholarship of the Historiographical Institute, it seems that Ienaga carried this trauma with him for a long time afterwards. In any case, Ienaga only worked for the Historiographical Institute for four years, until 1941. He eventually became a professor at the Tokyo Teacher's College after working at various places, including Niigata High School.

Immediately after the end of World War II, Ienaga began writing a textbook for middle school at the request of the Fuzanbō publishing company. This book was published as *Shin Nihon shi* (1947)[15] and was aimed at the general reader. It was the first postwar comprehensive history book written by a single individual. It is very interesting to note that *Shin Nihon shi* does not mention the rock garden at Ryōanji. Overall, rather than being a work of cultural history, it is an orthodox comprehensive history that reminds one of Kuroita, with an emphasis on politics and economics.

Twelve years after *Shin Nihon shi*, Ienaga wrote *Nihon bunkashi* (Japanese cultural history; 1959). In this book, Ienaga presents the rock gardens at Ryōanji and Daisen'in at Daitokuji as follows: "these gardens are also artistic expressions of the pantheistic philosophy of Buddhism, which tries to see the life of the entire universe even in a single atom."[16] By explaining the rock garden in terms of the Buddhist worldview, perhaps Ienaga was trying to emphasize the difference between his approach to history and that of the University of Tokyo.

Ienaga began his journey as a historian as a follower of the University

---

15. Ienaga Saburō, *Shin Nihon shi* (Tokyo: Fuzanbō, 1947).
16. Ienaga Saburō, *Nihon bunkashi* (Tokyo: Iwanami Shinsho, 1959), 152.

of Tokyo approach to history, which emphasized Japanese nationalism, but then broke away from it, spending the rest of his life traveling a different road. Buddhism was Ienaga's spiritual support in this situation, and it is likely that it was Ienaga's absorption in Buddhism that led him to emphasize Ryōanji. I think that it is probably this sort of background that lay behind Ienaga's enthusiasm for describing the rock garden at Ryōanji as "symbolizing the vastness of heaven and earth" when most high school textbooks during 1951–1952 treated it simply as "tiger cubs crossing the river."

Both before and after the war, Nishida continued to write about the rock garden at Ryōanji in school textbooks. *Nippon to sekai* (Japan and the world; approved in 1956) features a photograph of the rock garden with this caption: "in an area covered with white pebbles a few rocks are placed. The white pebbles are always raked so that a pattern is left. With only these things, an attempt is made to express a vast sea. This is commonly referred to as a rock garden."[17]

Quite a number of postwar middle school textbooks focus attention on Ryōanji, even if not to the extent of Nishida and Ienaga. In the final analysis, it can be said that at least as far as the rock garden is concerned, the postwar textbooks continued and amplified the prewar style of Nishida, who had been banned from holding any government position after the war. I cannot shake the feeling that the cultural history approach pioneered by Nishida was chosen to fill the void left after the view of Japanese history championed by the University of Tokyo, which glorified the Japanese empire, had been banished from Japanese textbooks.

UNSIGHTLY STONES AND A WEEPING CHERRY TREE

Leaving historians aside for the moment, I would like to address the question of what specialists in the history of Japanese gardens have said about the rock garden at Ryōanji. First, I would like to go back in history and trace the development of two discussions: that concerning who created the garden and that concerning its aesthetics, confining myself to the time up until the 1940s, before the view that "rock gardens = Zen" came to the fore.

Originally, a villa belonging to the aristocratic Tokudaiji family, for the

---

17. Nishida Naojirō and Suzuki Shigetaka, *Nihon to sekai* (Tokyo: Teikoku Shoin, 1956), 116.

use of the court nobility, was located on the land that now forms the precincts of Ryōanji. Hosokawa Katsumoto (1430–1473), a governor general under the Ashikaga shōgunate, took over the land in 1450 and built Ryōanji, installing a prelate from Myōshinji, Giten Genshō (1393–1462), as chief priest.

There are a number of theories regarding the identity of the rock garden's creator. The first candidate is the painter Sōami. While there is no corroborating evidence, Sōami is also said to be the creator of the rock garden at the Daisen'in, a sub-temple of Daitokuji in Kyoto. Among the seventeenth- and eighteenth-century documents that name Sōami as the creator of the garden are *Saga kōtei* (Journey to Saga; 1680),[18] *Kaiki* (The record of Sophora; 1729),[19] *Kyūai zuihitsu* (Dusty backpack essays; 1781–1788),[20] and the previously mentioned *Miyako rinsen meishō zue* (1799).[21]

The second candidate for creator of the rock garden is Hosokawa Katsumoto. The seventeenth- and eighteenth-century documents that name Katsumoto as the creator of the rock garden include *Tōzai rekiranki* (Record of journeys to the east and west; 1681),[22] *Yōshūfu shi* (Chronicle of Yōshūfu; 1682),[23] *Kyō habutae oridome* (Kyoto silk: the last volume; 1689),[24] *Sanshū myōseki shi* (Famous places of Sanshū; 1702),[25] *Wakan sansai zue* (The illustrated encyclopedia of Japan and China; 1712),[26] and *Miyako meisho zue*

18. Kurokawa Michisuke, *Saga kōtei* (1680), in *Kurokawa Michisuke kinki yūran shikō*, ed. Kamimura Kankō (Kyoto: Junpūbō, 1910): 43.

19. Yamashina Dōan, *Kaiki* (1729), in *Nihon koten bungaku taikei*, Vol. 96, ed. Nakamura Yukihiko et al. (Tokyo: Iwanami Shoten, 1965): 461.

20. Momoi Tōu, *Kyūai zuihitsu* (1781–1788), in *Nihon zuihitsu taisei dai 2 ki*, Vol. 12, ed. Nihon Zuihitsu Taisei Henshūbu (Tokyo: Yoshikawa Kōbunkan, 1974), 200.

21. I referred to the following books: Hisatsune Shūji, *Kyōto meien ki: Chūkan* (Tokyo: Seibundō Shinkōsha, 1968); Shigemori Mirei and Shigemori Kanto, *Nihon teienshi taikei*, Vol. 7, *Muromachi no niwa* (3) (Tokyo: Shakai Shisōsha, 1971).

22. Kurokawa Michisuke, *Tōzai rekiranki* (1681), in Kamimura, *Kurokawa Michisuke kinki yūran shikō*, 109.

23. Kurokawa Michisuke, *Yōshūfu shi* (1682), in *Shinshū Kyōto sōsho*, 2nd ed., Vol. 10, ed. Noma Kōshin (Kyoto: Rinsen Shoten, 1968), 307.

24. Koshōshi, *Kyō habutae oridome* (1689), in *Shinshū Kyōto sōsho*, 2nd ed., Vol. 2, ed. Noma Kōshin (Kyoto: Rinsen Shoten, 1976): 391.

25. Hakue, *Sanshū myōseki shi* (1702), in *Shinshū Kyōto sōsho*, 2nd ed., Vols. 15 and 16, ed. Noma Kōshin (Kyoto: Rinsen Shoten, 1976), 15:219.

26. Terajima Ryōan, *Wakan sansai zue* (1712), repr. in *Tōyō bunko*, Vols. 447, 451, 456, 458, 462, 466, 471, 476, 481, 487, 494, 498, 505, 510, 516, 521, 527, 532 (Tokyo: Heibonsha, 1985–1991), 498:98–99.

(Illustrated guide to noted Places in Kyoto; 1780).[27] Among these, *Saga kōtei, Tōzai rekiranki*, and the *Yōshūfu shi* were all written at about the same time by the doctor and Confucian scholar Kurokawa Dōyū (Michisuke) (d. 1691), yet they do not agree on who originally created the rock garden. As such, they cannot be relied upon.

Sōami and Katsumoto have always been considered the two people most likely to have created the rock garden. However, there is also another theory that a tea master named Kanamori Sōwa (1584–1656) designed it. This theory is based on the fact that Sōwa is named as the garden's creator in the *Ryōan shi* (Chronicle of Ryōan; 1744–1747) and the *Daiunzan shikō* (The record of Daiunzan; 1798)—both records of Ryōanji.

The names "Kotarō" and "Seijirō" (or Hikojirō) are chiseled on the rock nearest to the front wall as viewed from the abbot's quarters. These names are on the far side of the rock and the characters are quite weathered, so visitors to the garden cannot see them. There is one theory that Kotarō and Seijirō (or Hikojirō) themselves are the creators of the garden.

There are other theories too numerous to count, including the theory that the garden was created by Giten, the first chief priest of Ryōanji; by Shiken Saidō, the chief priest of Saihōji; or by Kobori Enshū (1579–1647). It is much too difficult to pursue all of the theories, so I hope that I can be forgiven for confining myself to the most commonly accepted ones.

At one point in history, there was a major event that changed the appearance of the garden—a fire that occurred in 1797. In the drawing of Ryōanji that appears in the *Miyako rinsen meishō zue* (figure 4), the abbot's quarters are not shown. This is because they had not yet been rebuilt following the fire. After the fire, the buildings of the Saigen'in, which had been located to the west, were reconstructed in a different location, and the abbot's quarters were rebuilt. These are believed to be the abbot's quarters which presently exist. There is a theory that when the abbot's quarters were rebuilt, there was a subtle change in the relative locations of the rock garden and the abbot's quarters. There is even a theory that when the abbot's quarters were rebuilt, the author of the *Miyako rinsen meishō zue* himself, a poet named Akisato Ritō, changed the placement of the rocks. All in all, this garden certainly seems to stir up the imagination.

Now, armed with the understanding that the placement of the rocks has not always been as it is now, we can try to go back and discover when the opinion that the garden is attractive was first voiced. Starting with

27. Akisato Ritō, *Miyako meisho zue* (Kyoto: Yoshinoya Tamehachi, 1780).

documents concerning the garden prior to the 1797 fire and then gradually moving closer to the present, I would like to explore the twin discussions that have taken place among students of stone gardens concerning the creator of the garden and its aesthetics.

The *Yōshūfu shi*, which names Katsumoto as the garden's creator, says the following: "The arrangement of the rocks is not the work of a common craftsman. Those who create such gardens take this as the example to follow."[28] Thus we can infer that already in the seventeenth century the garden was considered to be beautiful.

On the other hand, *Kaiki*, which considers Sōami to be the garden's creator, says that "The garden at Ryōanji is reputedly by Sōami. It is called 'tiger cubs crossing the river.' It is a noted garden, but I have no idea whether it is a fine garden or a poor one." This strikes me as a very honest opinion. The feelings of the author of *Kaiki* towards the garden are very similar to my own. However, there is no guarantee that the rock garden during this time was the same as it is now.

I would like to discuss one more document from the Edo period. The *Ryōan-shi*, written by a Rinzai Zen priest named Muchaku Dōchū (1653–1744), says the following: "There are a number of large and small unsightly stones in front of the abbot's quarters. They were placed there by the tea master Sōwa. They are called 'tiger cubs crossing the river.' Public opinion praises this garden as being skillfully executed." This passage names Kanamori Sōwa as the garden's creator and relates the esteem in which it is held, but the phrase "unsightly stones" (*shūseki*) troubles me.

If this sentence is understood in the normal way, it appears to be saying that Sōwa created the garden by skillfully arranging unsightly stones. However, people such as the modernist architect Horiguchi Sutemi (1895–1984) did not interpret it in this way. While the author of the *Ryōan-shi* may have used the phrase "unsightly stones" to mean precisely that, Horiguchi said that it is possible he used the phrase to mean "uncut stones of irregular sizes and shapes."[29]

Are the stones at Ryōanji really unsightly after all? Shigemori Mirei was a giant of landscape architecture who defined an epoch. In addition to personally creating many gardens, such as those at Tōfukuji and the Matsuo Grand Shrine in Kyoto, Shigemori also surveyed gardens all over Japan

28. Kurokawa, *Yōshūfu shi*, 307

29. Horiguchi Sutemi, *Niwa to kūkan kōsei no dentō* (Tokyo: Kashima Shuppankai, 1965), 179.

and was widely known as an independent historian of gardens. In his role as a researcher of garden history, he is also noted as the man who published the twenty-four volume *Nihon teienshi zukan* (Illustrated guide to the history of Japanese gardens; 1936–1939). To the end of his life, Shigemori unwaveringly held to the theory that the rock garden at Ryōanji had been created during the Muromachi period.

Shigemori was of the opinion that the stones used were not particularly good. In his major work *Nihon teienshi taikei* (A historical overview of Japanese gardens; 1971–1976) coauthored with his son Kanto,[30] Shigemori says, "as garden stones, the individual stones are by no means of high quality," but that since "the creator was of such high caliber" it was possible to create a garden of such excellence.[31]

It seems that professionals in the fields of architecture and gardens will go to great lengths to avoid associating the word "unsightly" with the rock garden at Ryōanji. Their conviction that the rock garden was beautiful perhaps led both Horiguchi and Shigemori to take the positions that they did.

The historian of Japanese gardens Ōyama Heishirō (1917–) was associated with Shigemori. He is an independent scholar known for such works as *Ryōanji sekitei nanatsu no nazo o toku* (Answers to the seven riddles of the rock garden at Ryōanji; 1970). Even Ōyama, who accepts the fact that the stones are "unsightly" in the sense that "considered individually the stones are neither particularly fine or exceptional," turns his whole argument on its end by concluding that "the fact that a superior rock garden was made using inferior stones just shows the genius of the garden's creator."[32] Ōyama unquestioningly bases his argument on the major premise that the garden is beautiful. In and of itself, this shows that he is starting from the conviction that the garden is beautiful.

It appears to me that the discussions regarding the creator of the garden and when it was made have proceeded from a certain fixed point of view that the garden is beautiful. A concrete example of this can be seen from closely examining the various interpretations of the incident of "Hideyoshi's Weeping Cherry Tree."

30. Shigemori changed his given name to "Mirei" after the artist Millet and named his son "Kanto" after the philosopher Kant.

31. Shigemori and Shigemori, *Nihon teienshi taikei*, 83.

32. Ōyama Heishirō, *Ryōanji sekitei nanatsu no nazo o toku* (Tokyo: Kōdansha, 1970), 100–1.

Apparently there was once a magnificent weeping cherry tree (*shidare zakura*) located in the front right hand side of the garden as viewed from the abbot's quarters. It is not clear how long the weeping cherry tree was there; one theory holds that it burned down along with the abbot's quarters in the fire of 1797. While it is not noticeable unless one looks closely, the remains of an old tree stump can still be seen.

In 1588, Toyotomi Hideyoshi (1537–1598), the general who brought the Warring States period to an end, visited Ryōanji, and upon seeing that even though it was spring the weeping cherry tree still had not bloomed and that there was snow on its branches, composed the following poem:

The unseasonal snow
fallen on the cherry branches
says "Flowers! You are late!"

toki naranu
sakura ga eda ni
furu yuki wa
hana o ososhi to
sasoi kinuran

At the time of his visit, Hideyoshi issued a decree stating, "it is forbidden to remove the stones and trees of the garden." These events are recorded in the historical document *Ryōanji monjo* (Documents of Ryōanji) preserved at the temple. One can clearly see that Hideyoshi was deeply moved by the elegance of Ryōanji.

In his voluminous work *Muromachi jidai teien shi* (History of Muromachi-period gardens; 1934), the authority on the history of Japanese gardens Toyama Eisaku says that it is inconceivable that in Hideyoshi's time the garden was as it is now, without a single tree or blade of grass.[33] (Toyama had already published this argument in the mid-1920s in the art history journal *Kokka*.[34]) Toyama said that since the cherry tree which was supposedly there in Hideyoshi's time no longer exists, it is most reasonable to assume that the garden was created in the Edo period by Sōwa, as recorded

33. Toyama Eisaku, *Muromachi jidai teienshi* (Tokyo: Iwanami Shoten, 1934), 647–48.

34. Toyama Eisaku, "Ryōanji teien no dentōteki setsumei o haisu (jō)," *Kokka* 35: 1 (1925): 26–30, idem, "Ryōanji teien no dentōteki setsumei o haisu (ge)," *Kokka* 35: 2 (1925): 58–64.

in the *Ryōan shi*. Moreover, Toyama also stated that the Sōami theory was a result of the sound of Sōwa's name being corrupted to "Sōami."

However, in opposition to Toyama, an art historian and professor at the Tokyo University of Art, Wakimoto Sokurō (1883–1963), advanced the theory that it was "Sōami" that was corrupted to "Sōwa" rather than the other way around.[35] He cited two reasons for this: first, it is not certain that the cherry tree that Hideyoshi saw was in the same place the garden is now, and second, the style of the garden is not consistent with Sōwa's taste.

Shigemori also disagreed with Toyama's theory. He held that since *Saga kōtei*, which states that Sōami created the garden, is an older document than the *Ryōan shi* (the first document to state that Sōwa created the garden), it makes more sense to believe that the "Sōa" of Sōami's name was corrupted to "Sōwa."[36] He also held that Hideyoshi's decree stating "it is forbidden to remove the stones and trees of the garden" did not mean that trees had been planted in the garden, but rather that it was forbidden to remove any trees found within Ryōanji's precincts; and the fact that a stone garden already existed during Hideyoshi's time can be proven by the edict containing the words "stones of the garden."[37] In sum, it appears that a thing can be whatever one wants it to be depending on how one looks at it.

In 1939, Mori Osamu (1905–1988), a historian of gardens and a student of Tamura Tsuyoshi, produced convincing proof that there had been a cherry tree in the rock garden. He publicized the fact that there was an old cherry tree stump on one side of the garden and a produced a drawing of Ryōanji's precincts showing that there had actually been a weeping cherry tree in that spot prior to the fire of 1797.[38]

According to Mori's theory, this demonstrates that in the past, the garden was an ensemble which consisted of the present stone garden paired with a weeping cherry tree, and that it was possible that this ensemble is what Hideyoshi had seen. While this somewhat weakens the theory that the rock garden was made in the Edo period by Sōwa, it does not completely negate Toyama's theory that the garden did not exist during Hideyoshi's time.

35. Wakimoto Sokurō, "Ryōanji no niwa," *Gasetsu* 5 (1937): 49–67.

36. Shigemori Mirei, *Nihon teienshi zukan* (Tokyo: Yūkōsha, 1938), Vol. 4, 41–42.

37. Ibid., 4, 48.

38. Mori Osamu, "Ryōanji teien no kenkyū," *Gasetsu* 33 (1939): 791–807.

A riddle still remains regarding the visit of Hideyoshi's entourage to Ryōanji. Hideyoshi composed a poem about the weeping cherry tree, but it appears that he was not moved by the rock garden which may have been right next to it. Hideyoshi was not the only one. The six men who accompanied Hideyoshi, including the famous commanders Maeda Toshiie (1538–1599) and Gamō Ujisato (1556–1595), all composed poems about the weeping cherry tree.

Basing himself partially on this event, in 1957, Nakane Kinsaku (1917–1995), an engineer with the Historical Properties Preservation Department of the Kyoto Educational Committee, proposed the theory that the rock garden did not exist in the time of Hideyoshi.[39] Nakane was himself a landscape gardener and was later president of the Osaka University of Arts. Nakane theorized that if the rock garden had been there, it is reasonable to assume that at least one out of the seven in Hideyoshi's party would have composed a poem about it. He also said that the "stones of the garden" in Hideyoshi's edict referred to a set of stones from the Muromachi period that Nakane himself had unearthed from the bottom of the pond behind the abbot's quarters, and that the rock garden had probably been created by "Kotarō (Kiyojirō)" in the Kan'ei era (1624–1644) of the Edo period.[40] What Nakane is saying is that if the rock garden had been there, Hideyoshi "ought to have been" enchanted by its beauty. For Nakane also, the assumed beauty of the garden is the major premise of his argument.

Garden scholars such as Tatsui Takenosuke immediately criticized Nakane's "ought to have been" theory.[41] Tatsui theorized that just because Hideyoshi's entourage had written poems on the theme of snow and the cherry tree not blooming in spite of it being spring, this does not prove that Hideyoshi did not notice the garden. It seems to me that even though Tatsui criticized Nakane, he, too, assumes the beauty of the rock garden.

Let us assume for a moment that Hideyoshi actually did not notice the rock garden. What would this mean? For those who assume the beauty of the rock garden, it would mean that Hideyoshi was a coarse boor with no eye for beauty who cared only about his great good fortune in life. Here

---

39. Nakane Kinsaku, "Ryōanji teien," *Shin kenchiku* 32: 10 (1957): 65–66.

40. Nakane Kinsaku, "Ryōanji no ikezoko no ikō to sekitei no sakutei nendai ni tsuite," *Zōen zasshi* 21:4 (1958): 1–8.

41. Tatsui Takenosuke and Ono Kazunari, "Nakane Kinsaku-shi no 'Ryōanji sekitei sakutei nendai' kōshō ronbun ni taisuru gimon," *Zōen zasshi* 22:1 (1958): 5–8.

again, the supposed beauty of the rock garden reasserts itself. The root of this problem is very deep indeed.

The conviction that the garden is beautiful can sometimes cause one to ignore what is right in front of one's eyes. In *Shinpan suishō Nihon no meien* (Admired and noted gardens of Japan, new edition; 1978), edited by the Kyoto Garden Association founded by Shigemori Mirei, the following passage can be found:

> In recent years someone has unearthed a tree root from one part of the garden and advanced the theory that the garden contained a weeping cherry tree, but the document says "in front of the garden," not "the front garden"; that is, this refers to outside of the wall. It is inconceivable that something like a cherry tree was planted in a *karesansui* garden depicting islands in the ocean.[42]

This sentence, which was most likely written by Shigemori, is probably criticizing Mori's research. The statement "in front of the garden," not "the front garden" here refers to the passage in the *Ryōanji monjo* that says that Hideyoshi came "on a day when the weeping cherry tree in front of the abbot's quarters garden was not yet in bloom." Based on this, Shigemori is saying that the cherry tree was "in front of the garden," that is, outside the wall. He also concludes that it is impossible that a cherry tree would have been planted in a *karesansui* garden in spite of the fact that the stump of an old cherry tree is actually right there next to the abbot's quarters. Once things have reached this point, it is no longer scholarship—it is something approaching religion.

The old stump to the side of the abbot's quarters can also be interpreted in myriad ways. Ōyama Heishirō says that the fact that a weeping cherry tree was planted in the constricted space in the corner of the garden is proof that there was a group of stones there and that entry into the garden was forbidden.[43] Ōyama even goes so far as to say that "considered from the perspective that the rock garden returned to its original condition, the fact that the cherry tree burned down is actually something to be welcomed."[44]

---

42. Kyōto Rinsen Kyōkai, *Shinban suishō Nihon no meien: Kyōto Chūgoku hen* (Tokyo: Seibundō Shinkōsha, 1978), 64.

43. Ōyama, *Ryōanji sekitei nanatsu no nazo o toku*, 150–52.

44. Ibid.

What if there had been a magnificent weeping cherry tree at the edge of the rock garden? It must have been a beautiful sight. In the past, young trees were reportedly planted as successive generations of the line of Hideyoshi's cherry tree. Today, there is a weeping cherry tree outside of the garden wall located at about the midpoint of the garden. When it is in bloom, people say that it captivates visitors to such an extent that the rock garden may as well be somewhere else.

Ōyama gives short shrift to the cherry tree that may have been in the garden for at least 210 years from the time of Hideyoshi's blossom-viewing excursion until the fire, simply declaring that the rock garden returned to "its original condition." Here can be seen the ideal beauty of the rock garden imagined by Ōyama.

Leaving aside the opinions of advocates like Ōyama, whose love for Ryōanji knows no bounds, there is some eye-opening testimony from a local gardener named Okuda Masatomo who is familiar with the rock garden as it was in the past. According to Okuda, the ground under the rock garden is full of tree stumps:

> "The rock garden at Ryōanji was not always like that. We dug up some stumps which made us think that there had been a lot of different kinds of trees planted between the rocks. There were still plenty of stumps left." I heard this story from some old gardeners I worked with at that time. I neglected to ask how big the stumps were, but if what they said is true, I think the rock garden at Ryōanji must have had a completely different appearance from what we think it had.[45]

Okuda's family has been in the gardening profession since his grandfather's time, and Ryōanji was Okuda's playground when he was a child. It is precisely testimony like Okuda's that is persuasive in a way that the words of the savants of garden history are not. People who were actually there know the truth better than scholars who think only in terms of documentation and theory. It may very well be that the rock garden at Ryōanji was once full of greenery. However, Okuda's testimony was not taken seriously in the subsequent research on the rock garden. While his story may have been credible, the image of a rock garden full of greenery was ignored.

---

45. Okuda Masatomo, "Sekitei no sugao," *Zen bunka* 64 (1972): 65.

SHIGA NAOYA AND MURŌ SAISEI

Ever since the Edo period, the rock garden at Ryōanji had been praised for the skill with which it was executed. However, during the Meiji period the rock garden succumbed to the influence of the anti-Buddhist sentiment of the times and people paid it little regard. Guidebooks of Kyoto from the Meiji period barely mention it at all.

Keika yōshi (The glories of Kyoto; 1895), published by the Kyoto Municipal Publishing Department, describes the rock garden as follows in the section which introduces the abbot's quarters at Ryōanji: "The famous front garden has no vegetation but only an arrangement of five or six curiously shaped rocks and is called 'tiger cubs crossing the river' after the fact that it resembles a mother tiger carrying her cubs across a mountain stream on her back."[46] *Keika yōshi* is a very thick official guidebook published by the city of Kyoto in commemoration of the 1,100th anniversary of the relocation of the capital from Nara to Kyoto and it had a great impact on subsequent books of that type. Even so, this is all it has to say about the rock garden. *Heian tsūshi* (Kyoto history; 1895),[47] another thick commemorative guidebook published in the same year as *Keika yōshi*, includes a brief description of Ryōanji, but the rock garden is not mentioned at all.

Travel guides from the Meiji period generally ignore the rock garden. For example, the *Kyoto meishō annai* (Guide to famous places in Kyoto; 1899), which is an all-inclusive introduction to the temples and shrines of Kyoto, says only the following, and does not mention the rock garden: "there is a pond on the temple grounds which attracts waterfowl during the winter. Prayers made here are efficacious."[48]

During the Meiji period, not only Ryōanji but Kinkaku and Ginkaku as well were neglected to the point of complete dilapidation. While old shrines and temples were treated with little regard, the people of Kyoto delighted in modern brick structures such as *kangyōjō* (industrial complexes) and the first ever Kyoto Station. People's taste in landscape is fickle. The trend today to value old architecture and attempt to restore it to its original state will probably be treated by history as just another phase in popular taste.

46. Kyōto-shi Hensanbu, *Keika yōshi: Jō* (Kyoto: Kyōto-shi Sanjikai, 1895), 231–32.
47. Kyōto-shi Sanjikai, *Heian tsūshi* 2:42 (Kyoto: Kyōto-shi Sanjikai, 1895), 19–20.
48. Kataoka Kenzō, *Kyōto meisho annai* (Kyoto: Fūgetsu Shōzaemon, 1899), 39–40.

Thanks to the sudden rise of research on Japanese gardens, which began in the 1920s, the gardens of Kyoto, once fallen out of fashion, again began to attract attention. In such an environment the rock garden at Ryōanji was naturally presented as something beautiful. However, if research into Japanese gardens is to be considered a field of scholarship, it is first of all necessary to be able to explain to everyone's satisfaction why the garden is beautiful.

One of the people in the 1930s who were interested in this question was Okazaki Aya'akira (1908–1995), a scholar of Japanese gardens. Okazaki later became a professor of the Faculty of Agriculture of Kyoto University. In a paper published in 1931, Okazaki said:

> The garden at Ryōanji is famous as the garden of all gardens, but just saying it is skillfully done or that it is a great garden does not give me any insight at all into why this should be so.
>
> Therefore, I would like to consider exclusively the following two points: what gives this garden its value as a famous garden? And what is so good about it?[49]

I will not focus on "what is so good about it," but regarding the question "what gives this garden its value?" Okazaki gave the following two reasons:

> The first reason is that prior to the appearance of the garden at Ryōanji, no one had even dreamed about creating a garden in this form. To put it another way, this garden created the pure "withered landscape-borrowed view" [kare-sansui shakkei] style of garden. . . . Next, more than the fact that this garden is so original, the second reason is the additional fact that it has such a high artistic value. That is to say, its value lies in the fact that none of the many similar gardens that came after it come anywhere near to approaching its level.[50]

Essentially, Okazaki is saying that the garden's value lies in the fact that it was the pioneer of the style of garden that contains no plants and that the reason the garden has a high artistic value is because many copies of it were later created.

49. Okazaki Aya'akira, "Ryōanji sekitei e no ichibetsu," Zōen zasshi 2:2 (1931): 50.
50. Ibid., 50.

The creativity, originality, and artistic value of a thing increase in accordance with the proliferation of imitations of it. The rock garden at Ryōanji gave rise to the creation of many similar gardens, and that is why it has a high artistic value—this is a very easy explanation to understand. Like the Mona Lisa, the value of the rock garden increased because of the plethora of copies that were made of it.

However, Okazaki's explanation was too dry and postmodern for the early 1930s. Luckily or unluckily, the mainstream of the garden discussion went in a more emotional and "damp" direction, so to speak. I would like to discuss two examples of this culled from the writings of that period.

The *ikebana* master Nishikawa Issōtei (1878–1938) had the following to say. Describing Sōami when he created the rock garden at the Daisen'in, a sub-temple of Daitokuji in Kyoto, as "using too many rocks and employing too much artifice," he contrasts this with Ryōanji:

> It is said that Sōami also created the garden at Ryōanji known as "tiger cubs crossing the river." Some say that someone other than Sōami created it, and comparing it to the garden at Daisen'in, I think that the theory that Sōami did not create it is probably correct. But assuming that it was Sōami who created the one at Ryōanji—he was much more relaxed and created a garden using so few stones that it is almost as though there are not enough of them.[51]

Nishikawa takes the position that since the style of the garden at Ryōanji is so different from that at Daisen'in he cannot believe that both of them are by Sōami. This is a classic example of the type of garden study that proceeds based on mutually supporting theories of creator and aesthetics.

At about the same time, the scholar of Japanese cultural history Mutō Makoto (1907–1995), who later became a professor at Kwansei Gakuin University, said the following:

> Among unnatural gardens, the garden at Ryōanji is probably the most unnatural . . . that it gives the viewer not the slightest feeling of unnaturalness in spite of its blatantly obvious separation from nature is due to the excellence of its artistry.[52]

---

51. Nishikawa Issōtei, "Kyōdō seisaku no niwa Ikkyūji no niwa to Daisen'in no niwa," *Heishi* (Autumn 1931): 41.

52. Mutō Makoto,"Geijutsu to shite no teien: Ryōanji no niwa to Saihōji no niwa," *Heishi* (Spring 1932): 41.

Mutō describes the rock garden as "art," but his explanation of why it is artistic is very abstract and hard to understand. It could be understood to mean that it just goes without saying that the garden at Ryōanji is artistic.

In this environment, where the theories about the garden's creator and its aesthetics both fused and clashed, statements about the garden by writers who were free of the restraints of scholarly conventions began to appear. Two prominent writers who wrote about the garden were Shiga Naoya (1883–1971) and Murō Saisei (1889–1962).

These two men, one a novelist and the other a poet, lived during the same era but had subtly different attitudes toward the rock garden. Shiga praised the garden without reserve, but Murō was ambivalent. I would like to examine the discussion, free of the rigidity of scholarship, that unfolded between these two men around their difference of opinion about the garden.

Shiga wrote an essay entitled "Ryōanji no niwa" (The garden at Ryōanji; 1924). In this essay, after stating summarily that Sōami created the garden, Shiga says the following:

> We see a wide sea dotted with islands and thick forests growing luxuriantly on these islands. Without a doubt, for Sōami, this was the only way to distill the essence of Mother Nature into an area of only fifty *tsubo* [150 square meters] or so.
>
> If we compare Enshū's garden at the Katsura Detached Villa to a masterpiece novel, then the rock garden at Ryōanji is like an even more magnificent masterpiece of short story writing. I do not know of any other garden that is so expansive and has such a strong feeling of vigor. However, this is not the sort of garden one can look at and enjoy on a daily basis. It is too austere for mere enjoyment. Moreover, as we gaze at the garden, our hearts feel strangely uplifted.[53]

Shiga goes on to say that the rock garden at Daisen'in was not as sophisticated as that at Ryōanji and stated his feeling that "if the garden at Ryōanji is by Sōami, then it was probably done in his later years."

During the same period, the poets Indō Masatsuna (1877–1944) and Sasaki Nobutsuna (1872–1963) collaborated on the following *tanka*

---

53. Shiga Naoya, "Ryōanji no niwa," in *Shiga Naoya zenshū*, Vol. 5 (Tokyo: Iwanami Shoten, 1999), 317–18.

(short poem) entitled "Kyōto Ryōanji no niwa" (The garden at Ryōanji in Kyoto; 1933).

> Looking deeply at this garden,
> the mind's eye
> can't taste the power of Sōami.

> *kokoro no me*
> *fukabuka to kono*
> *niwa ni sosogishi*
> *Sōami ga chikara o*
> *ajiwawa saruru*

> I look upon the vision of Sōami
> who created the garden
> without a single tree
> or blade of grass.

> *ichiju issō*
> *niwa ni mochiizute*
> *niwa o naseru*
> *Sōami ga me no*
> *okidokoro o omou*[54]

It seems as though it was already the commonly accepted opinion among writers of that time that Sōami was the garden's creator.

While Murō would later uncritically repeat Shiga's opinion that Sōami created the garden, he did not accept the garden without demur. Ten years after Shiga's essay, Murō wrote the following in his work *Kyōraku nikki* (Kyoto diary; 1934).

> In this, the king of rock gardens, the silent scene of the rocks deepens with each successive viewing. There is nothing but fifteen stones sunk into a space of sixty *tsubo* [180 square meters]. However, I felt oppressed as though the garden was forcing me to think about something, and the entire time I was in the garden this feeling bothered me to the point of distraction. As I

54. Taitō Shodōin, ed., "Kyoto Ryōanji no niwa," *Shodō* 2:9. Repr. in 1986 by Tōyō Shodō Kyōkai, p. 36.

thought about it by the light of my lamp back at my lodgings, it seemed as though the rock garden had mellowed and come into my mind. The feeling of rigid, stiff, formality gone to seed faded, my mind quieted, and I felt like I wanted to affectionately stroke the surface of each of the fifteen rocks.[55]

Murō's first impression of the garden was that it made him feel "oppressed as though the garden was forcing me to think about something" and that it had "a feeling of rigid, stiff formality." Murō is saying that it was a garden that entered the mind little by little as it was viewed repeatedly or as the viewer revisited it in his mind after some time had passed. In other words, the rock garden at Ryōanji cannot be understood unless one visits it repeatedly. Shiga's and Murō's manner of speaking, where they describe the garden through the senses, was easy for the general public to absorb.

Prior to the war, the temple office sold a one-page printed commentary on the garden that quoted writings by Shiga Naoya, Murō Saisei, Nishikawa Issōtei, and Sasakawa Rinpū (1870–1949; a critic and haiku poet).[56] It appears that the chief priest at the time, Ōsaki Ryōen, came up with the idea.[57] The commentary, which could be considered Ryōanji's official prewar guidebook, did not contain a single statement referring to the rock garden as a "Zen garden."

Upon discovering that Ryōanji had used his writing without his permission, Murō said the following: "Discovering that some old writing of mine had been quoted in Ryōanji's garden commentary made me feel awkward. I, having paid five sen [1/100 yen] without realizing this, felt all the more silly for buying my own commentary unawares."[58]

It may seem inconceivable to us today, but looking back on the 1920s and 1930s, there were a number of things written disparaging Ryōanji. Murō was involved in much of the criticism of the rock garden.

There is an interesting exchange in the spring issue of the garden and ikebana magazine Heishi (Flower vase chronicles), published in 1935. It is a discussion between Horiguchi Sutemi, who presupposes the garden's beauty on the one hand, and Nishikawa Issōtei and Murō Saisei, who

---

55. Murō Saisei, Murō Saisei zenshū (Tokyo: Shinchōsha, 1965), Vol. 5, 400–1.

56. Kyōto-shi Ukyō-ku Ryōanji, Sōami chikuzō Ryōanji hōjō no teien (tsūshō toranoko watashi).

57. Wakimoto Sokurō, "Ryōanji no niwa," Gasetsu 5 (1937): 55.

58. Murō, Murō Saisei zenshū, 5:401.

take the opposite position on the other. It is a bit long, but I would like to quote it in full:

HORIGUCHI: Doesn't Mr. Toyama take the position that the gardens at Daisen'in and Ryōanji are not by Sōami, but rather were made by Kanamori Sōwa? I haven't actually read his thesis, though.

NISHIKAWA: I don't think that Ryōanji was by Sōami. The feeling is totally different.

HORIGUCHI: But even if it was by Sōami, I think it is a phenomenal thing to have created a style of garden like that.

NISHIKAWA: You mean Ryōanji?

HORIGUCHI: Yes.

NISHIKAWA: I don't think it's that extraordinary. You don't agree?

HORIGUCHI: But there aren't any examples of anyone making a garden like that. If you look at it from the point of view of miniature tray landscapes, it is just a miniature landscape expanded to life size—what you could call a tray rock garden [*bonseki*]. It seems to me that it is a pretty tremendous thing to have created such a large tray rock garden.

NISHIKAWA: Really? To me it seems that the people who look at it are too impressed by it. [*to Murō:*] Have you seen it?

MURŌ: I like its childish quality.

NISHIKAWA: That's one way to look at it.

MURŌ: The stones are just put there without any logic, haphazardly, without that much thought. When I saw it for the first time it repelled me; somehow I found it irritating. . . .

NISHIKAWA: That's because people go overboard in treating it as a great garden.

MURŌ: Somehow, I felt the garden was really making a fool of me. Then when I went home and thought about it lying in bed, I felt like I came to understand it comparatively well, and now that I am away from it, completely. . . . It was a bit difficult to take to it right away, just going into the garden cold without any preparation. I really felt cramped, sort of like I was looking at a picture in my mind.

HORIGUCHI: What part of the garden did you feel was childlike?

MURŌ: How should I put this? It was just how the stones were lined up on the white sand, that is to say, the way the stones were arranged; that idea, well, you know, we played around doing that when we were kids; it just seemed that the idea behind the garden was like that . . . .

HORIGUCHI: Well, if you are going to look at it that way, perhaps you can

say that; but isn't the method of creating the tray landscape quite sophisticated?

MURŌ: That idea is something we conceive later, after pondering it over. I
have thought about it from many different angles, but that's all I come
up with, just a vague feeling. There is no logic to it or anything . . . .[59]

In this discussion, Murō is once again bringing up his perspective on
Ryōanji that he published the previous year in *Kyōraku nikki*. Horiguchi
persisted, insisting that even so, the rock garden was a sophisticated pre-
sentation; but Murō parried this by saying that his impression had "no
logic to it or anything."

This attitude of Murō's, where he talked about the garden in terms of his
sensory perception of it, seemed to have incurred the antipathy of the ratio-
nalists. In May of the year that the foregoing discussion was published, the
Yomiuri newspaper published something of a dispute between Murō and
Katsumoto Seiichirō (1899–1967), a literary critic and self-styled art expert. Katsumoto bemoaned the fact that the Japanese could only look at
Japanese gardens through the lens of how they were appreciated by foreigners. After touching upon such things as the fact that more and more Americans had recently been coming to see Japanese gardens, and that the prominent German architect Bruno Taut (1880–1938) had praised the Katsura
Detached Villa to the skies, Katsumoto threw down the gauntlet to Murō:

For the past couple of months, I have been reading Toyama Eisaku's *Muromachi jidai teien shi* bit by bit, and I am quite enjoying it. It has shown me
clearly just how shoddily the Japanese people have viewed Japanese gardens.
I regret to inform you that this book has completely discredited the theory
that you and Shiga Naoya have propounded—that Sōami created the garden at Ryōanji in his later years. Thanks to this book, I have come to clearly
recognize where your way of looking at gardens is to be placed in a historical
context. Your opinion is just that of a modern realist, isn't it?[60]

Judging from the fact that he was engrossed in Toyama's *Muromachi
jidai teien shi*, which is by no means light reading, it seems that Katsumoto
had quite a mania for gardens.

59. "Niwa o kataru zadankai," *Heishi* (Special Spring issue, 1935): 6–7.
60. Katsumoto Seiichirō, "Niwa no hanashi: Murō Saisei-shi ni kisu," *Yomiuri shinbun*
May 23, 1935.

Katsumoto was an adherent of Toyama's theory that the rock garden at Ryōanji was by Kanemori Sōwa and insulted Murō by saying, "I have come to clearly recognize where your way of looking at gardens is to be placed in a historical context." Considering the fact that subsequent research on gardens has relegated Toyama's Sōwa theory to the status of being just one more theory among many, Katsumoto's "historical context" is fairly worthless. This is both amusing and frightening at the same time.

Having been challenged in this way, Murō did not remain silent. The very next day, the *Yomiuri* newspaper carried his rebuttal. Regarding his support of the Sōami theory, Murō said that he had simply agreed with Shiga and that he did not know whether the garden was by Sōami or not. He then went on and compared the rock garden at Ryōanji to the one at Daisen'in:

Have you ever seen the rock garden at Daisen'in, which was also created by Sōami? Its layout, with a childlike landscape garden scene, has a completely different feeling from Ryōanji's tense, grim formality. There is a little brook running from the waterfall, with a stone bridge and stone islands made of similar looking boat-like stones, just like a "play" brook a child would make while playing in a dry river bed. Nowadays, when I think of the rock garden at Ryōanji, I get a headache for some reason, but when I think of the garden at Daisen'in, in spite of that profusion of stones arranged in such a jumble, I feel happy.[61]

It is still not clear whether or not the garden at Daisen'in is by Sōami. However, the way Murō compared Ryōanji to Daisen'in is intriguing. It appears that Murō vastly preferred Daisen'in over Ryōanji. Unfortunately, as a rebuttal, Murō's counterargument lacks punch. Murō did not meet Katsumoto's spoken daggers head on. The reason for this becomes clear when one reads the final lines of Murō's rebuttal:

You and I seem to meet in the strangest places. When I was looking for a house to rent in Ōmori, there you were. Near the Shinchō publishing offices, there you were on top of a car. On the street next to the Imperial Theater, two or three times in Tabata, and now you have jumped out and poked me in a very sensitive spot. . . . I wonder where and how we will meet next? Goodbye.[62]

61. Murō, "Zoku niwa no hanashi: Katsumoto Seiichrō-shi ni ohenji," *Yomiuri shinbun* May 24, 1935.
62. Ibid.

Murō knew what Katsumoto looked like. It seems as though Katsumoto was "stalking" Murō. What seems to be really going on here is that Murō had gotten tired of this and off-handedly turned the tables on Katsumoto just when Katsumoto thought he had Murō where he wanted him. Articles like this are proof that by around 1935 the Ryōanji discussion had begun to involve the general public.

What did some of the other participants in the discussion think about Murō's view of the rock garden? Regarding the feeling of pressure that Murō experienced, Wakimoto Sokurō said, "actually, that kind of pressure itself shows that the intention of the garden's creator is working. It is one of the fundamental things that causes us to see an ocean and caused people in the past to see tiger cubs crossing the river."[63] The attempt to explain the pressure that Murō experienced as the intention of the garden's creator is one of the strategies of the defenders of the rock garden's beauty. This is an all-embracing Buddhistic view typical of Ryōanji lovers.

For Murō, however, this reaction on the part of public opinion did nothing but increase the oppressiveness of the rock garden. Murō wrote a poem titled "Ryōanji no sekitei" (The rock garden at Ryōanji), which was included in *Insatsu teien* (Gardens in print), published in 1936:

> But I was, finally, shut out
> from the throng of countless stones.
> All the stones were burning with anger.
> All the stones were silent as the grave.
> All the stones were about to scream.
> Oh, all the stones were trying to return to Heaven![64]

The oppressiveness of the rock garden had finally exploded towards heaven. What Murō saw in the rock garden was nothing other than the image of the male sex organ. As though to underscore this fact, the *Tōkyō Asahi* newspaper published a piece by Murō in 1938 in which he put forth his "The Garden Stones = TesticlesTheory":

> I have been looking at garden stones for many years, but I have never felt that they had a particularly refined quality. As I looked at things like orna-

63. Wakimoto, "Ryōanji no niwa," 57.

64. Murō Saisei, *Nihon shijin zenshū*, Vol. 15: *Murō Saisei* (Tokyo: Shinchōsha, 1967), 145.

mental stones, paving stones for paths, and stone water basins where one crouches to wash one's hands, I felt more and more that they were very human, until finally I could not help but think they resembled a certain part of the human anatomy.[65]

Murō said that he was not speaking only of Ryōanji, but that it was usual for him to see "something like old wrinkled testicles in stones and such things" and "when I have Ryōanji or Daisen'in before me, what I see is something physical which invites all sorts of faraway thoughts." One can feel the physical sensations of Murō, who at that time was almost fifty years old. Once Murō's outlook on rock gardens had been reduced to using his own body as its reference point, it could no longer mesh with the theories about the garden's creator or its aesthetics. At this juncture, Murō retired from the rock garden dispute.

ARE ROCK GARDENS PRETTY?

Whether Shiga or Murō, the writings of professional writers are engaging, as is only to be expected. Whether praising rock gardens or disparaging them, their material evokes a response from the reader.

The *haiku* poet Yamaguchi Seishi (1901–1994) visited the garden and wrote his impressions in his work *Saihōji to Ryōanji* (Saihōji and Ryōanji; 1959):

I did not see any ocean or islands.

I did not see any ink painting of Northern Song.

I did not see any tray rock garden.

I did not see any Zen. . . . The white sand garden I saw was a flat plane.

The stones were "objects." I saw a relationship between stone and stone, between "object" and "object."

---

65. Murō Saisei, "Yomoyama banashi (1) Ishi no aijin," *Tokyo Asahi shinbun*, January 24, 1938.

That relationship is seen as a relationship between stone and stone, but in essence this is an abstract quality that cannot be seen by the eyes.

In this way, I saw abstract qualities in the rock garden at Ryōanji. And I was struck by its beauty.[66]

It sounds like Yamaguchi had made a rather thorough study of the various ways of looking at the garden. In the same work, Yamaguchi stated that he had read Shigemori Mirei's book. Disregarding the preconceived ideas he had gained through his study of the garden, Yamaguchi saw the abstract beauty of its composition.

I suppose there is nothing particularly wrong with this. However, the issue here is *when* Yamaguchi wrote these words. *Saihōji to Ryōanji* consisted of photographs by Domon Ken (1909–1990) with commentary by Yamaguchi. It was published in 1959, when Yamaguchi was fifty-eight years old. Judging from the content of the text, it is likely that it was written just before publication of the book.

Yamaguchi was born in the Okazaki district of Kyoto. He moved to Sakhalin when he was ten years old but returned to Kyoto when he was a middle school student and graduated from the Number Three College. Even though Yamaguchi had an intimate relationship with Kyoto, he did not see Ryōanji until he was an adult—his words make this fact quite clear. Ironically, his appreciation of the rock garden's structural beauty, and what might be called his previous "nonappreciation," since he did not see it until the publication of his book, seem to coexist like two sides of the same coin.

Another professional writer, Inoue Yasushi (1907–1991), had a different sensibility about the garden. Inoue gathers his impressions of the rock garden, with which he was intimately familiar, in his poem "Sekitei" (Rock garden), written in 1946. This is one stanza from the poem:

> I wonder who first said that the garden here at Ryōanji was beautiful?
> People always come here and are convinced their worries are as nothing,
> Are comforted, are made to feel warm, and then
> They just leave, under the illusion that the garden is beautiful.[67]

66. Domon Ken, Yamaguchi Seishi, and Fukuyama Toshio, *Saihōji, Ryōanji* (Tokyo: Bijutsu Shuppansha, 1959), 5.

67. Inoue Yasushi, *Utsukushii mono to no deai* (Tokyo: Bungei Shunjūsha, 1973), 126.

Inoue's poem forsakes the discussion of the garden's creator and takes the form of a conversation between the poet and himself, where he makes the shocking statement that visitors "leave under the illusion that the garden is beautiful."

When he was a student, Inoue lived near Ryōanji, and during his walks he would often go to the rock garden. Remembering those times, Inoue says:

> Thus, I was quite familiar with both Ryōanji and the rock garden there. At that time, the rock garden was not as famous as it is now. A few people knew about it, but it was very rare to meet anyone there.
>
> There was no entrance fee or anything like that. You would just go to the entrance of the priests' quarters and call. If someone was there, you would let him know you wanted to come inside; if no one was there you would remove your shoes on the dirt floor, go inside, and walk directly out to the veranda by the abbot's quarters. If you went at nightfall, there were swarms of gnats and mosquitoes, so if you weren't careful you could really get in trouble.
>
> There was not the slightest feeling that you were being shown something extraordinary like there is now.[68]

The reason that Inoue could make a bold statement like "under the illusion that the garden is beautiful" in his poem is precisely because there was no "feeling that you were being shown something extraordinary like there is now." To put it another way, if one does not have the preconceived idea that one is "being shown something extraordinary," it is fairly easy to say that the beauty of the garden is an "illusion."

There are other statements like Inoue's that do not simply praise the rock garden at Ryōanji. A participant in the Conference for the Appreciation of Noted Gardens of Kyoto, sponsored by the Japan Garden Association in 1936, recorded his impressions of the rock garden:

> I had long been aware of Ryōanji's "tiger cubs crossing the river" garden from books and photographs, but the first instant I saw it I thought that the sand looked rather dirty, perhaps because I had imagined that it would be a prettier white color. However, the more I looked at it, the more I came to like it.[69]

68. Ibid., 119.
69. Yamamoto Hikaru,"Kyōto meien kanshōkai kansō," *Teien* 18:1 (1936): 19.

Since a member of the Japan Garden Association wrote this, I think it is safe to assume that the author had a certain degree of knowledge about gardens and an eye for appreciating their beauty. Yet he lets slip his honest impression that "the first instant I saw it I thought that the sand looked rather dirty." He tries his best to recover from this by saying, "the more I looked at it the more I came to like it," but it appears to me that he is trying to force himself to like the garden. This seems like another example of a person being intimidated by the supposed beauty of the rock garden.

There is an even more extreme statement from the landscape gardener Hisatsune Shūji (1911–), which was published in the art news magazine *Geijutsu shinchō* in 1953:

> Just what is so special about this garden? Is it the striking novelty of its unique style that uses only rocks with no trees or greenery? To state my honest opinion, there are any number of old gardens still existing in Kyoto that are vastly superior to this one.[70]

Statements like this that forthrightly disparage the rock garden are rare. Normally, people use a more moderate tone when discussing the garden, even if they are dissatisfied at how it is being treated. Tatsui Matsunosuke is an example of this.

Tatsui, a scholar of gardens, graduated from the History Department of Tokyo Imperial University when Kuroita Katsumi was teaching there, and he later took up research on the history of gardens. He is the father of Tatsui Takenosuke, whom I quoted earlier, and was very active in the effort to designate and preserve gardens as cultural assets of Japan. Tatsui had this to say about the rock garden at Ryōanji:

> The garden at Ryōanji is a famous garden known all over Japan, and at this point in time needs no introduction. However, there is something about the way it has been presented up to now which leaves me strangely dissatisfied. . . . I believe, rather, that this type of garden was not at all rare for its time. That is, looking at the way the stones are handled in this garden, it seems to me that it is simply an imitation of a miniature tray stone garden — surely the most common thing that anyone would think of for a Muromachi-

70. Hisatsune Shūji, "Ryōanji sekitei no kachi," *Geijutsu shinchō* 4:11 (1953), 152.

period garden. However, while there is absolutely no doubt that the placement of the stones is masterful, there is also no doubt that many *shoin* had gardens of grouped stones in the tray stone garden style. It just happened that since one example of this type of garden survives at Ryōanji, and since it is such an excellent garden, we landscape gardeners who came later mistake it for something extremely rare.[71]

Tatsui is saying that while the rock garden at Ryōanji is certainly beautiful, the design was probably very common in the Muromachi period. While Tatsui is by no means denying the beauty of the garden, he does not completely accept it either. It seems that he simply was not completely satisfied with the way the rock garden at Ryōanji had been treated.

After the war, it became increasingly common to hear people praise the garden excessively without any regard for logic. I would like to give three examples of this. The first is a conversation that took place on the veranda of the rock garden between Tatsuno Yutaka (1888–1964), a scholar of French literature and professor at the University of Tokyo, and the writer Osaragi Jirō (1897–1973); it was published in the magazine *Shūkan Asahi* (Asahi weekly) in 1947.

TATSUNO: This garden is wonderful. . . .

(Dr. Tatsuno seemed to moan as he said this and continued to stand at the edge of the veranda. Mr. Osaragi sat in the middle of the veranda facing the garden and drank in the garden without moving.)

TATSUNO: Osagari-san . . . you don't get tired of it, do you? It's a big tray garden. If it were a painting it would be a still life. . . .

OSARAGI: No, you don't get tired of it. And I've seen it I don't know how many times.

TATSUNO: Somehow, I want to argue with the garden. I feel like it would make a fool of me if I didn't. . . .

OSARAGI: It's a garden that makes you think.

TATSUNO: It reminds me of a *shōgi* [Japanese chess] player who coughs before he makes a tactical move.

71. Tatsui Matsunosuke, "Kyōto no meien o mite," *Teien to fūkei* 14:10 (1932): 316–17. *Shoin* is a traditional style of Japanese residential architecture, including a reception hall and private study.

OSARAGI: Each and every stone is alive. Murō [Saisei] said that this garden
was the king of rock gardens . . . yes, it's alive.

TATSUNO: Do you think that foreigners with a highly developed appreciation for beauty would understand it?

OSARAGI: Oh, I don't think so. But maybe a few, perhaps.[72]

This conversation scene is like a picture, so much so that there are some
who count it as one of postwar Japan's most famous conversations. Tatsuno, intimidated to the point of wanting to argue with the garden; Osaragi who said that foreigners could not understand its beauty—it seems
like both of them had fallen into a state where their thought processes had
almost come to a complete halt. It may be, however, that this was the first
step towards infusing the garden with its Zen flavor. Of course, it goes
without saying that Osaragi's impression that foreigners could not understand the rock garden was mistaken.

Perhaps basing himself on this experience, Osaragi had Moriya Kyōgo,
the hero of his story *Kikyō* (Return to the capital), which was serialized
in the *Mainichi* newspaper in 1948, say, "Westerners, unless they're special, can't understand the beauty of this garden." *Kikyō* earned Osaragi the
Japan Art Academy Prize. Tatsuno wrote the letter recommending Osaragi
for this prize.

The second example was written by the literary critic Komiya Toyotaka
(1884–1966), and appeared in *Geijutsu shinchō* in 1950:

I think that the garden at Ryōanji is probably at its most beautiful on a rainy
day when the stones and the sand are moist. Unfortunately, I have never been
to Ryōanji on such a day. However, over and above everything, the most cru-
cial thing is that this garden expresses the *idée* of its creator, who pushed his
art to the absolute limit until it reached a point where it could go no further.[73]

Finally, the third example. This was written in 1955 by Naramoto Tatsuya.

The grouped stones are magnificent. If you say only that, maybe nothing
else needs to be said . . . in any case, this was created as a garden. It is not a

72. Tatsuno Yutaka, "Tatsuno Yutaka rensai taidan wasureenu kotodomo dai 7 kai
Osaragi Jirō," *Shūkan Asahi*, December 7, 1947, 18.

73. Komiya Toyotaka, "Ryōanji no niwa," *Geijutsu shinchō* 1:9 (1950): 56.

painting or a sculpture, nor is it anything like philosophy or religion, and it is most certainly not artifice.[74]

Even though they both praise the garden, Komiya and Naramoto approach it somewhat differently. Komiya exclusively pursued the philosophical issue, the *idée* of the garden's creator. Naramoto, on the other hand, is saying that the garden should not be viewed through the lens of painting, sculpture, philosophy or religion, which all have an aura of the West about them. The garden is a garden, and has a beauty unique to Japan that flowered during the medieval period.

In contradistinction to these men, there is someone who said clearly that he did not know whether the garden was pretty or not. He was the historical scholar Nakamura Naokatsu (1890–1976). Nakamura led the Japanese History Department at Kyoto Imperial University (with Nishida Naojirō, Naramoto's teacher) before and during World War II; and after the war, he was banned from public office together with Nishida. Nakamura's specialty was looking at history from the perspective of the life and culture of the common people. There are many modern historians who were influenced by Nakamura's style of scholarship. Nakamura had this to say:

Is the rock garden at Ryōanji unconditionally beautiful?

Apparently so. Apparently there is nothing to say. But is it really that good?

Do people praise it because the Japanese are so polite that they feel they must agree with foreigners who say that it is wonderful, perhaps? Or is it because its transcendence is so beyond our ability to see it that we simply decide it is wonderful without understanding why?

To tell you the truth, its beauty is lost on me.[75]

It seems to me that Nakamura may have had Nishida and Naramoto in mind when he wrote this. Influential scholars coming from the same Japanese History Department of Kyoto University assessed the rock garden at Ryōanji in all manner of different ways. When Nishida was a professor of

74. Naramoto Tatsuya, *Kyōto no niwa* (Tokyo: Kawade Shinsho, 1955), 14–15.
75. Nakamura Naokatsu, *Kyō no miryoku* (Kyoto: Tankō Shinsha, 1959), 130.

Japanese history at Kyoto University, Nakamura was an associate professor, but it seems that their scholarship differed considerably.

For some people, their vague and inexpressible dissatisfaction with
the garden made them avoid daring to voice a clear opinion about it. The
woodblock print artist Ikeda Masuo (1934–1997) is an example of this:

> I visited the rock garden for the second time a number of years ago with
> Yōko, who is now my wife, and even though I had gotten accustomed to it a
> bit, no feeling of excitement came welling up from the depths of my heart.
> Perhaps somewhere in my mind I was aware of the fact that I was trying to
> figure out the garden and this prevented me from simply experiencing it nat-
> urally. While I may work in a different field, I am a professional artist and I
> still find the rock garden hard to understand. Or rather, that is to say, I can't
> decide if this garden is a great garden or a worthless one, basically.[76]

I do not understand what stopped a man like Ikeda, who introduced a
daring hypothesis on the true identity of the enigmatic eighteenth-century
woodblock print artist Sharaku, from deciding how he felt about the rock
garden. I suspect that Ikeda really wanted to make a clear statement to
the effect that the garden was not so great. But he could not do it. What
crossed his mind at that moment? Was it the idea that the garden had to
be beautiful? Or was Ikeda afraid of being labeled an artist who did not
understand the garden that expressed Zen?

POPULARIZATION AND THE EXPRESSION OF ZEN

At the risk of being overly repetitive, I want to reiterate that it was only
after World War II that the description of the garden as being an expression of Zen became widespread. It was the addition of the Zen element
that solidified the reputation of the garden once and for all. This does not
mean that the opinion that the garden was an expression of Zen was completely absent prior to the war. Already in the 1920s, Tatsui Matsunosuke
had written that the rock garden at Ryōanji had a Zen flavor, for example.[77]
Tamura Tsuyoshi, in a paper from 1936, wrote that "one can detect a Zen-

76. Ikeda Masuo, "Ikite iru ishi," in *Nihon no teien bi*, Vol. 4: *Ryōanji* (Tokyo: Shūeisha,
1989), 52.

77. Tatsui Matsunosuke, *Nihon meien ki* (Tokyo: Takayamabō, 1924), 106.

like style there."[78] However, both Tatsui and Tamura only refer to the rock garden and Zen in the most modest way.

Many historians, beginning with Kuroita Katsumi and Nishida Naojirō, have said that the culture of the fifteenth and sixteenth century itself was a Zen-style culture. However, there is a great difference between saying the culture at the time had a Zen atmosphere and saying that the formation of the rock garden at Ryōanji expressed Zen thought itself. When and in what way did this leap occur?

Let us not forget that the rock garden at Ryōanji was popularly known as the garden of the "tiger cubs crossing the river." "Tiger cubs crossing the river" has nothing to do with Zen. Also, prewar garden historians were very careful about connecting the rock garden to Zen. The reason for this is that it is unclear when the rock garden at Ryōanji was created. While some held to the theory that Sōami created the garden in the sixteenth century, there were also authorities such as Toyama Eisaku who believed that it was made in the Edo period by Kanamori Sōwa. It is not possible to just casually assert that the rock garden at Ryōanji = sixteenth-century culture = Zen.

After World War II was over, the opinion that the rock garden was an expression of Zen was on everyone's lips, and its popularization as a tourist destination soared. Actually, it was the cinema that contributed to the popularization of the rock garden. Once again, let us look at the reminiscences of Ikeda Masuo:

> I'm sure that I must have first learned of the existence of the rock garden from an art history textbook or some other book, but I really first became aware of it when I saw the scene in Ozu Yasujirō's film *Banshun* [*Late Spring*] where Ryū Chishū and Hara Setsuko are sitting on the veranda by the abbot's quarters looking at the rock garden. According to what someone from the temple told me, *Banshun* was the first time the rock garden was featured in a film.[79]

Ikeda says that the rock garden at Ryōanji became instantly famous as a result of being the setting for *Banshun*, made by Shōchiku Studios in 1949. It would be more correct to say, however, that it was only used very slightly, since the rock garden scene lasts one minute and forty-five seconds in a

---

78. Tamura Tsuyoshi, "Nihon teien ni okeru hiraniwa no ishō," *Zōen kenkyū* 17 (1936): 3.
79. Ikeda, "Ikite iru ishi," 51.

film that is almost one hour and fifty minutes long. Also, Ikeda's memory is playing tricks on him: Hara Setsuko does not appear in the rock garden scene. The scene actually shows a father, a professor at the University of Tokyo played by Ryū Chishū, sitting on the veranda by the abbot's quarters with his friend, a professor from Kyoto University, looking at the garden as they discuss his feelings about marrying off his daughter, played by Hara Setsuko.

How was the rock garden portrayed in *Banshun*? Seeing as how it appeared as the setting for a conversation between a professor from the University of Tokyo and a professor from Kyoto University, perhaps Ozu was trying to portray it as an out-of-the-way place known only to the intelligentsia. The two professors are not meditating as they look at the garden, much less are they discussing Zen. Ozu is obviously using the "tiger cubs crossing the river" image of a mother tiger carrying her cubs across a river on her back as a metaphor for the feelings of a father sending off his daughter in marriage. In short, the rock garden in *Banshun* was the garden of "tiger cubs crossing the river," not a Zen garden.

The statement that the movies made Ryōanji famous also appears in the recollections of Tōkai Sekimon, who was a junior to Matsukura Shōei when both of them were trainee monks. To repeat, when Matsukura became chief priest in 1948, the temple was unimaginably poor when viewed from the perspective of its present-day prosperity, and visitors to the rock garden were rare.

> The appearance of the rock garden in the movie *Return to the Capital* brought Ryōanji to national prominence, and from that time forward it became one of Kyoto's famous tourist destinations and has continued to be so down to the present day.[80]

Ryōanji does not appear in the Shōchiku film *Kikyō* (Return to the capital) (1950), which was based on the story by Osaragi Jirō and directed by Ōba Hideo (1910–). Tōkai probably confused *Kikyō* with *Banshun*. Be that as it may, it seems like there is little doubt that the popular medium of the movies brought about a Ryōanji boom and helped to fix the rock garden in the consciousness of the general public.

At the end of the 1950s, all of a sudden the opinion that the rock gar-

80. Tōkai Sekimon, "Ryōanji zen jūshoku Matsukura Shōei oshō no senge o itamu," *Zen bunka* 110 (1983): 128.

den at Ryōanji was an expression of Zen was heard everywhere. Among garden industry professionals, Nakane Kinsaku began to vigorously promote the relationship of the garden to the world of Zen:

> As this kind of Zen view of nature and the world penetrated deeply into the consciousness of society, it influenced art and entertainment and had a profound effect on landscape gardening, eventually giving birth to a specific kind of garden characterized by abstract structure and expression. These gardens do not have even the slightest degree of the kind of sensual splendor seen in gardens that are bedecked with ponds, artificially created hills, blooming trees, flowers, and greenery; rather, transcending sensual [beauty], they express what is called the beauty of the Void [*mu no bi*].[81]

These words appeared as the caption for a large photograph of the rock garden that appeared in *Shin kenchiku* (New architecture), a journal devoted to modernist architecture. It is not clear who wrote this commentary, but judging from the fact that an article by Nakane appears in the magazine directly following this caption and that Nakane used very similar expressions in his subsequent writings, it seems reasonable to assume that Nakane was the author. For modernist architects, the fact that structures made using very simple elements, like the rock garden at Ryōanji, had long existed in Japan was a big "discovery."

The problem is Nakane's article, which follows this commentary. In it, Nakane claims that his own archaeological survey showed that the rock garden did not exist in the time of Hideyoshi.[82] Nakane believed that the garden was created in the early Edo period. In spite of this, in this caption in the very same issue of the same magazine, he writes about the garden as though it were the crystallization of the climate of Zen spirituality of the fifteenth and sixteenth centuries. This seems like quite a contradiction.

Subsequent to this, Nakane began to mass-produce statements about the Zen nature of Ryōanji's rock garden, such as the following:

> In this garden there is not the slightest bit of the gaudy beauty seen in gardens that are ornamented with blossoming trees, flowers, and greenery. While it appears to be nonchalant and artless, nevertheless the beauty of the Void is expressed within a perfectly seamless austerity. The beauty of this

---

81. "Ryōanji sekitei," *Shin kenchiku* 32: 10 (1957): 61.
82. Nakane, "Ryōanji teien," 65–66.

garden has the quality of the quiet, elegant, and simple beauty found in the spirit of the tea ceremony and the austere, simple, and elegant beauty that *noh* drama tries to achieve.[83]

In 1963, the same year that Nakane wrote these words, he also wrote a pocketbook called *Kyō no meien* (Famous gardens of Kyoto). This book was one of a series of books published by the Hoikusha publishing company called Color Books. What makes these books unique is that they are like mini-encyclopedias on various fields, filled with beautiful color pictures, and small enough to fit in one's pocket. This series is still being published today, and the appeal of the books lies in the fact that they can be carried along wherever one goes and consulted on the spot. These books have provided the general public in Japan with a great deal of educational information.

In *Kyō no meien*, Nakane describes the rock garden at Ryōanji as follows:

> The rock garden at Ryōanji is a *karesansui* [withered landscape] garden which was influenced by the thought of the Zen sect of Buddhism. . . . It does not have the superficial magnificence of gardens created with ponds, brooks, flowers, and trees; rather, it transcends the sensual, expressing what is called the beauty of the Void. There are few gardens the spirit of whose creation was so influenced by Zen thought as this one.[84]

It is obvious at a glance that this has been copied from a part of the commentary that Nakane wrote for *Shin kenchiku* (New architecture). The fact that the rock garden was explained in this manner in the Color Books, a long-lived series that has seen many reprintings, had a great impact on the general public in Japan.

That being said, how did Nakane come to arrive at "the beauty of the Void" (*mu no bi*)? Was it because he had passed forty and settled into a mature middle age free of doubts? Here, one can make out the shadow of Matsukura Shōei, the postwar chief priest of Ryōanji, hovering in the background. It was Matsukura who asked Nakane to do the archaeological survey mentioned above. Those people who wanted to discuss Ryōanji, including Nakane, probably visited Ryōanji and were influenced in no small measure by Matsukura's lectures about it.

83. Nakane, *Nihon no niwa* (Kyoto: Kawahara Shoten, 1963), 94.
84. Nakane, *Kyō no meien* (Tokyo: Hoikusha, 1963), 16–17.

Both Matsukura and the previous chief priest, Ōsaki Ryōen, also influenced Shigemori Mirei. Shigemori wrote the following, presenting it as Ōsaki's words:

> He said, "when I sit here [in an interior room] and listen to the footsteps of the visitors on the wooden floor as they leave, I can tell who has really understood the garden well and who is leaving without understanding it at all. It's a pretty frightening thing to be able to understand that just from the sound of a person's footsteps, you know."[85]

It is said that an experienced Zen master can understand a person's state of mind from the sound of his footsteps. In the Rinzai Zen tradition, trainees are given *kōans*. During the daily meditation sessions, the trainee meets with the master one on one and tells him his answer to the *kōan* he has been given. If the trainee has not understood the *kōan* sufficiently, the master will be able to detect this just from the sound of the trainee's footsteps as he comes to meet with him. Chief priest Ōsaki was probably able to do the same thing.

If one stops to think about it, it is perfectly natural for a Zen priest to discuss the rock garden in Zen terms. Prior to Ōsaki, however, there is no proof of anyone from Ryōanji having done so of their own accord. This is only to be expected, of course, since up until Ōsaki's appointment in 1907, Ryōanji had not had a chief priest for close to three hundred years. It is likely that both Ōsaki and Matsukura lectured Shigemori on Zen during the years before and after the war as he sat looking at the garden. Already in a paper from 1947, Shigemori was bringing Zen into the discussion: "This kind of symbolic expression is quite characteristic of Zen and was born from a background of Zen thought."[86] In *Nihon teienshi taikei* (A historical overview of Japanese gardens; 1971), the Zen interpretation of the rock garden is even clearer:

> In general, most people say that they cannot understand the garden at Ryōanji. . . . The only way to a enjoy a garden like the one at Ryōanji is to discard all of one's preconceived notions and confront the garden head on in

85. Shigemori and Shigemori, *Nihon teienshi taikei*, 81–82.
86. Shigemori Mirei, "Ryōanji to Daisen'in no sekitei bi," *Shiseki to bijutsu* 17:4 (1947): 147.

all of one's nakedness . . . when one looks at the garden, one ought to be at a loss for words; and until one can silently meditate on it, until one can hear the sound of waves emanating from the entire garden, one has not understood the garden at Ryōanji.[87]

Shigemori considered the *karesansui* garden to be the pinnacle of the Japanese garden, and his evaluation of Ryōanji is written in that context. I do not know what is behind his outlook on gardens, but it may be connected to the fact that as a landscape gardener, Shigemori's patrons consisted primarily of Zen temples and tea ceremony practitioners.

Was the idea that the form of the rock garden expressed the spirit of Zen itself initiated from the Ryōanji side during the era of chief priests Ōsaki and Matsukura? The source of this idea is unclear, but it appears that authoritative garden researchers such as Nakane and Shigemori agreed with it and that when the rock garden became famous during the 1960s, this explanation was disseminated as a form of edification for the general public.

It is possible to see the influence of chief priest Matsukura even in the "unsightly stones" theory of Ōyama Heishirō, discussed earlier. As befits a Zen priest, Muchaku Dōchū, the author of *Ryōanshi* (Chronicle of Ryōan), said bluntly that "the stones are unsightly"; and when Ōyama heard chief priest Matsukura refer to the garden in the same way, he says that he was "profoundly impressed." Expressing how moved he was, Ōyama said, "Listening to the words of the Zen master who calmly dismissed the stones as 'unsightly' even though he was fully aware that popular opinion praised them as being pleasing to the eye, I felt that I was in the presence of a truly enlightened Zen priest."[88]

The ultimate explanation equating the rock garden and Zen was put forth by the sculptor Mizuno Kinzaburō. Mizuno is known for having practiced Zen assiduously from a young age. He seems quite pleased with his own research on the rock garden at Ryōanji, praising it as "a quest for the fountainhead of ultimate beauty."[89] Mizuno explained the structure of the garden in the form of a *kōan*. Here, I will reconstruct the questions and answers from Mizuno's article that appeared in the magazine *Zen bunka*

87. Shigemori and Shigemori, *Nihon teienshi taikei*, 81–82.

88. Ōyama, *Ryōanji sekitei nanatsu no nazo o toku*, 101.

89. Mizuno Kinzaburō, *Zen to geijutsu no setten* (Tokyo: Kondō Shuppansha, 1983), 1.

(Zen culture), the house organ of the Institute for Zen Studies at Hana-
zono University in Kyoto.

QUESTION: What is the meaning of the rock garden of Ryōanji?
ANSWER: That which forms an arc like water flowing in three points re-
sembles a sickle for cutting grain.
QUESTION: Do not speak in riddles.
ANSWER: I do not speak in riddles.
QUESTION: What is the meaning of the rock garden of Ryōanji?
ANSWER: Like a cross-hook three point moon, like a star.[90]

Mizuno seems to have created this *kōan* in imitation of the well-known
"The Oak Tree in the Courtyard" *kōan* from the *Wu-men kuan* (The gateless barrier), a collection of Zen *kōans* compiled in the thirteenth century,
where a monk asks Chao-chou, "What is the meaning of Bodhidharma's
coming from the West?" and Chao-chou answers, "The oak tree in the
courtyard."[91] I am not competent to pass any judgment on its quality as a
kōan, but I can say that Mizuno came to the following conclusion about
the *kōan* he created:

I think that it can now be understood without a doubt that the rock garden
at Ryōanji was created with a Zen *kōan* as its subject.
Moreover, as a classic form that magnificently fuses the points of contact
between Zen and the arts, it is truly unparalleled.[92]

Mizuno says that the relationship between the *kōan* and the rock garden "can now be understood without a doubt," but in reality this is not
anything even vaguely resembling proof. Saying that the rock garden is
Zen simply because one can liken it to a *kōan* is nonsense. I feel sorry for
Mizuno for having to say this, but his obsession is too extreme. However,
it is true that this kind of single-minded fantasy can come to be a common way to frame an opinion. I suppose that any faith is prone to this,
not just Zen.

90. Mizuno Kinzaburō, "Ryōanji no sekitei to kashiopea za," *Zen bunka* 91 (1978): 53–54.
91. *The Gateless Barrier: The Wu-men Kuan (Mumonkan)*. Trans. with commentary by
Robert Aitken (New York: North Point Press, 1990), 226–30.
92. Mizuno, "Ryōanji no sekitei to kashiopea za," 54.

PROOF OF BEAUTY

Is the rock garden at Ryōanji really pretty? For many of the people discussed previously in this chapter, the beauty of the garden is a self-evident fact. However, simply asserting that its beauty is self-evident is not universally convincing. After all, it is also a fact that there were influential people involved in the discussion who found the rock garden unattractive. For devotees of the rock garden, the desire to somehow prove that it is beautiful must be very strong.

However, is it really possible to prove that something is beautiful? In the final analysis, beauty is nothing more than that which is seen in the eye of the beholder at the time he beholds it. Something that is beautiful to one person is not beautiful to another; something that was once thought to be beautiful ceases to be beautiful with the passage of time— this is the natural course of things.

Many people, including the garden historians discussed previously, thought that even if beauty cannot be completely proven, it should be possible to rationally explain it to a degree if only a good method for doing so could be devised. The method they used relied on precise measurements and visual analysis. This method appears to have been influenced by the theory of Constructivism that was popular in art and architecture circles beginning in the 1920s.

Equilibrium and dynamism—the interpretation of the rock garden according to Constructivism can be summarized in this way. I would like to review the attempts of this faction from the 1920s to the present to explain the beauty of the rock garden at Ryōanji so that we can see whether or not what they said really proves that the rock garden is beautiful.

The first diagram (figure 6) was created in 1923 by Saitō Katsuo, a student of Tamura Tsuyoshi of Tokyo Imperial University.[93] Already from this time Saitō was describing the rock gardens at Ryōanji and Daisen'in as the epitome of the "Zen garden." At a time when the rock garden at Ryōanji was only described as the garden of "tiger cubs crossing the river," Saitō can be considered the first person who saw Zen in the garden.

Even so, Saitō also described modern gardens as "embracing one in the great universe" and "guiding the contemplation of the viewer deep and far into the metaphysical realm." It does not appear that he intended to

93. Saitō Katsuo, "Ryōanji no ishigumi 'toranoko watashi' no kaibō," *Teien* 5: 8 (1923): 7.

Figure 6. Sketch of garden by Saitō (1923).

state that it was only the garden at Ryōanji that was particularly philosophical. Saitō said the rock garden had "spirit-harmony" and "vitality of movement."[94] He tried to explain this by means of the directional axes of the stone groupings. He analyzed the stones by categorizing them as vertically placed stones (イ in figure 6), horizontally placed stones (リ, ヌ, カ, ヨ), and obliquely placed stones (ロ, ハ, ニ, ホ, ヘ, ト, チ, ル, ヲ, ワ) and pointed out that the vertical stone is in the center, the horizontal stones are on both edges toward the front, and the oblique stones are placed so as to fill in the gaps between the vertical and horizontal stones. Saitō said that the overall dynamism of the groups of stones gives "the garden a very ambitious appearance with a faint tinge of lustful passion, bringing it to the edge of vulgarity,"[95] but that the vertical and horizontal stones maintain the dignity of the garden.

As an explanation, this is rather ambiguous. However, considering the fact that this was done at a time when even a decent surveyor's diagram of the rock garden did not exist, I suppose it is unavoidable that this was the best diagram that could be made. In any case, it seems that Saitō was trying to explain the beauty of the garden by means of its vertical, horizontal, and oblique lines as seen from a bird's-eye view.

A man named Tanaka Sansetsu objected to Saitō's theory, saying that the design of the rock garden at Ryōanji included the weeping cherry tree that Hideyoshi loved and that Saitō's calculations did not include it.[96] It appears that Tanaka was also quite enamored of the garden himself. He

94. The characters used here, 気韻躍動, are similar to the phrase 気韻生動, which appears in the Chinese painting treatise *Guhua pinlu* (Classification of ancient painters) by Xie He.

95. Saitō, "Ryōanji no ishigumi 'toranoko watashi' no kaibō," 8.

96. Saitō Katsuo, "'Ryōanji niwa ni taisuru ichi shiken' o yomite," *Teien* 24:1 (1942): 32–33.

wrote the following prose piece for the magazine *Teien* (Gardens), which reads like a passionate love letter:

> How beautiful is the golden light of a late autumn morning as it plays on the surface of the garden! Ah, why do you rend my heart so? When I came to see you last February on a cold day when the powdery snow was falling, you seemed as cold as the moonlight. But when I took your hand you were passionate enough to melt my heart. Yet today, why do you now greet me with the blood-red color of love burning in your face?[97]

To anthropomorphize the garden to this extent is quite incredible. Saitō responded to Tanaka as follows:

> If so, then, in response to the structural question of whether the stones in the garden by the abbot's quarters at Ryōanji were grouped with a weeping cherry tree as part of the design, I can, without hesitation, answer with an unequivocal "no".... For a person who does not really understand the garden's vigor, nothing would be better than to have him study stone arranging for ten or twenty years; but even without going that far, if he were to pay close attention to stone arranging for about three years and watch how a master gardener arranges stones, I think that he would naturally come to understand it.[98]

Saitō is saying, "Oh, Tanaka, you really don't understand the vigor of stone arranging, do you? Go and study some more!" This is nothing but a children's squabble. Whatever happened to analyzing the garden's beauty?

Let us go on to the next diagram. The diagram in figure 7 was drawn in 1931 by Okazaki Aya'akira.[99] Using this diagram, Okazaki pointed out that the central space was shifted somewhat to the left. Then, by comparing it side by side with a diagram showing the groups of stones labeled III and IV shifted somewhat to the right, which gives the garden an enlarged central space, he attempted to show how skillfully the stones in the actual rock garden had been placed.

To really assert that the present placement of the stones is the optimum arrangement, it would be necessary to arrange the fifteen stones randomly

97. Tanaka Sansetsu, "Ryōanji niwa sōken," *Teien* 24: 12 (1942): 514.

98. Saitō, " 'Ryōanji niwa ni taisuru ichi shiken' o yomite," 32–33.

99. Okazaki Aya'akira, "Ryōanji sekitei e no ichibetsu," 50–52.

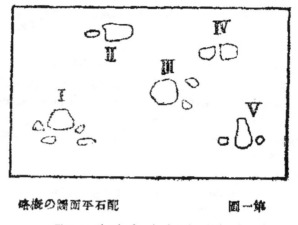

配石平面圖の概略   第一圖

Figure 7. Sketch of garden by Okazaki (1931).

in every possible way and then to evaluate the arrangements subjectively. In that sense, it is quite a simple thing to point out the inadequacy of the rhetorical device that Okazaki used to make his case. This is because his method of comparison is primitive and is nowhere near to being "scientific."

Shigemori Mirei also published a diagram of the garden in 1933 called *Ryōanji sekitei ishigumi no kōsei bi sankō zu* (Reference diagram of the structural beauty of the grouped stones in the rock garden at Ryōanji; figure 8).[100] Shigemori himself did not provide a detailed explanation of this diagram. However, it seems as though he was trying to make the point that the groups of stones fit into an area defined by the horizontal line, the two oblique lines that cross at almost right angles at the stone by the edge of the wall, and the lines that run parallel to the oblique lines. Shigemori was the first person to explain the stone groupings using supplemental lines, a practice which subsequently became fashionable.

The diagram in figure 9 was created in 1935 by Eyama Masami (1906–1978).[101] In 1933, prior to the publication of Eyama's paper, the Gardening Laboratory of Kyoto University made a surveyor's diagram of the rock garden at Ryōanji. Eyama's drawing is based on that diagram.

---

100. Amanuma and Shigemori, *Kyōto bijutsu taikan*, 19.

101. Eyama Masami,"Taisū teki kinsei ni yoru Ryōanji teien no kōsei ni tsuite,"*Zōen zasshi* 2:2 (1935): 111.

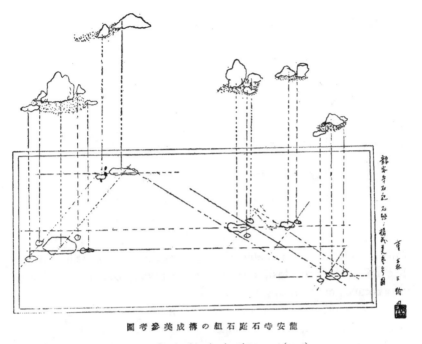

龍安寺石庭石組の構成美参考圖

Figure 8. Sketch of garden by Shigemori (1933).

Using this surveyor's diagram, Eyama explained the rock garden as follows. Symmetrical beauty, like that seen in the forms of plants or the shape of a conch shell, can be explained by means of logarithmic rules. This is the theory of naturally occurring logarithms propounded by the scholar J. Hanbidge in 1920. If one adds suitable supplementary lines to the surveyor's diagram of the rock garden, a number of rectangles with a vertical-to-horizontal ratio of about 1 to $\sqrt{6}$ appear. Eyama focused on this and said that the design of the rock garden at Ryōanji was based on the $\sqrt{6}$ logarithmic standard, and that this is what makes it beautiful.

Eyama's thesis was the first to examine the beauty of the rock garden using mathematical principles. It appears to have had considerable impact in garden history circles. Encouraged by this, the following year Eyama published a thesis on the rock garden at Daisen'in that employed the same method.[102] However, the rock garden at Daisen'in is more compli-

102. Eyama Masami, "Daisen'in teien kōsei ni kansuru Dynamic Symmetry teki ken-kyū," *Zōen zasshi* 3:2 (1936): 97–107.

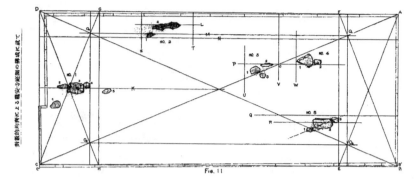

Figure 9. Sketch of garden by Eyama (1935).

cated, and Eyama was not able to produce as clean a result as he did with Ryōanji. Eyama's conclusion was that the garden at Daisen'in was based on a composite $\sqrt{2}$ rectangle.

Among garden historians of the time, it appears that those scholars who were searching for a verifiable method of proving the beauty of the garden were excited by Eyama's thesis. Mori Osamu, who was working on a method that combined documentary data and archeological surveys, was one of those who was encouraged by Eyama's work. However, while praising Eyama's Ryōanji thesis as being "extremely interesting and truly admirable in the deftness of its logical exposition," Mori faulted it for assuming that the abbot's quarters and the earthen wall had always been in the same positions in which they were presently located and for ignoring the existence of the weeping cherry tree.[103] What Mori is saying is that, looking at figure 9, if the weeping cherry tree which was in the lower right corner is taken into consideration, a different set of lines can be drawn. We must remember here that it was Mori himself who pointed out that the stump of an old cherry tree was in that location. It is easy to understand Mori's desire for his discovery to be reflected in the analysis of the garden.

Let us stop here for a moment and think. Does Eyama's logarithmic theory really explain the beauty of the rock garden? Compared to a simple subjective assertion that the garden is beautiful, the argument that the logarithmic theory conforms to the laws of natural beauty and therefore the rock garden is beautiful seems to have an aura of objectivity about it. However, is it really appropriate to accept the logarithmic theory unques-

103. Mori, "Ryōanji teien no kenkyū," 791–807.

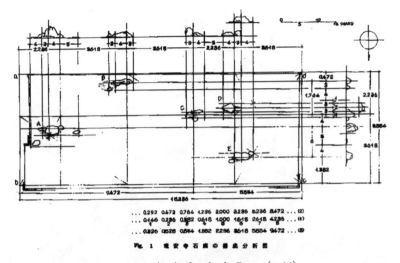

Figure 10. Sketch of garden by Eyama (1966).

tioningly? All Eyama is saying is that the garden fits into the 1 to root-whatever law. Does that make it beautiful?

After World War II, in 1966, Eyama himself retracted his logarithmic theory. He said, "the research on Ryōanji that I originally published was clearly immature and incoherent, and even though it is full of errors it was quoted a number of times in publications in the field and has continued to be used without being publicly criticized."[104] Rather than being pleased that his work was being discussed at scholarly conferences, it appears that he was unhappy about it.

What Eyama replaced the logarithmic theory with was the well-known "golden ratio" (figure 10). Eyama assumed a fundamental progression based on the golden ratio and created another progression consisting of the fundamental progression multiplied by two, to which alternating terms in the basic progression had been added. He then claimed that the rock garden fit this standard. However, as one can see immediately when one looks closely at figure 10, there are a number of lines that look out of place. It appears as though they were squeezed in to make it easier to explain the rock garden according to the golden ratio. However, garden history circles in 1966 probably welcomed this argument as a novel way of explaining the garden's aesthetics.

104. Eyama Masami, "Ryōanji teien no kōsei ni tsuite," *Zōen zasshi* 30: 2 (1966), 2.

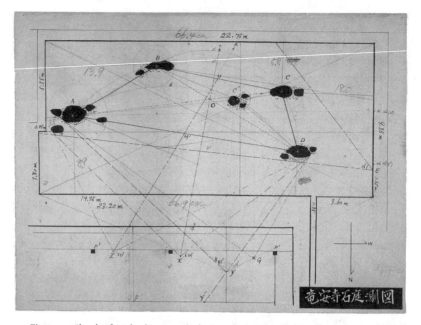

Figure 11. Sketch of garden by Kitawaki (ca. 1939). Collection of the National Museum of Modern Art, Tokyo.

Let us return to the prewar period for a moment. The surrealist painter Kitawaki Noboru (1901–1951) created a drawing called *Ryōanji sekitei sokuzu* (Survey diagram on the stone garden of Ryōanji; figure 11), reportedly in 1939. It looks quite similar to the Kyoto University surveyor's diagram, but the measurement units used for the vertical lines are different. The story behind the creation of this diagram is unclear, but it seems that Kitawaki did the measurements himself.

In 1941, Kitawaki painted an oil painting based on his diagram called *Ryōanji sekitei bekutoru kōzō* (The vector structure of the rock garden at Ryōanji). It is a fairly un-surrealist painting and looks like an extremely simplified version of his diagram. Perhaps Kitawaki felt that the situation prevailing during wartime was no longer compatible with surrealism and so he decided to try to change his style.

Turning to postwar diagrams, figure 12 is well known. It appears in the book *Ryōanji sekitei nanatsu no nazo o toku* (Answers to the seven riddles of the rock garden at Ryōanji) written by Ōyama Heishirō, who was men-

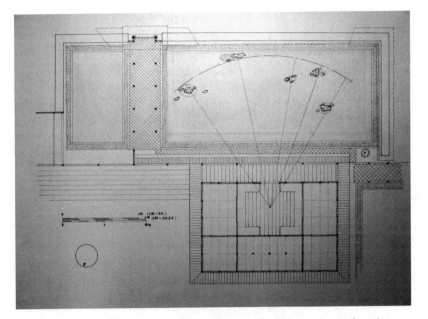

Figure 12. Drawing of garden by Ōyama (1970). Reprinted by permission from the Ōyama Collection, Research Center for Japanese Garden Art & Historical Heritage, Kyoto University of Art and Design.

tioned previously.[105] It is a commonly held belief that if one looks at the garden while walking on the veranda in front of the abbot's quarters, only fourteen stones are visible at any one time, even though the garden contains fifteen stones. People say that this shows the skill with which the stones were arranged. This explanation seems easy for middle school and high school students to understand. If one listens to how the guides explain the garden to the students they bring to Ryōanji on field trips, one always hears them tell the students that one stone is hidden.

The point of Ōyama's book was that the stones are arranged like a fan opening around the center of the abbot's quarters. He says that according to his diagram, all fifteen stones can be seen from the center of the abbot's quarters and that this is the point from which the garden is intended to be viewed. He also says that even if one does not go all the way to the center, all of the stones can be seen from a point three meters inside the abbot's

105. Ōyama, *Ryōanji sekitei nanatsu no nazo o toku,* 63.

quarters. Of course, it is forbidden to enter the abbot's quarters, so there is no way for an ordinary person to verify Ōyama's theory.

In reality, however, even without entering the abbot's quarters, there is a point on the veranda where it is possible for one to see all of the stones, if just barely. This is something that I "discovered" at the site. As insignificant as it is, this is, perhaps, the only "new theory" about Ryōanji that can be found in this book.

What Ōyama really wanted to present in his book *Ryōanji sekitei nanatsu no nazo o toku* was his new theory that Shiken, who designed the gardens at Reiun'in within the Myōshinji temple compound, was the creator of the rock garden at Ryōanji. Ōyama cited a number of things as the basis for his belief, such as the style in which the garden was made, the types of stones used, and, furthermore, the fact that the same person was chief priest at both Reiun'in and Ryōanji.

It appears that Mori Osamu thought Ōyama was going too far. Mori criticized Ōyama's position, saying, "Even if there are a few points of similarity between the grouped stones in the garden at Reiun'in and the rock garden at Ryōanji, I think that more scientific data and a longer period of careful research are necessary before it can be definitely determined that they were both created by Shiken."[106] This sounds like a scholar disparaging a layman's "scholarly theory."

While this garden research dispute was going on there were people who watched with exasperation. One of these was Sasaki Kōzō (1928–), an art historian at Waseda University. Sasaki wrote the following in the magazine *Geijutsu shinchō*:

> The discussion of the rock garden at Ryōanji is still filled with riddles. This is not because there is insufficient documentary data or because garden research is still immature . . . the fault lies with a generally low-level method of research characterized by an old-fashioned outlook, where researchers make it their life's work to determine when and by whom the garden was built.[107]

There is little doubt that Sasaki wrote these words with Ōyama's *Ryōanji sekitei nanatsu no nazo o toku* in mind. The book had been published the previous year and caused something of a stir. It would not have been un-

106. Mori Osamu, "Ryōanji sekitei ni tsuite," *Zen bunka* 64 (1972): 51.

107. Sasaki Kōzō, "Ryōanji sekitei no nazo," *Geijutsu shinchō* 22: 9 (September 1971): 127.

reasonable for Sasaki to become exasperated with the incorrigibility of garden historians who seemed never to tire of coming up with one "new theory" after another.

What Sasaki wrote seems to have cut Ōyama to the quick. The following year Ōyama published a paper in *Zen bunka* in which he refuted Sasaki quite bluntly. In his rebuttal, Ōyama stated his belief that his style of research, which concentrated on determining the identity of the creator of the garden and the year of its creation, was the "essence" of the garden history field; and he denounced Sasaki's position, which belittled that approach, as amounting to a "declaration that research should be abandoned."[108]

However, Ōyama was under a misapprehension. He mistook Sasaki, who was actually an art historian, for a garden historian, and so he interpreted Sasaki's words as being yet more of the abuse that he had suffered from people in his own field. In his rebuttal of Sasaki, Ōyama inadvertently exposed the situation in the field of garden history scholarship, saying it "is not completely free of difficult-to-eradicate unscholarly barriers, such as artificial factions divorced from pure scholarship trying to consolidate false theories."[109] As an independent scholar not affiliated with any of the old imperial universities, this is probably how Ōyama really felt.

The next diagram I would like to discuss (figure 13) was published in 1980 by the landscape gardener Ono Masa'aki (1947–).[110] Based on Shigemori's surveyor's diagram, Ono discovered that the rock garden contained what he called the "15-*shaku* standard."[111] Almost all of the stone groupings in the garden are ensconced in a harmonious relationship of a distance from one another of 15 *shaku*, half of that (7.5 *shaku*), or one third of that (5 *shaku*). The only stones that are outside of this relationship is the grouping deep in the interior of the garden on the right as seen from the abbot's quarters (labeled "E" in figure 13). Ono states that this group of stones, which is outside the 15-*shaku* relationship, was not there when the garden was built. Ono hypothesizes that Akisato Ritō moved the group of stones labeled E to their present location from another area of the temple grounds. This sounds somewhat suspicious to me, but I have no grounds on which to refute such a theory.

108. Ōyama Heishirō, "Ryōanji sekitei ni kansuru nana shō (ge)," *Zen bunka* 67 (1972): 66–71.

109. Ibid., 67.

110. Ono Masa'aki, "Ryōanji hōjō nantei II: Shōzen," *Rinsen* 320 (1980): 3–5..

111. A *shaku* is a traditional Japanese unit of measurement roughly equal to one foot.

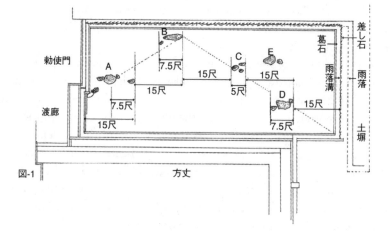

Figure 13.　Sketch of garden by Ono (1980). Reprinted in Ono (2003).

With the appearance of Ono's theory, it seems that the attempt to prove the beauty of the rock garden at Ryōanji came to a halt for quite some time. However, in 2002, Gerte J. Van Tonder, who had been a graduate student at Kyoto University, used a computer-based calculation called medial axis transformation to show that the visual axis of the rock garden passes through the center of the abbot's quarters (figure 14).[112] When these findings were published in *Nature*, the most authoritative science journal in the world, all of the newspapers in Japan featured this story en masse, creating something of a sensation.

This research was still fresh at the time this book was written, so while I do not want to rush to judgment, I would like to raise just two points. First, Van Tonder's conclusion, which was to give a privileged position to the center of the abbot's quarters because of the arrangement of the stones, is no different from Ōyama's 1980 theory. Other than the fact that he used a computer and complicated calculations, it does not seem to me that there is any particular difference between the two. Second, I want to emphasize that here again we can see the Japanese penchant for setting a high value on the fact that a foreigner discovered the beauty of Japan and that this theory was well regarded by a foreign science journal. After all,

112. Gert J. Van Tonder, Michael J. Lyons, and Yoshimichi Ejima, "Visual Structure of a Japanese Zen Garden," *Nature* 419 (2002): 359.

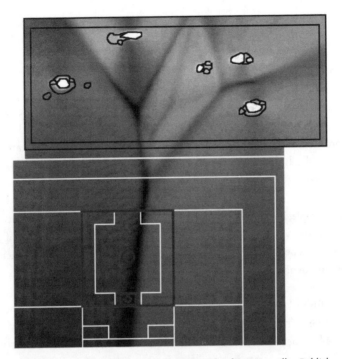

Figure 14. Graphic by Van Tonder. Reprinted by permission from Macmillan Publishers Ltd.:
Nature © 2002.

if the rock garden at Ryōanji had been unknown outside of Japan, *Nature*
would never have been interested in Van Tonder's thesis. For now, I would
like to conclude by pointing out that research which is considered science
with its universal applicability really only becomes meaningful within the
historical dynamic.

Van Tonder's thesis was the first new theory about Ryōanji to appear in
almost two decades, but it represents research in the scholarly field of visual data processing, which is unrelated to the history of gardens. To what
conclusion, then, did the majority of garden historians come regarding
the beauty of the rock garden? I think that this is summed up by the following words of Shigemori Mirei, from his *Nihon teienshi taikei*:

> The finest artwork is that in which, depending on the viewer's feelings, a
> great number of different themes can be discovered. In this sense, there is
> no garden with depths as unplumbed as the garden at Ryōanji. It is a garden

which one can view scores, no, hundreds of times without wearying of it. For a person who has seen the garden once or twice to say, "I understand this garden well now," is the height of absurdity.[113]

From before World War II, Shigemori had been repeatedly saying that a person without an eye for beauty could not understand the rock garden at Ryōanji. For example, as early as 1935, Shigemori wrote the following in his commemorative message for the inaugural issue of *Rinsen* (Landscape gardens), the house publication of the Kyoto Garden Association, which he founded:

> For example, if a person can see a different kind of great natural beauty in the finished work despite the fact that a completely unnatural mode of expression is being used, as in the gardens at Ryōanji and Daisen'in, such a person can, in general, be said to have the ability to appreciate gardens.[114]

This line of argument is truly vexing, because it just goes around in circles, like this: if a person does not understand the rock garden, that is because he does not have the ability to appreciate it; and if a person has the ability to appreciate it, he will understand the merit of the rock garden. It seems as though Shigemori had no choice but to give up on trying to explain the beauty of the rock garden. All he could do was to simply keep on repeating that one could not appreciate its beauty after only seeing it once or twice.

Not only Shigemori but Ōyama Heishirō also came to follow the same course. In *Nihon teien shi shinron* (New theories on the history of Japanese gardens; 1987), Ōyama concluded that the rock garden was excellent because "it combined all of the elements necessary for excellence."[115] Ōyama named three things as "the elements that make the rock garden excellent": the absence of a single tree or shrub; the thoroughness of its symbolic representation; and the superiority of its spatial composition.

Let us stop here and think a moment. Are there any gardens other than Ryōanji, and the gardens it has influenced, that are devoid of trees or shrubbery, are symbolic, and have skillfully executed spatial compositions? It really seems that Ōyama is simply listing the qualities that the

113. Shigemori and Shigemori, *Nihon teienshi taikei*, 84.
114. Shigemori Mirei, "Nihon teien no kanshō hō (2)," *Rinsen* 2 (1935): 58–59.
115. Ōyama Heishirō, *Nihon teienshi shinron* (Tokyo: Heibonsha, 1987), 827–32.

rock garden at Ryōanji possesses and saying that since these are excellent qualities, the garden is excellent. This is not proof of anything at all. In logic, this is called a tautology. A tautology may exist in rhetoric, but there is no way to prove the truth or the falsehood of it.

One night Ōyama saw the rock garden, illuminated by the full moon, shrouded in a bluish white, glimmering mist the shade of oxidized silver. He said, "Seeing this unexpected mystical scene, I felt an excitement throughout my whole body that took my breath away, and I continued standing lost in quiet contemplation, oblivious to the increasing lateness of the hour."[116]

This is something of a digression, but Kitagawa Momoo (1899–1969), who is famous for translating D. T. Suzuki's *Zen and Japanese Culture* into Japanese, also spoke about the beauty of the rock garden in the moonlight in *Sekitei rinsen* (Rock and landscape gardens; 1954), saying, "it displayed a strange beauty, if that is the right word, that makes one feel a kind of bleak desolation."[117] I am sure that the rock garden under the moonlight is quite pretty. There is no doubt that the more times a person has seen the garden, the more its beauty will sink into his consciousness.

Shigemori said that in order to understand the true beauty of the garden one had to see it scores of times. Ōyama said that the true beauty of the rock garden is revealed only under the moonlight. However, only a local person with a great deal of leisure time at his disposal could afford to visit the rock garden the number of times Shigemori requires; and except for special occasions, a person would not be able to see the rock garden under the light of a full moon.

These two distinguished authorities, even though they lived in the mundane world, had fallen into a dimension where they searched for the beauty of the rock garden in a world that only they knew and that everyday people could not experience. In the end, in trying to explain the reasons why the rock garden at Ryōanji was beautiful, all they did was emphasize their own privileged position.

116. Ibid., 834.
117. Kitagawa Momoo, *Sekitei rinsen* (Tokyo: Chikuma Shobō, 1952), 37.

6 Looking at the
Mirror's Reflection

ANOTHER JAPAN EXPERIENCE

Exactly how have *kyūdō* and Ryōanji been introduced in foreign countries? The popular conception is that they are both connected to the essence of Zen. However, as we have seen, this image has a specific origin that is fairly recent, and it is an image created with a specific intention in mind.

Knowledge of *kyūdō* and Ryōanji spread in foreign countries during the 1950s. This is closely intertwined with the great Zen boom that occurred in Europe and the United States at that time. In the midst of this Zen boom, the twin images of Herrigel as the first Westerner to embody Zen through the practice of *kyūdō* and of the rock garden at Ryōanji as the icon of mysterious Zen thought spread far and wide.

I would like to look primarily at the process of how, from the 1950s onward, Herrigel and Ryōanji became intertwined in the context of Zen and how this was received in Japan and foreign countries. In foreign countries, the leading roles in this process were played by Bruno Taut, Isamu Noguchi, Arthur Koestler (1905–1983), and Alan Watts (1915–1973). When the opinions of these men were reimported back into Japan — that is, when the Zen community, the *kyūdō* community, the garden history community, and the Japanese intelligentsia saw their self-image reflected in the mirror—how did they react?

Before I go into this subject, however, I would like to talk about a man named William R. B. Acker (1907–1974), someone who is practically unknown. Acker was a researcher at the Freer Gallery of Art, one of the constituent museums of the Smithsonian Institution. From 1933 until 1937, while he was still in his twenties, he lived in Kyoto and conducted research on Asian art while practicing *kyūdō*.

Why is Acker important? The book he wrote, *The Fundamentals of Japanese Archery*[1] (1937), is the oldest serious English-language book about *kyūdō* among those that are presently known. It was published eleven years earlier than Herrigel's *Zen in the Art of Archery*. However, Acker did not write it by himself. Only 250 copies were originally printed, and up until the mid-1990s, the first edition was considered to be a phantom book. As far as I have been able to determine, there are only six copies of the first edition still in existence: two in Holland, two in the United States, one in Belgium, and one in Japan. This book was reprinted in 1965 by Tuttle and is now available in paperback.[2] As a result, Acker's book is fairly well known among foreign *kyūdō* practitioners. However, it was not widely read by people who do not practice *kyūdō* themselves. In this respect, it is completely different from Herrigel's book.

In spite of the fact that Acker's book was published eleven years earlier than Herrigel's book, it was not popular among the general public. Why was this? The reason is very simple: it was too specialized. All Acker did was explain the shooting method of *kyūdō* in plain and simple language, faithfully adhering to the teachings of a traditional school. There is practically no trace whatsoever of the mysticism and Zen found in Herrigel's book. This is not because Acker did not understand Japanese culture; it is because this is the kind of book that will naturally result if the author has a normal understanding of *kyūdō*.

What sort of a person was Acker and what was he doing in Japan? I would like to give some background on him while contrasting him with Herrigel. Acker was born in New York on October 17, 1907. He was twenty-three years younger than Herrigel, who was born in 1884. Acker majored

1. Nasu Munekazu and William R. B. Acker, *Fundamentals of Japanese Archery*, Vol. 1 (Kyoto: Shikisha, 1937).

2. William R. B. Acker, *Japanese Archery* (Rutland, VT and Tokyo: Tuttle, 1965).

in Chinese studies at Harvard University, and became a researcher at the Freer Gallery of Art in 1929. He was posted to Japan by the gallery from 1933 until 1937. He received his PhD from the University of Leiden in Holland in 1940. He retired from the Freer Gallery in 1946. Subsequently, after working at the University of Leiden library and in various other capacities, he became a professor at the University of Ghent in 1959. He died of illness in Antwerp in 1974.

It seems as though Acker had a playful and mischievous character. The Freer Gallery has kept much of the correspondence that Acker wrote to his superiors, and from these letters it is possible to get an idea of his personality. For example, on a trip to Paris when he was twenty-two, he suddenly decided to get married, only to face the bitter opposition of his superiors; and on one occasion he even sent his supervisor a picture of himself cooling off, sitting naked in a tub in his study while reading, inscribed in Chinese with the legend "*zhizhe leshui*" (a man of wisdom enjoys water).[3] According to a person who has met Acker's wife, Acker was fond of drinking from a young age, and it seems that he died from an illness brought on by alcoholism.

Acker's field was East Asian art history, and most of his achievements were in this area. His main work was a serious scholarly treatise with the title *Some Tang and Pre-Tang Texts on Chinese Painting* (1954).[4] This book consists of English translations, with notes and commentary, of three representative treatises on painting from the period ending with the Tang: *Guhua pinlu* (Classification of ancient painters) by Xie He, *Xuhua pin* (A sequel to the evaluation of paintings) by Chun Yaosui, and *Lidai minghua ji* (Record of famous painters of all dynasties) by Zhang Yanyuan. *Lidai minghua ji* is a particularly important document in the field of the history of Chinese painting, and translating such a number of works in their entirety into English is a tremendous accomplishment. In the field of Japanese art, Acker also translated and published *Hōryūji hekiga no kenkyū* (1932; *The Wall-Paintings of Horyuji*, 1943) by Naitō Tōichirō (1897–1939).[5] Acker worked on these translations while he was in Japan.

3. 知者樂水. This four-character phrase appears in *The Analects* by Confucius (551 BC–479 BC).

4. William R. B. Acker, *Some T'ang and Pre-T'ang Texts on Chinese Painting* (Westport, CT: Hyperion Press, 1954).

5. Naitō Tōichirō, *Hōryūji hekiga no kenkyū* (Osaka: Tōyō Bijutsu Kenkyūkai Ōsaka Shibu, 1932; trans. William R. B. Acker as *The Wall-Paintings of Horyuji* [Baltimore: Waverly Press, 1943]).

Acker came to Kyoto on February 10, 1933. He was keenly interested in Zen and had read the well-known Zen text *Bi Yan Lu* (*Blue Cliff Record*) in English translation. It seems as though Acker had already decided to live in a Zen temple when he came to Japan, and he took up lodgings at Enpukuji as soon as he arrived in Kyoto. One does not hear of this sort of thing much today, but in the past in Kyoto, regular people could rent land and buildings at famous temples and live there just as they would live anywhere else.[6] The actor Tsugawa Masahiko (1940–) said that when he was a child, he lived at Ryōanji on rented land.[7]

Acker describes his life at Enpukuji as follows:

> Living in Enpukuji was somewhat strenuous. Breakfast was at five in the morning, and was preceded by a long chanting of the scriptures, the monks all sitting huddled on the *tatami* of the chapel, shivering in the early morning frost. The chanting would have been more impressive had any two of them sung in the same key, and I could not help wishing that the rhythms maintained by the drum and gong would come a bit nearer to synchronizing.... More chanting, and then the meal, eaten in perfect silence. Rice gruel and *daikon* [Japanese radish], nothing further. The other meals were exactly the same except that you got a sort of red bean soup with the rice and *daikon*. Lunch was at ten, and dinner at four.[8]

Acker's description of the meals and the chanting of the sutras at a Zen temple is quite vivid. It seems as though he was delighted with his new experience of living at a Zen temple. He did not stay long at Enpukuji, however, and he next moved to Fukōin, a sub-temple of Shōkokuji. Acker lived there until he left Japan in 1937 and completely immersed himself in traditional Zen temple life. This was completely different than Herrigel, who tried to approach Zen in a roundabout way.

6. An article in the *New York Times*, dated December 25, 1932, reported: "American seekers after the 'Light of Asia' can now study Zen, or meditative Buddhism, at a hostel which has been specially built for foreign comfort and dedicated in the name of world peace to foreigners in search of the wisdom of the East. It is attached to the Empukuji [*sic*] Temple in Yawata.... They will be guided in their meditations by Chief Priest Kotsuki and his sermons will be interpreted once a week by Dr. Daisetsu Suzuki."

7. Tsugawa Masahiko, "Watashi to Ryōanji," in *Daiunzan Ryōanji* (Kyoto: Saikōsha, n.d.).

8. Letter from William R. B. Acker to John Lodge, March 4, 1933, William R. B. Acker's Personal File, Collection of Smithsonian Freer Gallery of Art.

There is one more difference between Herrigel and Acker. Herrigel came to Japan looking for Zen. Acker, however, did not come to Japan for Zen; he came to Japan to conduct research on Asian art. Through living in a Zen temple, he became familiar with the world of Zen in a completely natural way.

The decisively different ways in which Herrigel and Acker came into contact with Zen resulted in great differences in their encounter with *kyūdō* and what each of them learned from it. In Herrigel's case, on the advice of an acquaintance he began studying *kyūdō* as a shortcut to Zen. In Acker's case, how he came to *kyūdō* is rather surprising: he was out on a stroll and he simply happened to pass by a *kyūdō* training hall. He talks about it in this excerpt from a letter dated June 2, 1933:

On May twelfth, I went around to the Butokuden to see the fencing and *jūdō*. While there I stumbled upon the archery grounds, went into the building, and sat down to one side to look on at the shooting.

Got into a conversation with one of the people there, Mr. Nasu—and first thing I knew I had a bow in my hands and was shooting at a straw barrel, with him showing me how to hold the string with my thumb—nock the arrow etc.

I asked if foreigners could join, and he said yes. Took me right over to the office where I became a Butokukai member in about five minutes for as many yen.

Thence we went to his home where he showed me swords, one of them over five hundred years old. When I left, he presented me with a couple of sword guards and some old Japanese iron arrowheads. He came round to call next day, and I gave him one of the Chinese composite bows I had brought back with me from China, together with some arrows.

Since that time, he has come around every morning and stayed from eight to ten instructing me in the art. Isn't getting anything for it but the pleasure of spreading knowledge of *kyūdō* which is a religion to him. He speaks not a word of English—and talks steadily all the time—so I couldn't possibly have better practice in conversation, and what's more I get good exercise.

We practice in the garden back of the Fukōin.[9]

9. Letter from William R. B. Acker to John Lodge, June 2, 1933, William R. B. Acker's Personal File.

An affable Japanese befriends a foreigner who wandered into the training hall and then goes to his house every day to teach him *kyūdō*. This really evokes a nostalgic scene from times gone by. It seems to me that Japanese people are not that friendly anymore.

The Japanese named Nasu was the Kyoto archer Nasu Toshisuke (Munekazu, 1901–1978). He is also, with Acker, the coauthor of *The Fundamentals of Japanese Archery*. There are a lot of things we do not know about Nasu. In an issue of the magazine *Kyūdō* from 1965 there is a photograph of Nasu attempting the *tōshiya* at Sanjusangendō. According to the magazine, Nasu held the rank of *renshi*, sixth degree,[10] and belonged to the Ishidō Chikurin-ha, a traditional school of *kyūjutsu*. The shooting technique described in *The Fundamentals of Japanese Archery* conforms to the Chikurin-ha tradition. However, in the foreword, Acker describes Nasu as the student of Ichikawa Kojirō (Nobumitsu, 1846–1925), who was an archer of the Yamato-ryū.[11]

It appears that Nasu subsequently taught *kyūdō* at the American School in Kyoto, and an English-language book that he coauthored, *A Syllabus on Japanese Archery* (1949),[12] is still extant. However, the shooting technique described in this book is neither that of the Yamato-ryū or the Chikurin-ha. Nasu described himself as a twenty-sixth-generation descendent of Nasu no Yoichi (a famous archer of medieval Japan), but of course there is no proof that this is actually true. In any case, while there are many things about him that are unclear, he seems to have been a cheerful, normal Japanese person one cannot help but like. He was very different from Awa Kenzō, who conducted himself as though he was a religious figure.

Both the Yamato-ryū and the Ishidō Chikurin-ha are traditional schools several hundred years old with documented lineages, and so regardless of the school to which he belonged, what this means is that Nasu received instruction from a legitimate successor to his school's lineage. On this point also he was very different from Awa, who studied a branch of a traditional school and then created his own individual style of *kyūjutsu* from what he had learned. While it is not possible to state categorically that one way is better than the other, it is clear that Nasu was much closer to the mainstream of Japanese archery than was Awa.

10. *Renshi* is a teaching certification.

11. Yamato-ryū is a traditional *kyūjutsu* school founded by Morikawa Kōzan in 1652.

12. Nasu Toshisuke, and Betty Hornish, *A Syllabus on Japanese Archery* (Kyoto: Kyoto American School, 1949).

Nasu did not talk to Acker about Zen. *The Fundamentals of Japanese Archery* says that we can see an influence of Zen Buddhism in the breathing during shooting, but that is the extent of it. Nasu did not use any of the mysterious figures of speech that Awa loved. Acker includes a very long footnote in *The Fundamentals of Japanese Archery* regarding breathing where he speculates that the breathing of *kyūdō* might be related to Zen. However, he does not say anything further than this regarding *kyūdō* and Zen. Acker chose to live in a Zen temple and became intimately familiar with Japanese culture through his art research; but even so, he did not discover Zen in *kyūdō*. This is not because he overlooked something important. It is because at that time, *kyūdō* and Zen were two separate things.

In a letter of Acker's dated January 24, 1934, he included a chart showing his weekly schedule. According to this schedule, his weekly routine included *kyūdō* practice with Nasu on Tuesday, Wednesday, and Saturday for two hours each day. This is more practice than the average modern *kyūdō* practitioner puts in. Of course, it is also far more practice than Herrigel, who only trained with Awa once a week.

There is a Chinese archery text from the Ming period called the *Wujing shexue zhengzong* (The orthodox study of archery in the military classics). While it is very long and difficult to understand, serious modern Japanese *kyūdō* practitioners read it avidly, even today. It appears that Acker and a friend of his were translating *Wujing shexue zhengzong* into English. In the foreword to *The Fundamentals of Japanese Archery*, Acker says that "I hope to complete and publish it at some future time."

There is probably no doubt that Acker really was translating *Wujing shexue zhengzong* into English. I say this because when Acker's book collection found its way into a used book store in London in 1996, the catalog describing the contents included *Wujing shexue zhengzong* (three volumes), *Wujing shexue zhengzong zhimi zhu* (The orthodox study of archery in the military classics, instructional texts; five volumes), and *Wakun shagaku seisō* (Japanese gloss of the orthodox school of shooting). Unfortunately, the price for these books was exorbitant, and I was not able to examine them. Acker kept these books his entire life. He must have always hoped to translate and publish them, yet he died without being able to accomplish his goal. One can feel Acker's passion for *kyūdō* from the fact that he would attempt to translate such a long and difficult text as *Wujing shexue zhengzong*. I do not think that it can be said that there was any difference between Acker and Herrigel in their desire to understand *kyūdō*.

Acker made the following wry observation in a letter dated November 21, 1937, as the time of his departure from Japan approached.

> The last month has of course been unusually expensive—that little pamphlet on archery cost me all in all about 500.00 yen to put out, and so far I have been giving copies away and haven't sold one. I had 250 copies printed—or rather multigraphed—and hope to be able to sell them for about $1.00 apiece to American archers. Most of that 500.00 yen was spent about 6 months ago for paper, binding, etc., which partly explains the indebtedness to the Gallery. Archery has been a very expensive pastime: had I known how expensive, I would never have let myself in for it. But as a matter of fact, most of these Japanese pastimes [dōraku] are expensive. The equipment [dōgu] always turns out to be far more expensive than you could have dreamt—and each exam to get an additional grade [kyū] or rank [dan], you get an additional gratuity [orei] to pay—"it gradually runs over the budget" [dandan ashi ga deru], as the Japanese say.[13]

This kind of concern with everyday, worldly things is completely absent from Herrigel's book. While it may sound rather mercenary, such things are very common in Japanese society. However, it is somewhat embarrassing for Japanese to be shown this kind of self-image by a foreigner. Japanese would, after all, prefer to see the noble image of the Japanese that Herrigel showed them. Thus, they have been continually making this kind of unconscious choice.

Herrigel took a Daishadōkyō rank test, and with one word from Awa he was given a fifth-degree ranking on the spot. Acker, on the other hand, took his rank tests from the Butokukai, the national kyūdō organization that existed at that time. He got his first-degree ranking on his second attempt and received his second-degree ranking before he left Japan. To a modern-day kyūdō practitioner, this is an easily understandable, average rate of advancement for a person who has been practicing for four years.

Acker is an interesting case, being a member of the foreign intelligentsia who was interested in Zen and Japanese culture, and who, after coming into contact with a traditional school of kyūjutsu in Kyoto, left such a book and

13. Letter from William R. B. Acker to John Lodge, November 21, 1937, William R. B. Acker's Personal File.

letters for posterity. Nevertheless, the difference between Acker's book and Herrigel's *Zen in the Art of Archery* is astonishing. The important point, however, is that the Japanese did not want to look into the mirror called Acker.

BRUNO TAUT AND RYŌANJI

The rock garden at Ryōanji is similar to *kyūdō* in the sense that the aura of Zen surrounding it was not as strong in the past as it is now. *Kyūdō* and Ryōanji are also similar in that until around 1930, few if any foreigners knew about them. However, Ryōanji was not unknown because no foreigners visited Kyoto. According to the book *Kyoto* (1910), the numbers of foreigners who visited Kyoto during the years 1905 through 1908 were 6,166, 7,373, 6,823 and 6,368 respectively.[14] This cannot be compared to the numbers who visit today, but considering the fact that there was no air travel then, these are respectable numbers. However, it was rare for any of these foreign tourists to visit Ryōanji.

Ryōanji was simply not popular with tourists. As I mentioned earlier, Ryōanji was rarely mentioned in Japanese-language guidebooks from the late nineteenth century. The same was true of English-language guidebooks to Kyoto.

Let us look at a few examples of English-language guidebooks. Ryōanji does not appear in *The Guide to the Celebrated Places in Kiyoto & The Surrounding Places for the Foreign Visitors* (1873).[15] Even though Ryōanji also has a stone garden, the stone garden at Daisen'in is mentioned instead. *Illustrated Guide To Kyoto & Its Suburbs* (1891)[16] also features Daisen'in and omits Ryōanji. The tendency to feature Daisen'in and ignore Ryōanji can also be seen in *Kyoto, Japan (with 120 Illustrations)* (1903),[17] compiled by the Kyoto City Council. In this book, not only is there no text discussing Ryōanji, the accompanying map does not even show that there is a temple where Ryōanji is located.

14. Niwa Keisuke, *Kyoto* (Kyoto: Kyoto Exhibitor's Association to the Japanese-British Exhibition, 1910), 30.

15. Yamamoto Kakuma, *The Guide to the Celebrated Places in Kiyoto & The Surrounding Places for the Foreign Visitors* (Kyoto: Niwa, 1873).

16. Yoshii Tsunetarō, *Illustrated Guide to Kyoto & Its Suburbs: with Map, an Entirely New Work* (Osaka: T. Nakashima, 1891).

17. Kyōto-shi Sanjikai, *Kyoto, Japan (with 120 illustrations)* / compiled by the Kyoto City Council (Kyoto: K. Azumae, 1903).

When foreign visitors came to Kyoto, one of the places they usually stayed was the Miyako Hotel. However, *The Miyako Hotel Guide to Kyoto and the Surrounding Districts* (1908),[18] a small booklet published by the hotel, contains no mention of either Ryōanji or Daisen'in. As we can see, guidebooks for foreigners ignored Ryōanji.

Prominent foreigners who wrote about Japanese gardens after the late nineteenth century rarely touched on Ryōanji, nor did they say that Japanese gardens had a Zen air about them. For example, while the zoologist Edward Morse (1838–1925), who is famous for the excavation at Ōmori Kaizuka,[19] recognized the artistry of Japanese gardens in his book *Japanese Homes and Their Surroundings* (1885),[20] he viewed them only as "decorations."

The architect Josiah Condor (1852–1920), who designed the Rokumei Hall,[21] wrote a book called *Landscape Gardening in Japan* (1893), in which he explained Japanese gardens from a professional point of view while quoting from classical texts. While he described Ryōanji by saying, "Abstaining from employing even a single tree, [Sōami] combined clipped shrubs and bushes with rocks of fantastic shapes to represent the forms of ocean islands,"[22] he did not equate this with Zen.

In his essay "In a Japanese Garden" (1894),[23] Lafcadio Hearn (1850–1904) also minutely described the garden at his home in Matsue, and while he spoke of "the beauty of the stones," he did not call this Zen.[24]

The situation began to change on October 3, 1933 when the German architect Bruno Taut visited Japan and was taken to see Ryōanji by his Japanese hosts. The entry in Taut's diary for this day contains the following words:

18. *The Miyako Hotel Guide to Kyoto and the Surrounding Districts* (Kyoto: Nishimura Jinbei, 1908).

19. The shell mounds of Ōmori, said to be the birthplace of Japanese archeology.

20. Edward S. Morse, *Japanese Homes and Their Surroundings* (New York: Harper & Bros., 1885).

21. This Western-style hall, constructed in Tokyo in 1883, became a symbol of Westernization in Japan.

22. Josiah Condor, *Landscape Gardening in Japan* (Tokyo: Kelly & Walsh, 1893), 17.

23. Lafcadio Hearn, "In a Japanese Garden," in *Glimpses of Unfamiliar Japan* (New York: Houghton, Mifflin, 1894).

24. Suzuki Makoto, *Nihon jin no teien kan* (Tokyo: Tōkyō Nōgyō Daigaku Zōen Gakka, 1997); Katahira Miyuki, "*Nihon teien*" *zō no keisei to kaishaku no kattō: eigo ken no manazashi to Nihongawa no ōtō (1868–1940)* (Kanagawa: Sōgō Kenkyū Daigakuin Daigaku Hakase Ronbun, 2004).

This is the panorama of the garden commonly referred to as the "tiger cubs crossing the river," said to be by Sōami. This garden demands of the viewer that he quiet his mind and contemplate it with the utmost absorption. Each small stone, chosen with the utmost care, seems as though it is alive, and the stones have the appearance of crags in a great sea. Still, it has a Japanese appearance after all.[25]

Taut, who had discovered the beauty of the Katsura Detached Villa, also found a kind of Japanese quietude in the rock garden at Ryōanji and seems to have been quite absorbed by it for a while. There was a reason for Taut to feel this way. On the previous day, October 2, he went to the Takarazuka Theater and saw a musical variety show put on by an all-female cast. He did not enjoy it. He particularly disliked the Western-style revue and criticized it harshly, calling it a "complete burlesque," "kitsch," and "an insult to the Japanese people." The visit to Ryōanji took place the next day. In contrast to the clamor of the Western-style women's musical variety show, he must have felt that it was remarkably quiet and very Japanese.

The people who planned Taut's Ryōanji visit were two Japanese Modernist architects, Ueno Isaburō (1892–1972) and Kurata Chikatada (1895–1966). Ueno invited Taut to Japan and arranged his visit to the Katsura Detached Villa, which took place the day after he arrived. Ueno's house was only a stone's throw from Ryōanji. I do not know whether this was because he liked the rock garden or for some other reason. In any case, Ueno was in a position to be able to visit the rock garden any time he felt the desire to do so. Taut often stayed at Ueno's house when he visited Kyoto, so his visit to Ryōanji on October 3, 1933, may not have been the only time he went there.

Kurata had a particular regard for Ryōanji. He describes his feelings about the rock garden in an essay he wrote in 1927:

I can look at this garden for any length of time, and as I do so, all sorts of images float into my mind one after the other and then disappear, just as if I were viewing a perfect natural scene which human hands could do nothing to improve.[26]

25. Bruno Taut, *Nihon Tauto no nikki 1933 nen*, trans. Shinoda Hideo (Tokyo: Iwanami Shoten, 1975), 263–64.

26. Kurata Chikatada, "Ryōanji sonota," in *Kindaiteki kakudo* (Tokyo: Shinyūdō Shoten, 1933), 263. I thank Professor Inoue Shōichi for introducing me to this book.

However, as can be seen from reading Kurata's words, he is not trying to achieve "emptiness" as he views the garden, nor is he saying that the garden is Zen. Kurata was a Modernist, and for him the garden was a model from which he drew inspiration.

Actually, the simple structure of the rock garden at Ryōanji was a perfect match with the Modernist architectural ideal. The aim of Modernism in Japan was not only to imitate Western architecture but also to carry on the Japanese tradition. The rock garden, along with the Katsura Detached Villa, was a concrete example of the form needed to build the argument to support this approach.

Kurata recorded what happened when Taut visited Ryōanji for the first time:

> When Mr. and Mrs. Taut came to Kyoto again, I met them and we walked around Kyoto visiting various gardens. At that time the four of us, including Mr. Ueno, went to Ryōanji. Taut had praised the Katsura Detached Villa, and I was rather hoping that he would also see the merit that we saw in the rock garden at Ryōanji and was wondering how he would express it. However, from start to finish Taut did nothing but view the garden from one different vantage point after another, all the while saying not a single word, seemingly lost in thought. This whole time Taut was frightfully serious, his broad brow furrowed like that of a philosopher.
>
> To the last, he said nothing while at the garden, but on the way home he said, "to a European, that garden is extremely foreign (*fremde*, in German)" and then lapsed back again into thought. Subsequently, in his book *Houses and People of Japan*, Taut did not interpret the rock garden at Ryōanji aesthetically, but rather, spiritually, citing it as a good example of "an Embodiment of the *Zen* spirit."[27]

Houses and People of Japan was written in German in 1936 and published the following year in English by Sanseidō. According to Kurata, in this book Taut referred to the rock garden at Ryōanji as "an Embodiment of the *Zen* spirit." It is very rare for writings from this period, including those written by Japanese, to explicitly link Zen and the rock garden. A book written by a person of Taut's stature must have had a great impact.

27. Kurata Chikatada, *Burūno Tauto* (Tokyo: Sagami Shobō, 1942), 138–39 (original emphasis).

In Taut's *Houses and People of Japan*, there is a photograph of the rock garden at Ryōanji with the caption "an Embodiment of the *Zen* spirit."[28] However, Taut only used the word "Zen" in the caption of the photograph, and "Zen" is not to be found in the important part of the book—the text itself. All of the photographs were removed from the Japanese-language version of *Houses and People of Japan* published by Iwanami Shoten in 1966, so the phrase "an Embodiment of the *Zen* spirit" is also missing. Parenthetically, however, the following short passage can be found in the main body of the text:

> The garden became a medium of philosophical thought; it had to encourage deeply contemplative moods by reminiscences of natural scenes, or even to produce them. In Ryuanji [*sic*] near Kyoto there is a garden done only in stones on sandy ground without trees and water. Thus, on garden art as on architecture, demands were made which were alien to its being.[29]

Taut's main point was that gardens of the fifteenth and sixteenth centuries were intended to illustrate philosophical ideas, and that in Ryōanji's case, this was expressed in white sand and oddly shaped stones. Compared to this judiciousness found in the text itself, the caption "an Embodiment of the *Zen* spirit" seems somewhat unexpected.

There are a lot of statements from garden historians from this same period, but it is rare to find any that directly connect the rock garden and Zen. If that is the case, where did Taut get his ideas about the rock garden and Zen? One possibility is that the Modernist architects Kurata and Ueno had already interpreted the rock garden in this way. However, this seems unlikely, since, as we saw from Kurata's reminiscence that I quoted earlier, he seemed to be struck by Taut's statement that the rock garden was "an Embodiment of the *Zen* spirit." Why was Taut able to connect the rock garden and Zen? The more one thinks about it, the deeper the mystery becomes. In this connection I have to wonder how the chief priest at that time, Ōsaki Ryōen, explained the garden to Taut, but there is no data that could bring this to light.

Another possibility has to do with when *Houses and People of Japan* was published. Taut completed the manuscript during his stay in Japan, deliv-

28. Bruno Taut, *Houses and People of Japan* (Tokyo: The Sanseido Co. Ltd., 1937), 147.
29. Ibid., 146–47.

ered the photographic negatives and the manuscript to the publisher, and then left for Istanbul without waiting for the book to be printed. Consequently, there is some doubt as to how deeply Taut himself was involved in the photo captions. It may very well be that the editors wrote captions for the photographs without Taut's approval. At the least, this possibility cannot be discounted.

In any case, the caption of the photograph in Taut's book directly linked Zen and the rock garden at Ryōanji. Once this happened, this opinion took on a life of its own. This is seen, for example, in the following passage from Ōyama Heishirō's book, *Ryōanji sekitei nanatsu no nazo o toku*:

> The famous German architect Bruno Taut called the rock garden at Ryōanji "The Philosophical Garden." Was this because he was able to discern the fact that it combined a deep spirituality, an exalted artistry, and a distinct law hidden in its depths?[30]

This statement is misleading. Taut never called Ryōanji "The Philosophical Garden." He made a general statement to the effect that the gardens of the fifteenth to sixteenth century had a tendency to be "mediums of philosophical thought or to encourage deeply contemplative moods." The fact that Ōyama altered the information and gave it his own slant is, in itself, an interesting phenomenon.

THE PEOPLE WHO INTRODUCED ZEN AND RYŌANJI TO THE WEST

Beginning in the mid-1930s, when Taut came to Japan, English-language introductions to the gardens of Kyoto, including Ryōanji, became increasingly popular. There was a specific motivation for this. In 1935, 120 members of the Garden Club of America visited Japan and toured gardens all over the country. The group arrived in Yokohama on May 13, and beginning with a visit to Meiji shrine the following day, they toured gardens in Tokyo, Nikkō, Hakone, Nagoya, Kyoto, and Nara, until their departure from Japan on June 2. They visited Ryōanji on May 22.[31]

---

30. Ōyama Heishirō, *Ryōanji sekitei nanatsu no nazo o toku* (Tokyo: Kōdansha, 1970), 252.

31. *A Photographic Diary of the Visit of the Garden Club of America to Japan* (Tokyo: Beikoku Teien Kurabu Shōtai Iinkai, 1935).

For the garden community in Japan, this inspection tour by the Garden Club of America was a major event. They must have had a lofty goal for the tour, hoping that the Americans would understand how wonderful Japanese gardens were and that this would open the road of friendship between Japan and the United States. Unfortunately, I was unable to find any record of the group members' raw impressions of Ryōanji. There are, however, two English-language books explaining the Japanese garden that were prepared for the visit of the Garden Club and distributed to the members of the tour. These books were written by Tamura Tsuyoshi and Tatsui Matsunosuke. Let us see how Ryōanji is described in these books.

Tamura's *Art of the Landscape Garden in Japan* (1935) describes Ryōanji as follows:

> Let us now discuss the other of the two types originated in the Ashikaga period [ca. 1336–1573], that is, the Flat Garden, by taking individual specimens, most of which are also found in the great Zen temples of Kyoto.
>
> The most famous of the kind is the Stone Garden of the Ryoan-ji [*sic*] . . . and this Ryoan-ji garden is especially noted for its originality of design and perfect beauty of composition. . . . Here one sees the most artistic attitude man can attain toward stones.[32]

The temple of Saihōji in Kyoto, famous for the Kokedera (Moss Temple) on its grounds, has a pond shaped like the Japanese character for "heart" or "mind" (*kokoro* 心). Taking this pond as an example, Tamura says: "The heart-character is often used as the ultimate symbol of Zen thought, and so it is a splendid idea to shape the lake of a Zen temple in the form of this symbolic character, for surely it is conducive to meditation."[33] Following this passage he discusses Ryōanji. This indicates to me that Tamura wanted to imply that the rock garden at Ryōanji was a Zen-style garden. However, I must emphasize that Tamura did not say that the garden was Zen itself.

Tatsui's *Gardens of Japan* (1935) is a lavish, folio-sized book. In it, while asserting that the *karesansui* (withered landscape) garden was influenced by Zen, Tatsui describes the rock garden at Ryōanji as follows: "For instance, the flat garden of the Ryūan-ji [*sic*] Temple in Kyoto, very famous

32. Tamura Tsuyoshi, *Art of the Landscape Garden in Japan* (Tokyo: Kokusai Bunka Shinkokai, 1935), 21–22.

33. Ibid., 21.

from olden times, was certainly laid out according to the same technique as that of the tray-landscape."[34] Thus for Tatsui, what was essential at Ryōanji was not what it was expressing, but the fact that it used the technique of a tray landscape garden. Not only that, the large photo of the rock garden at Ryōanji in his book shows a garden rank with weeds and lacking the famous flowing water pattern in the sand.

In *Japanese Gardens* (1934), an English-language pocketbook that Tatsui published at about the same time as his *Gardens of Japan*, Ryōanji is described very simply: "A flat garden, oblong in shape, enclosed by earthwork walls. Five groups of either two, three or five stones, totaling fifteen stones in all, are arranged, and white sand spread over the whole ground. The ensemble suggests a 'tray landscape.' Attributed to Sōami."[35]

There was another Japanese who introduced Japanese gardens in English even earlier than did Tamura and Tatsui.[36] His name was Harada Jirō (1878–1963), a translator and art historian who was active from the early twentieth century until after World War II. In his book *The Gardens of Japan* (1928),[37] written in masterful English, Harada states that Zen and the tea ceremony (*chanoyu*) brought about a revolution in gardens. In the English-language *Official Catalogue* (1910)[38] of the Kyoto Merchandise Showroom, thought to have been written by Harada, he expresses the same view, describing Ryōanji as follows:

> A rare specimen is found at Ryoanji [*sic*], where, enclosed by low walls on three sides, there are simply fifteen rocks of varying sizes wonderfully grouped on a flat piece of ground covered with sand. This unique garden by So-ami [*sic*] (some say by Zen-ami), is said to illustrate the story of a tiger fleeing from one island to another with its three cubs.[39]

Even for Harada, who insisted that Zen had changed the Japanese garden, the rock garden at Ryōanji did not depict Zen thought but was the "tiger cubs crossing the river" found in the Chinese classics.

34. Tatsui Matsunosuke, *Gardens of Japan* (Tokyo: The Zauho Press, 1935), 7.

35. Tatsui Matsunosuke, *Japanese Gardens* (Tokyo: Maruzen Co., 1934), 67.

36. Katahira, "*Nihon teien" zō no keisei to kaishaku no kattō: eigo ken no manazashi to Nihongawa no ōtō (1868–1940)*.

37. Harada Jiro, *The Gardens of Japan* (London: The Studio Limited, 1928), 4.

38. Niwa Keisuke, *The Official Catalogue* (Kyoto: Kyōto Shōhin Chinretsusho, 1910), 37. I thank Dr. Katahira Miyuki for the reference to this book.

39. Harada, *The Gardens of Japan*, 23.

Aside from Taut, what did other foreigners who saw Ryōanji in the 1930s think of the garden? Loraine E. Kuck was one of the foreigners who came to Japan early on and studied Japanese gardens. She lived in Kyoto and learned about Japanese gardens from Harada Jirō, Tamura Tsuyoshi, Tatsui Matsunosuke, Toyama Eisaku, and Shigemori Mirei. She also wrote an English commentary on Japanese gardens for the visit of the Garden Club of America and subsequently wrote a book based on this commentary called *One Hundred Kyoto Gardens* (1936). In this book, Kuck describes the Ryōanji rock garden as an "esoteric Zen temple garden" and that "the creator of this garden was a follower of Zen."[40]

Kuck clearly puts a Zen interpretation on the rock garden at Ryōanji. In her book *The Art of Japanese Gardens* (1940), she is even more hyperbolic in the way she connects the rock garden and Zen. She devotes an entire chapter, "Sermon in Stone," to Ryōanji wherein she delivers the following panegyric: "undoubtedly this garden is one of the world's great masterpieces of religiously inspired art."[41]

This seems strange, considering that in the 1930s, the garden historians Harada, Tamura, Tatsui, Toyama, and Shigemori, from whom Kuck learned so much, were not advocating the idea that the rock garden was Zen with any particular vigor. Who taught Kuck this Zen interpretation of the rock garden at Ryōanji?

According to the scholar of Japanese gardens Wybe Kuitert, the idea of landscape gardens being expressions of Zen philosophy does not appear until after the beginning of the twentieth century. He says that Kuck's book was the first English-language publication to describe Ryōanji in these terms and that this was due to the influence of Daisetsu T. Suzuki.[42] I agree with Kuitert.

In the foreword to *The Art of Japanese Gardens*, Kuck thanks Suzuki, calling him the "noted Zen scholar, who greatly aided my understanding of that difficult philosophy." In the acknowledgments in a different book she published in 1968,[43] she refers to Suzuki as her "neighbor who discussed

40. Loraine E. Kuck, *One Hundred Kyoto Gardens* (London: Kegan Paul, Trench Trubner, 1936), 111–12.

41. Loraine E. Kuck, *The Art of Japanese Gardens* (New York: John Day, 1940), 156.

42. Wybe Kuitert, *Themes, Scenes, and Taste in the History of Japanese Garden Art* (Amsterdam: J. G. Gieben, 1988), 152.

43. Loraine E. Kuck, *The World of the Japanese Gardens* (New York and Tokyo: Weatherhill, 1968).

Zen." Suzuki published his thesis on the relationship of Japanese culture and Zen—*Zen and Japanese Culture*—in 1938, which coincides with the time that Kuck was in Japan. It seems that Kuck lived near Suzuki's house and that he taught her about Zen along with his view of Japanese culture that he was spreading, one element of which was the idea that Japanese gardens were also Zen.

Thus, in Kuck's book from the 1930s, we can see signs of the rock garden at Ryōanji being introduced as Zen. However, I would like to emphasize the strong possibility that this was due not to the influence of scholars of garden history, but rather to the influence of D. T. Suzuki.

ISAMU NOGUCHI

With the war and its aftermath, the 1940s were a chaotic period that saw little of note in the way of cultural exchanges between Japan and the West concerning Zen. Zen, *kyūdō*, and Ryōanji began to travel back and forth beyond the borders of Japan beginning in the 1950s when Japan's economic recovery was well underway.

To limit the discussion to Ryōanji, the person most responsible for publicizing the rock garden overseas was the avant garde artist Isamu Noguchi. The Zen scholar Yanagida Seizan (1922–2006) also says that Noguchi is the one who taught him that the rock garden is the artistic expression of Zen.[44] Inasmuch as it seems as though Yanagida referred to Noguchi's opinion in order to lend authority to the idea that the garden was beautiful, it is necessary to know who Noguchi was.

Noguchi's father was a Japanese poet and his mother was an American. Born out of wedlock in Los Angeles, Noguchi lived in the United States with his mother, who had been abandoned by his father, eventually becoming a successful artist. In 1950, Noguchi returned to Japan after an absence of nineteen years. He stopped in Japan on his way back to America from India, partly to visit the grave of his father, who had passed away three years earlier. While the Japanese art world was in a fever of excitement over the visit of the world-famous Noguchi, Noguchi himself had a pleasant trip, quietly experiencing his personal roots in Japanese culture.

In the beginning of June, Noguchi spent two weeks in Kyoto. Noguchi

---

44. Yanagida Seizan, *Zen to Nihon bunka* (Tokyo: Kōdansha Gakujutsu Bunko, 1985), 9.

chose the abstract painter Hasegawa Saburō (1906–1957) to be his guide
on the trip. Hasegawa had studied art history at Tokyo Imperial University.
An idiosyncratic artist who was a pioneer of abstract art in Japan, he was
also a person who lived in the junction between Japan and America, traveling back and forth between the two countries.

In preparation for his trip, Noguchi apparently read and reread D. T.
Suzuki's *Zen and Japanese Culture* and books by Bruno Taut.[45] In Kyoto,
Noguchi spent most of his time eagerly visiting Zen temples. Among the
many famous gardens, it was the rock garden at Ryōanji that most capti-
vated him. Hasegawa recollects what happened at that time: "Noguchi had
taken great delight in the beauty of the Katsura Detached Villa, but what
really struck him strongly was the extreme terseness and deep spirituality
of the rock garden at Ryōanji."[46]

This was not the first time Noguchi had seen the rock garden at Ryōanji.
He had also seen it when he went to Japan in 1931 at the age of twenty-
seven. However, it seems as though Noguchi was not particularly moved
by the rock garden at that time. Dore Ashton, the author of *Noguchi: East
and West* (1992) describes Noguchi's encounter with Ryōanji as follows:

> Noguchi remarked that nobody ever went there, which was certainly true
> in 1931. The legendary gardens were generally neglected, as were impor-
> tant architectural structures, many of which were rotting away. He saw the
> most celebrated garden of Ryoanji [*sic*], for instance, at a time when it had
> just been rediscovered by a few aesthetes, mostly European, and its stone
> and gravel arrangements were in disarray. (The sixteenth-generation gar-
> dener Touemon Sanō [*sic*] from Kyoto who assisted Noguchi years later at
> UNESCO's headquarters in Paris, creating a garden, remembered playing
> freely in the enclosure as a child.) The wild and disheveled appearance of
> many of the temple gardens made a deep impression on Noguchi, who, at
> the end of his life, complained that they had been "cosmeticized."[47]

It would be interesting to discuss Sano the gardener, but let us concentrate on Noguchi. Ashton states that at the time of Noguchi's first visit
in 1931, the rock garden was in disarray. However, in 1950, Matsukura

45. Dore Ashton, *Noguchi: East and West* (New York: Knopf, 1992), 96.
46. Hasegawa Saburō, "Noguchi Nippon," *Bijutsu techō* 33 (1950): 59.
47. Ashton, *Noguchi: East and West*, 43.

Shōei had just replaced Ōsaki Ryōen as the head priest and the temple was at its absolute postwar nadir. It is hard to imagine that the rock garden could have been in its present neat and tidy state. Noguchi must have seen essentially the same rock garden both in 1931 and 1950. If that is so, then why on his second visit was he so moved by the rock garden that it changed his subsequent life as an artist?

Two things were decisively different in 1950 as compared to 1931: D. T. Suzuki's book and the presence of the talkative Hasegawa. It is also possible that Noguchi had read Kuck's *The Art of Japanese Gardens*, with its Zen interpretation of Ryōanji. Hasegawa was familiar with Zen through the temple of Engakuji, which is located in Kamakura, where he lived. It is probable that as they viewed the garden, Hasegawa told Noguchi about Zen in his own way. In addition, it is unthinkable that Matsukura, the chief priest, was not present for the visit of such a famous artist as Noguchi. It is probable that Hasegawa translated Matsukura's lecture for Noguchi. Noguchi describes his impression of the rock garden at Ryōanji:

> The garden itself is small, about 24 by 9 meters. Perfectly flat, it is covered with a fine white gravel out of which rise 15 rocks arranged in five main clusters . . . . In viewing this garden one has the sense of being transported into a vast void, into another dimension of reality—time ceases, and one is lost in reverie, gazing at the rocks that rise, ever in the same but different spot, out of the white mist of gravel. . . . Here is an immaculate universe swept clean.[48]

From this point onward, Noguchi began to build gardens that imitated the rock garden at Ryōanji. The following year, in 1951, Noguchi was asked to build a garden at the Tokyo branch of the Reader's Digest building in Takebashi (this is now the Palaceside building, and Noguchi's garden is no longer there). Noguchi constructed a garden with a small artificial hill and running water. He also intended to build a large iron fountain and place large stone sculptures shaped like *kokeshi* dolls in the garden. Neither of these things were in the original order and so payment for them was refused, but Noguchi did make the fountain.

Regarding this project, Noguchi said, "Here was an opportunity to learn from the world's most skilled gardeners, the common Uekiya [gar-

48. Ibid., 111.

dener] of Japan. Through working with them in the mud, I learned the rudiments of stone placing."[49] For Noguchi, the Reader's Digest project was valuable practice.

In 1956, Noguchi was entrusted with creating the garden for the headquarters of UNESCO, which was being built in Paris. In order to compensate for an insufficient budget, Noguchi traveled to Kyoto in hopes of getting donated stones from Japan for the garden. He was hoping to get the great Shigemori Mirei to help him. Shigemori took Noguchi to Shikoku and they selected the stones together.

Although the stones were transported to Paris without incident, there was another problem: there were not enough skilled artisans to do the work. Once again, Noguchi appealed to Shigemori for help. In response to Shigemori's entreaties, Sano Kiichi (1928–) went to Paris. Sano was born into a family that had been garden craftsmen for generations, and he later became the sixteenth-generation Sano Tōemon.[50] Every day Sano and Noguchi were at loggerheads about how the work should be done. For Sano, coming as he did from a long line of traditional garden craftsmen, Noguchi's way of thinking seemed strange; and for Noguchi, Sano appeared to be simply a craftsman who did not understand his art.

In the end, their collaboration was exceedingly unpleasant. Regarding the UNESCO project, Sano said that it "was not what you would call a good experience," and as for Noguchi, "he never again attempted to embrace orthodoxy even partially in his large projects."[51] In the end, the UNESCO project also turned out to be Noguchi's experiment, and it was not well regarded.

About six years after the completion of the UNESCO project, in 1964, Noguchi finished his masterpiece, which he saw fit to call "my Ryūanji [sic], as it were."[52] This is the Sunken Garden in the plaza of the Chase Manhattan Bank building that I introduced at the beginning of this book. About this garden, Noguchi says, "The chief interest here is the use of rocks in a non-traditional way."[53] Noguchi had sublimated the rock garden

49. Isamu Noguchi, *Isamu Noguchi: A Sculptor's World* (London: Thames & Hudson, 1967), 163.

50. In such traditional craft families, the successor to the family line takes on the name of his predecessor, so that the name is continued throughout the generations.

51. Ashton, *Noguchi: East and West*, 147.

52. Noguchi, *Isamu Noguchi*, 171.

53. Ibid.

at Ryōanji in his own unique way and planted it in New York. In this way, Noguchi played a role in exporting Ryōanji overseas. Subsequent to this, Noguchi recorded the following reminiscence:

> I remember a conversation I once had with Suzuki Daisetsu, the great Zen expositor, on the train from Kyoto to Tokyo. I had said that in the West the ideal was to triumph over gravity, and that in doing a rock garden in America it would be logical to have the rocks themselves levitate (as I was then doing in the Chase Manhattan Garden). He replied, "Ah, that is why they will eventually have to come back to us." Did he include me in "us"?[54]

Reading these words, I can feel the lingering pain of Noguchi, born as an illegitimate child of mixed parentage, as he groped for his identity in the interstice between Japan and America. In a way, the garden at the Chase Manhattan Bank, which for Noguchi was "my Ryōanji," was an illegitimate mixed-race child with a Japanese father and an American mother. I think that it was something that expressed Noguchi's own fate. When they gaze at this illegitimate child of mixed race, how do Japanese people feel, I wonder?

HOW *ZEN IN THE ART OF ARCHERY* AND RYŌANJI WERE RECEIVED

The year 1953, when Isamu Noguchi began imitating Ryōanji, was also the year that the English version of *Zen in the Art of Archery* was published. It was after the publication of this English version that Herrigel became world famous. D. T. Suzuki provided a foreword for this English version, an excerpt of which follows:

> In this wonderful little book, Mr. Herrigel, a German philosopher who came to Japan and took up the practice of archery toward an understanding of Zen, gives an illuminating account of his own experience. Through his expression, the Western reader will find a more familiar manner of dealing with what very often must seem to be a strange and somewhat unapproachable Eastern experience.[55]

54. Ibid., 40.

55. Herrigel, *Zen in the Art of Archery*, repr. without the author's preface (New York: Vintage Books, 1999), x.

Perhaps because it was not included in the first German edition, Suzuki's introduction did not appear in the Japanese version of *Zen in the Art of Archery*. For Japanese, this could be called the "phantom introduction."

In the midst of the Zen boom taking place in Europe and the United States, *Zen in the Art of Archery* appeared in the English-speaking world with the imprimatur of the great D. T. Suzuki. The impact of this is incalculable. With its reliability completely unchallenged by anyone, *Zen in the Art of Archery* became part and parcel of the Zen boom. However, how did Suzuki really feel about the foreword that he wrote? In a conversation with the Zen scholar Hisamatsu Shin'ichi (1889–1980) in 1959, Suzuki divulged his true feelings:

HISAMATSU: What about Herrigel?
SUZUKI: Herrigel is trying to get to Zen, but he hasn't grasped Zen itself.
Have you ever seen a book written by a Westerner that has?[56]

Belying the credibility that his introduction gave to *Zen in the Art of Archery*, here Suzuki says that "Herrigel . . . hasn't grasped Zen itself." In this same conversation, the moderator, Fujiyoshi Jikai (1915–1993), of the Institute for Research in Humanities, Kyoto University, asked Suzuki why he had written the introduction to *Zen in the Art of Archery*. In response to Fujiyoshi's question, Suzuki went so far as to say, "I was asked to write it so I wrote it, that's all." As befits a Zen person, Suzuki displays what might be called a lack of attachment, perhaps, or, shall we say, a supreme indifference.

Looking at this a bit more closely, we find that the teacher of the teacher of Ōhazama Shūei, who taught Herrigel about Zen, was Suzuki's own teacher, Shaku Sōen. That is, for Suzuki, Herrigel was the disciple of one of his brother disciples. Both Suzuki and Herrigel must have known that they had this mutual connection. Suzuki's introduction to *Zen in the Art of Archery* probably contained a certain amount of flattery of Herrigel, who was Suzuki's kinsman in a religious sense.

Under these circumstances, Kyōdō Publishing released the Japanese version of *Zen in the Art of Archery* in 1956, three years after the English edition appeared. This Japanese edition made its debut accompanied by the plaudits of the foreign intelligentsia who held the book in high es-

56. Suzuki Daisetsu and Hisamatsu Shin'ichi, "Taidan: Amerika no zen o kataru," *Zen bunka* 14 (1959): 28.

teem. This was before Japan had entered its period of rapid growth, and foreign things were particularly appreciated.

In 1957, a short treatise entitled "Zen Mysticism"[57] was published in *Zen bunka*, the official journal of the Rinzai Zen sect. It was written by Gilbert Hyatt (1906–1978), a professor of classical studies at Columbia University in New York, and was serialized in two issues of the journal. In it, Hyatt quotes the contents of *Zen in the Art of Archery* profusely and goes on at great length about how what Herrigel wrote captures the essence of Zen.

This article was originally a radio lecture that was later published by Oxford University. What this means is that by 1957, Herrigel had become sufficiently well known to be featured on a mass medium like radio.

More than a few Zen practitioners harbored misgivings about the fact that, unbeknownst to much of the Zen community in Japan, Zen was spreading arbitrarily in this fashion in foreign countries. Even the translator of Hyatt's article, Kobori Sōhaku of Ryōkōin at Daitokuji in Kyoto, said the following:

> The fact that Zen has attracted sufficient attention in the West to be featured on the radio is, I think, the fruit of the efforts and the great vows of Mr. Suzuki and other pioneers to spread the message of Buddhism to the world. On the other hand, however, we must be strictly on our guard against the tendency in the West for people to prefer a Zen that ignores hands-on training and study and is only absorbed through the eyes and ears.[58]

This can be read as a veiled criticism of Suzuki. However, it seems that even Kobori, who feared that a Zen devoid of actual training and consisting only of theory would spread in the West, could not bring himself to completely deny Suzuki's achievements.

However, the situation in the world at large involving Zen took the direction that Kobori had feared. An example of this is one of the driving forces behind the Zen boom in America: Alan Watts. Beginning with *The Spirit of Zen* (1936),[59] Watts wrote more than twenty books on Zen, psychology, and religion before his death in 1973. His activities were centered

---

57. Girubāto Haietto [Gilbert Hyatt], "Zen no shinpi," trans. Kobori Sōhaku, *Zen bunka* 7 (1957): 23–29; "Zen no shinpi," trans. Kobori Sōhaku, *Zen bunka* 9 (1957): 7–13.

58. Haietto, "Zen no shinpi," *Zen bunka* 9 (1957), 13.

59. Alan W. Watts, *The Spirit of Zen* (London: Murray, 1936).

on the West Coast of the United States, and he also had a big impact on the counterculture of the 1960s. In Watts's *The Way of Zen* (1957), both Ryōanji and *kyūdō* are introduced as symbols: the rock garden at Ryōanji as the icon of Zen, and *kyūdō* as Zen physical culture leading to enlightenment:

> This spirit is seen at its best in the great sand and rock gardens of Kyoto, of which the most famous example is the garden of Ryoanji. It consists of five groups of rocks laid upon a rectangle of raked sand, backed by a low stone wall, and surrounded by trees. It suggests a wild beach, or perhaps a seascape with rocky islands, but its unbelievable simplicity evokes a serenity and clarity of feeling so powerful that it can be caught even from a photograph . . . .
> Every one of the arts which have been discussed involves a technical training which follows the same essential principles as training in Zen. The best account of this training thus far available in a Western language is Eugen Herrigel's *Zen in the Art of Archery*, which is the author's story of his own experience under a master of the Japanese bow.[60]

Here, the rock garden at Ryōanji and Herrigel's *kyūdō* are deftly connected within the context of Zen. The fact that this was written by Alan Watts, the most successful Western Zen ideologue at that time, had a great impact.

The ensemble of Zen, rock gardens, and *kyūdō* also came to be repeated iconographically. Among the English editions of Herrigel's *The Method of Zen*, there is one which, while it is not Ryōanji, has a cover decorated with a photograph of a rock garden.[61] The voluminous work *Zen-Unterweisung* (Zen instruction)[62] by the German Hugo M. Enomiya-Lasalle (1898–1990), a member of the Catholic Society of Jesus who became absorbed in Zen, makes use of photographs of *kyūdō* and rock gardens.

If one thinks about it, there are not that many ways to express the world of Zen graphically. There are either rock gardens or *kyūdō*, and if these are not used, we are left with nothing except perhaps ink blots or Zen pictures done by Zen priests. Perhaps it is not so unreasonable for a publisher to use rock gardens and *kyūdō* as visual elements when making a book about Zen.

60. Alan W. Watts, *The Way of Zen* (London: Thames & Hudson, 1957), 194–95.

61. Eugen Herrigel, *The Method of Zen*, trans. Richard F. C. Hull (London: Arkana, 1988).

62. Hugo M. Enomiya-Lassalle, *Zen-Unterweisung* (Munchen: Kösel, 1988).

A man named Christmas Humphries (1901–1983), the chairman of the London Buddhist Church, contributed greatly to the postwar dissemination of Zen and Buddhism in England. He was also legal advisor to the British royal family. Humphries wrote the introduction to an English-language reprint edition of Robert Linssen's *Essais sur le Bouddhisme en général et sur le Zen en particular* (*Living Zen*), where he mentions Herrigel: "I understand that the late Eugen Herrigel's *Zen in the Art of Archery* is in the opinion of Zen experts in Japan the best such work so far produced."[63] Parenthetically, a photograph of *kyūdō* is shown on the cover of the French-language edition of *Living Zen*,[64] and the cover of the 1988 reissue of the English edition shows a photograph of the rock garden at Ryōgen'in at Daitokuji in Kyoto. Here again, the ensemble of Zen, rock gardens, and *kyūdō* is repeated.

In Humphries's own work, he discusses the assessment of Herrigel by the "Zen experts in Japan" in the following way:

> Yet, these Eastern teachers alike criticise the West for being too intellectual. Herrigel alone, they seem to say, in his *Zen in the Art of Archery*, has caught the spirit of Zen, but then he learnt it from a Master of Zen in Japan. This rules out my own *Zen Buddhism*, Benoit's *The Supreme Doctrine*, and Robert Linssen's *Living Zen*. It also rules out Alan Watts' *Spirit of Zen* and his new book, his *magnum opus* on the subject, *The Way of Zen*.[65]

The "Zen experts in Japan" praise Herrigel without reservation, but the other side of this is that they do not recognize the books about Zen written by Humphries or other Westerners. Humphries must have found this hard to bear. But to whom, precisely, is Humphries referring when he says "Zen experts in Japan?" Certainly one of them must be D. T. Suzuki. Other famous Zen priests who supported Herrigel were Yamada Mumon (1900–1988) of the Rinzai sect and Ōmori Sōgen (1904–1994).

It seems as though Mumon would occasionally talk about *Zen in the Art of Archery* in conversation and in his religious lectures.[66] For example,

63. Robert Linssen, *Living Zen*, trans. Diana Abrahamas-Curiel (New York: Grove Press, 1960), 7.

64. Robert Linssen, *le Zen* (Verviers: Gerard, 1969).

65. Christmas Humphreys, *Zen Comes West* (London: George Allen & Unwin Ltd., 1960), 30.

66. Yamada Mumon, "Zeni to zen," in *Mumon hōwashū* (Tokyo: Shunjūsha, 1963), 63–85.

when the prime minister of Canada came to visit EXPO '70 in Osaka, Mumon told him about *Zen in the Art of Archery*:

> When you see a flower and you become the flower; when you see the moon and you become the moon; when you see the target and you become the target; when there ceases to be any distance between you and all of creation, this is Zen. When the pain of the people of Canada becomes your pain, when you can see the happiness of the people as your happiness, at that moment you will have become one with the Void.[67]

Mumon referred to this conversation he had with the prime minister of Canada at a talk he gave in Mexico in 1972. It seems that when addressing foreigners, Mumon frequently mentioned that there had been a Westerner named Herrigel who had a deep understanding of Zen. Without a doubt, the recommendation of a high-ranking priest like Mumon raised the credibility of *Zen in the Art of Archery* to new heights.

Ōmori Sōgen, the author of such books as *Ken to Zen* (The sword and Zen; 1966)[68] was well known as an advocate for Zen and the martial arts. He wrote an article called "Zen to kyūdō" ("Zen and *kyūdō*"),[69] which appeared in the book *Gendai kyūdō kōza* (Lecture series on modern *kyūdō*; 1968). In this article he expresses his endorsement of Herrigel, saying, "judged from the standpoint of a veteran Zen practitioner, both Master Awa's method of instruction and Professor Herrigel's experience are quite admirable."

What was behind Sōgen's authorship of this article? Sōgen, while maintaining that "I am completely ignorant of the internal affairs of the *kyūdō* world," says the following:

> Above all, *Zen in the Art of Archery* is a famous work, which was translated into many languages and became a bestseller not only in Japan, but in countries such as Germany, America, and Italy. In spite of this fact, for some reason there are many people among Japanese *kyūdō* practitioners who scorn this work as immature.
>
> I am completely ignorant of the internal affairs of the *kyūdō* world, but

---

67. Yamada Mumon, "Kokoro no kiyoki mono," *Zen bunka* 65 (1972): 7.

68. Ōmori Sōgen, *Ken to zen* (Tokyo: Shunjūsha, 1966).

69. Ōmori Sōgen, "Zen to kyūdō" (1968), in *Gendai kyūdō kōza*, 2nd ed., Vol. 6: *Kyūdō bunka hen* (Tokyo: Yūzankaku, 1982), 159–75.

it would indeed be a great shame if even the slightest feelings of factionalism regarding the fact that Professor Herrigel was the disciple of Master Awa
Kenzō were behind the desire to disparage this book.[70]

It is unnatural for Sōgen to say, on the one hand, "I am completely ignorant of the internal affairs of the *kyūdō* world," and to then go on about
"feelings of factionalism." It sounds to me that when Sōgen was asked to
write this article, someone from the *kyūdō* world must have spoken to him
and prevailed upon him to present Herrigel in a positive light.

Sōgen did not actively pursue writing this article of his own volition.
It seems as though he tried to excuse himself from writing it a number of
times, saying that he had no *kyūdō* experience. However, in the end, he endorsed Herrigel. Sōgen's article, appearing as it did in *Gendai kyūdō kōza*,
a commemorative series of books consisting of articles written by well-
known *kyūdō* masters of the time, had a great impact.

I would like to direct the discussion back to rock gardens. None of D. T.
Suzuki's main works, beginning with *Zen and Japanese Culture*, discuss
Ryōanji to any great degree. However, in Hisamatsu's *Zen to bijutsu* (Zen
and the fine arts; 1958), Ryōanji is presented in a Zen light:

> In this sense, although the term *seki-tei*, or "stone garden," is perfectly ap-
> propriate for this garden, I prefer the term *kū-tei*, "empty garden." The term
> "empty" refers to the depth of the garden, the depth of the Fundamental Sub-
> ject that is Nothing, of the Formless Self. The Ryōan-ji [*sic*] garden, in that
> sense, is incomparably expressive of the Formless Self of Zen. The profundity
> of the garden is felt all the more because of the sparseness of the rocks.[71]

From this we can see that Hisamatsu was the original inspiration for the
term "empty garden," used in the introduction to the rock garden hanging
on the wall at Ryōanji, which was cited at the beginning of the previous
chapter.

Hisamatsu lists the following things as the seven characteristics of Zen
culture: asymmetry, simplicity, austere sublimity or lofty dryness, natural-
ness, subtle profundity or deep reserve, freedom from attachment, and
tranquility. In addition to Ryōanji, Hisamatsu identifies as Zen culture

70. Ibid., 160.
71. Hisamatsu Shin'ichi, *Zen and the Fine Arts*, trans. Tokiwa Gishin (Tokyo: Kōdansha
International Ltd., 1971), 88.

such things as the *raku* ware tea bowl "Masu," the painting *Persimmons* by Mu Qi (Mokkei, in Japanese), and "Shōkintei," the tearoom at the Katsura Detached Villa, since they fulfill these requirements.

However, there is a rhetorical trick at work here: these seven character-istics of Zen culture obviously were not present from the start. They were introduced by Hisamatsu, who inferred them from such things as the rock garden at Ryōanji and *raku* ware tea bowls. Something that was originally only inferred is presented as being a preexisting condition, and is then used to define Zen culture. This kind of bait and switch is a trick com-monly used by cultural theorists.

However, we must not assume that we have now figured everything out. The issue goes even deeper. The entire concept of "Zen culture" itself has been created using just this sort of rhetorical sleight of hand. The view of Japanese culture that today is taken to be axiomatic is that Zen is a spiri-tual culture emblematic of Japan and that almost all of Japanese culture is permeated with Zen elements. If one traces this idea to its source, one will find that it originated with Suzuki and Hisamatsu. Suzuki and Hisamatsu, among others, created the theory of Zen and Japanese culture around the middle of the twentieth century in just this way.

In this intellectual climate, the artist Will Petersen wrote an article entitled "Stone Garden" that appeared in 1957 in the American literary magazine *Evergreen Review*, which was aimed at a counterculture audience. Quoting Suzuki's *Zen and Japanese Culture* and Kuck's *The Art of Japanese Gardens*, Petersen described the rock garden at Ryōanji in the following manner:

> Like all great art, the garden is perhaps a "visual koan [*sic*]." It remains in the mind, and, if it can be likened to anything, rather than "islands in the sea," it is the mind. It does not matter, therefore, what materials the garden is com-posed of; what is important is the mind that interprets the essentials. The garden exists within ourselves; what we see in the rectangular enclosure is, in short, what we are.[72]

I do not know which of them came first, but it is clear that Petersen and Watts were looking at Ryōanji along the same lines. This view of Ryōanji was the standard among American New Age devotees.

72. Will Petersen, "Stone Garden," *Evergreen Review* 1:4 (1957): 137.

In her excellent anthology *The World of Zen* (1960), the American scholar Nancy Wilson Ross (1901–1986), while quoting from Petersen, says:

> One of the truest expressions of the Zen way with garden designing may be seen in the famous Kyoto garden of Ryoanji [sic], . . . Today—their eyes opened by abstract art—many Western visitors find at Ryoanji something deeply satisfying; subtle qualities that remain in their memories long after other more colorful Japanese scenes have faded.[73]

In *The World of Zen*, Ross excerpts and collects noted passages from such people as D. T. Suzuki, Alan Watts, Okakura Tenshin (1862–1913), Robert Linssen, and Eugen Herrigel. Ross quotes Petersen along with them, and she speaks of Ryōanji with unbounded admiration. The unbroken chain of quotes from D. T. Suzuki to Kuck, from Kuck to Petersen, and then from Petersen to Ross is as plain as day.

DOES ZEN STINK?

As Zen spread around the world, not every member of the intelligentsia in the West championed it. There were some who criticized Zen sharply, thereby incurring the wrath of Suzuki and his supporters. The Hungarian-born author Arthur Koestler is one of the best examples of this. In addition, there were those whom Suzuki frowned upon for spreading Zen in their own way, even if they did not criticize it. People like Alan Watts fall into this category.

In the sense that they both had their own self-made version of Zen, I do not see that much difference between Herrigel and Watts. Why, then, did Herrigel find favor with Suzuki and his circle of Zen culture theorists while Watts was disliked? I have a feeling that some secret pertaining to the ideal image the Japanese have of themselves is hidden somewhere in this dichotomy.

In 1960, Koestler published *The Lotus and the Robot*. Based on his experiences in India and Japan, it spoke quite critically of the cultures of both countries, so much so that it was banned in India because of its negative portrayal of Gandhi. Koestler's criticism of Japan centered mainly on Zen.

73. Nancy Wilson Ross, ed., *The World of Zen* (New York: Vintage Books, 1960), 100–1.

In this book, Koestler spent an entire chapter entitled "Delusion and Self-Delusion" criticizing Herrigel, saying, "Zen started as a de-conditioning cure and ended up as a different type of conditioning. The cramp of self-critical watchfulness was relieved by the self-confident ease of exercising an automatic skill. The knack became a comfortable substitution for 'It.'"[74] Koestler did not deny the existence of "It" and appeared to interpret the study of *kata* (form) as an "automatic skill."

The Lotus and the Robot also discusses the rock garden at Ryōanji. After quoting from a section of a guidebook, he dismisses the garden with nothing but a brusque "I stood in that famous garden, but could neither hear the sound of the waves nor feel the weight of the iceberg against the escaping tiger."[75]

At the same time as the publication of *The Lotus and the Robot*, Koestler published an article entitled "A Stink of Zen: The Lotus and the Robot" in the journal *Encounter*.[76] Suzuki did not hide his anger and displeasure at the scathing criticism of Zen displayed in the article, and this led to the famous "Koestler-Suzuki Controversy." Here I would like to outline the gist of Koestler's article.

After first criticizing Japan's family-centrism, male chauvinism, age-based social hierarchy, and the vagueness of the distinction between objectivity and subjectivity in Japanese society, Koestler said:

> Zen is to religion what a "flat garden" is to a garden. It knows no god, no afterlife, no good and no evil, as the rock garden knows no flowers, herbs, or shrubs. It has no doctrine or holy writ, its teaching is transmitted mainly in the form of parables as ambiguous as the pebbles in the rock garden which symbolise now a mountain, now a fleeing tiger.[77]

Here we can immediately see that Koestler is using Ryōanji as a metaphor for Zen itself. Koestler continued, saying that "this cult of the absurd," where students are struck and abused, was an important factor in maintaining the ambiguity of thought in the Japanese social structure and that

---

74. Arthur Koestler, *The Lotus and the Robot* (London: Hutchinson, 1966), 264.

75. Ibid., 194.

76. Arthur Koestler, "A Stink of Zen: The Lotus and the Robot (II)," *Encounter* 15:4 (1960): 13–32.

77. Ibid., 15.

"Zen was the *tanki* (as the Japanese call their tranquillizer pills) of feudal Japan."[78]

Koestler also directed his arrows of criticism at Suzuki, saying such things as "Dr. Suzuki, the *sensei* of Zen *senseis*, comments with a lucidity which is quite unusual in his voluminous writings . . . ." It is only natural that this would make Suzuki angry.[79]

Regarding the influence of Zen on Japanese culture, Koestler also said the following:

> A little later it also became the dominant influence in painting, landscape-gardening, flower arrangement, tea ceremony, firefly hunting, and similar nipponeries on the one hand—of swordsmanship, wrestling, Judo, archery, dive-bombing, on the other.[80]

While I would really like to know how and where firefly hunting and Zen are connected, this is not so important. The fact that Koestler mentions *kyūdō* suggests that Herrigel was somewhere in his mind.

Regarding the relationship of Zen to the war, Koestler concluded that because of Zen's "ethical relativism" and "a misguided tolerance," it "had become indistinguishable from passive complicity" in Japanese nationalism.[81] It seems to me that this observation of Koestler's is, in some deep way, connected to the fact that Herrigel was judged to be a *Mitlaüfer* at his denazification trial. It is difficult to distinguish between Zen's characteristic of constant mutability on one hand and conformity to a social or political system on the other.

Koestler did not base his criticism of Zen only on what he had read in books. He relates that his experience of going to Kyoto and engaging in discussions with Zen monks at one of Kyoto's five main Rinzai temples, together known as Kyoto's *gozan* (Kyoto's five most prestigious Zen temples), only served to reinforce the conclusions he had arrived at on his own. Koestler and the monks repeatedly engaged in "meaningless exchanges," where Koestler would ask a question, the monks would respond

---

78. Ibid., 16.
79. Ibid. Here, *sensei* refers to "master."
80. Ibid., 19.
81. Ibid., 31.

with a parable, and when Koestler would respond in his turn with a parable, the monks would ask for a question.

> The abbots were delightful, but after two days of talking, we felt discouraged and dejected. The one significant remark we got out of them was: "When you ask these logical questions, we feel embarrassed."[82]

At the end of his difficult discussions with the Zen monks, Koestler came to the following conclusion regarding the spiritual nature of Japan:

> whose mentality, for all their Western ways, is so alien to us. But it is precisely this marriage between opposite extremes—the Lotus and the Robot; Confucius and Zen, rigid perfectionism and elastic ambiguity—which has such a profound fascination. Unable to achieve a synthesis, they rejected compromise, and settled for the juxtaposition of extremes.[83]

This idea of a "marriage of extremes" strikes me as a very interesting theory of Japanese culture. Had Koestler developed this theory of Japanese culture without criticizing Zen, he might have been lionized in Japan and not incurred the wrath of such an authoritative figure as Suzuki. However, Koestler made the mistake of directing the barbs of his criticism at Suzuki. The following year, Suzuki published an anger-filled rebuttal in *Encounter*.

In his rebuttal, Suzuki said, "I was again reminded of the difficulty of imparting the knowledge of Zen to Western people who have no such tradition in their cultural history,"[84] and that "Mr. Koestler himself is to be blamed if he cannot extricate himself from the metaphysical entanglements or mental contortions which are his own creation."[85]

Suzuki also directed his criticism at the monks who had engaged in the discussion with Koestler:

> Wonderful is the stupidity of those high-ranked abbots of Zen! Why did they not give Mr. Koestler Rinzai's *"Kahtz!"* or Tokuzan's stick and chase him out

---

82. Ibid.
83. Ibid., 32.
84. Suzuki Daisetsu, "A Reply from D. T. Suzuki," *Encounter* 17:4 (1961): 55
85. Ibid., 56.

of the temple? He would never have written the article in which Zen stinks altogether too much in the wrong way![86]

While his imagery is somewhat violent, Suzuki's anger can also be clearly felt through his words. Still, the difference in heat between Suzuki, the Zen layman who zealously preached his theory of Zen culture, and the monks, who were part of the legitimate line of transmission of Kyoto's "Five Zen Temples," is an interesting phenomenon. Suzuki closed his rebuttal with an abusive parting shot, saying that Koestler, who could not escape from the two-dimensional Western idea of subject and object, "unfortunately, seems not to be cognizant of 'the stink' radiating from his own 'Zen.'"[87]

Suzuki's rebuttal, while attempting to remain logical, was emotional from start to finish. It would not have been so bad if Suzuki had contented himself with just this rebuttal, but he repeatedly criticized Koestler in various other venues, attempting to bury him once and for all. For example, in *Chūgai nippō* (a newspaper for a Buddhist audience), Suzuki continued his attack on Koestler:

Mr. Koestler came to Japan this spring and caused a bit of a ruckus with the Pen Club . . . . He seems to be an impulsive person who is not afraid of saying whatever is on his mind . . . . If something does not fit perfectly into a logical framework, he discards it as nothing but some kind of joke. This is how a majority of Westerners think . . . . It seems to me that Mr. Koestler needs a thwack with Tokuzan's stick.[88]

The year after writing this, Suzuki wrote the following in *Chūo kōron*:

A recent example is Arthur Koestler, who resides in London now. One of his recent publications is called *The Lotus and the Robot*. In it, there is a section where he touches on Zen. His observations are not uninteresting, but as a criticism of Zen they are completely off the mark. His remarks are very typical of this genre. Another person who says he understands Zen but is completely off target is Alan Watts.[89]

86. Ibid.
87. Ibid., 58.
88. Suzuki Daisetsu, "Zen to ōbei no hitobito—satori," *Chūgai nippō*, October 1 and 2, 1960.
89. Suzuki Daisetsu, "Gendai sekai to zen no seishin," *Chūō kōron* (August 1961): 64–77.

Koestler made no particular response to Suzuki, and so the controversy ended without going any further.

I would now like to turn my attention to Alan Watts, whom Suzuki criticized by name as being "completely off target." In 1959, Hisamatsu Shin'ichi wrote the following about the influence Watts had in America at the time:

> In America there is a man named Alan Watts whom I suppose can be called an American scholar of Zen. He is the foremost authority on Zen in America and has written many books and given a lot of lectures. At the invitation of the Buddhist church, he gave a series of lectures in London in mid-April, and it was reported that the hall was filled to overflowing and so they had to switch to another larger hall since the scheduled hall could not hold everyone. This shows the high degree of interest in Zen in America and England. In addition, a German named Eugen Herrigel has written a book called *Zen in the Art of Archery*, and this book is being very widely read both in the U.S. and the U.K.[90]

Watts quoted Herrigel quite a bit in his lectures and publications.[91] He felt that reading Herrigel was a natural part of the education of any Westerner interested in Zen. In his lecture "The Democratization of Buddhism," which touched on Herrigel, Watts also referenced Ryōanji in support of his thesis, saying, "consider the famous Ryōan-ji [*sic*] Garden in Japan."[92] Here again, the ensemble of Zen, rock gardens, and *kyūdō* makes its appearance.

While this is something of a digression, Watts also was friendly with Hasegawa Saburō, who was then living in San Francisco. This is the same Hasegawa Saburō who took Isamu Noguchi to Ryōanji. There is the following story related about them: one day, Hasegawa gave a book he had written to Watts as a present. Watts said that D. T. Suzuki was coming, and that he would point it out to him, and Hasegawa said that he would be so happy if Suzuki would walk by it without noticing it.[93] This is very

90. Hisamatsu Shin'ichi, "Zen no sekaiteki shimei," *Zen bunka* 17 (1959): 9.

91. Alan W. Watts, *Beat Zen, Square Zen, and Zen* (San Francisco, CA: City Lights Books, 1959).

92. Alan W. Watts, "The Democratization of Buddhism," in *Zen and the Beat Way* (Boston: Tuttle, 1997), 79.

93. Mark Watts, introduction to Watts, *Zen and the Beat Way*, xix.

enigmatic, resembling a Zen *mondō* (an exchange of questions and answers between Zen master and pupil), but from it we can understand the delicate relationship between Watts, Suzuki, and Hasegawa.

Despite his popularity in Europe and the United States, Watts had a poor reputation in Japan. The reason that Watts was unpopular in Japan was because he had only an intellectual and theoretical understanding of Zen and had little or no real Zen training. Fujiyoshi Jikai, who met Watts in the United States, said that "while his knowledge and understanding of Zen is broad, I felt that he was weak in the area of practical experience."[94]

The German theologian Ernst Benz writes about this reputation that Watts had among Japanese Zen teachers in his well-known book *Zen in westlicher Sicht* (Zen: from east to west):

> I had the opportunity to discuss the Zen boom in Europe with a number
> of Zen teachers in Japan. Individually, all these teachers assured me that,
> indeed, Herrigel alone was the only Westerner who had grasped the true
> nature of Zen and been touched by the breath of its essence. Most of the
> Japanese with whom I spoke, when they praised Herrigel in this way, would,
> politely to be sure but without exception, habitually speak of other European
> writers who had written about Zen in an unmistakably critical fashion. For
> example, a *rōshi* from Shōkokuji pointed out the big gap between Herrigel's
> book on Zen and Watts' writings about Zen and said that compared to Her-
> rigel, Watts was like a painter who had tried to paint a tiger but "was only
> able to draw a cat."[95]

This statement expresses the contrasting opinions held by the Japanese regarding Herrigel and Watts. The Zen teachers with whom Benz spoke were D. T. Suzuki and those Zen teachers who accepted Suzuki's evaluation of Herrigel at face value. In this way, Herrigel's high reputation in Japan took firm root in the form of a contrast with Watts's obviously self-taught Zen.

The same opinion can be seen in a discussion among D. T. Suzuki, Nishimura Keishin (1933–), and Kimura Shizuo, which appeared in *Zen bunka* in 1963:

NISHIMURA: For example, I went to a seminar in America given by Alan
    Watts, "the noted Zen commentator." Watts was discussing Zen with a

94. Fujiyoshi Jikai, "Ōbei zengyō angya," *Zen bunka* 14 (1959): 42.
95. Ernst Benz, *Zen in westlicher Sicht* (Weilheim: O. W. Barth-Verlag, 1962), 15.

cigar in his mouth seated in front of a picture of a man-made satellite. This Watts is very popular in America. What disappointed me about his seminar was that a certain atmosphere of solemnity, the feeling of Zen-like excitement found at a lecture given by a teacher in Japan, was completely lacking.

SUZUKI: Oh, that guy Watts is a fake. He is in Japan now, so it's a good opportunity. If we could just find some way to guide him on the right path I'm sure he would improve. I'm sure that an opportunity to turn him around will come. He is still young, so if he trained for ten years he would get better. If he doesn't do that, there's no hope for him. Still, it's probably useless from the start to hope for him to do that.

KIMURA: Right now, he is completely uninterested in seeking out and trying to understand traditional Zen.[96]

Watts was extremely well versed in Zen as a kind of intellectual knowledge. However, he did not study the practical side of Zen by seeking out a Japanese master under whom to train in meditation.

What about Herrigel on the other hand? Prior to coming to Japan, Herrigel had learned about Zen from the Japanese overseas students in Heidelberg, so his knowledge of Zen was by no means weak. The decisive difference between Herrigel and Watts is that Herrigel came to Japan and undertook some practical training. This is one of main reasons for Herrigel's popularity in Japan. However, as we have seen, the practical training Herrigel had was not in Zen but in Awa's own personal philosophy. Not only that, but a language barrier existed between Herrigel and Awa. We have also seen that *Zen in the Art of Archery* even contains things that are, more or less, Herrigel's own fabrications.

In spite of all that, many Japanese would probably prefer Herrigel to the cigar-chomping Watts who talked about Zen to hippies. This is because Herrigel showed us the traditional attitude toward training and the spirituality that we prefer. Herrigel told us that he had actually experienced the good old traditional Japan that we hold up as our ideal. This is the beautiful self-image for which many Japanese, somewhere in their hearts, are searching.

The main source for understanding Zen for Westerners, Herrigel and Watts included, is D. T. Suzuki. However, the greater part of Suzuki's thought was formed as a response to Western philosophy—Robert H.

96. "Zadankai: Zen no kokusai-sei ni tsuite," *Zen bunka* 29 (1963): 35–36.

Sharf points this out in his well-known essay "The Zen of Japanese Nationalism."[97] Without the West, Suzuki's ideas would never have existed. Even more fundamentally, without the wave of Westernization that swept Japan, Suzuki's whole life as a college-educated person who preached about Buddhism, even though he was only a layman, would have been completely impossible. Sharf has the following to say about the Zen that, through Suzuki, caused such a mania in the West.

> The irony, as we have seen above, is that the "Zen" that so captured the imagination of the West was in fact a product of the New Buddhism of the Meiji. Moreover, those aspects of Zen most attractive to the Occident— the emphasis on spiritual experience and the devaluation of institutional forms—were derived in large part from Occidental sources. Like Narcissus, Western enthusiasts failed to recognize their own reflection in the mirror held out to them.[98]

If the Zen that Westerners saw in Japan was nothing more than their own image reflected in a mirror—what then? In my mind's eye, I can see a cartoon where Japan and the West are facing each other through a strange magic mirror—now a mirror, now a pane of plain glass.

KYŪDŌ, ZEN, AND THE OLYMPICS

What was happening in the *kyūdō* world when *Zen in the Art of Archery* was becoming popular? I would like to discuss this, focusing on the vicissitudes of *kyūdō* and archery and the contrasts between them.

While this may seem surprising, it is not that long ago that *kyūdō* and archery came to be clearly distinct from a conceptual point of view. This is proven by the fact that in the beginning, the All Nippon Kyūdō Federation (ANKF) was the organization that represented archery in Japan (both Western archery and *kyūdō*) to the International Archery Federation (FITA). Up until 1968, when the right to represent Japan to FITA was transferred from the ANKF to the All Japan Archery Federation (AJAF), *kyūdō* was trying to merge with archery.

97. Robert H. Sharf, "The Zen of Japanese Nationalism," *History of Religions* 33:1 (1993): 1–43.

98. Ibid., 39.

The Tokyo Olympics, which took place in 1964, are indispensable to a discussion of the relationship between *kyūdō* and archery. In 1957, archery was recognized as a new Olympic event for future Olympic games, starting in 1964. From that point on until 1968, when the right to represent Japan to FITA was transferred from the ANKF to the AJAF, it was hoped that Japanese archery could defeat Western archery in a head-to-head competition. This proved to be impossible, and this experience strengthened the tendency to describe *kyūdō* as Zen, to emphasize its spirituality, and to refrain from modifying the equipment. To state the case even more strongly, *Zen in the Art of Archery* and the Zen boom in Europe and the United States are very closely related to the separation of *kyūdō* and archery.

Let us trace the historical development of this situation.[99] The first people to introduce Japanese archery overseas were Japanese *kyūdō* aficionados who had immigrated to the West in the early 1920s. There is a record of a practice hall for Japanese archery existing at a private Japanese home on Long Island in New York in 1931. In 1932, an archery tournament where Western archers and *kyūdō* practitioners competed together was held in New York. Through this sort of interaction, many Americans became interested in Japanese archery, and vice versa.

In 1937, the first Japan-America Friendship Archery Tournament was held in New York with *jūdō* master Kanō Jigorō as the guest of honor. The American side competed according to the point system, shooting at a target 120 centimeters in diameter from a distance of 36 meters. The Japanese side competed according to the *kyūdō* hit-or-miss system, shooting at a standard 36-centimeter-diameter target from a distance of 28 meters. Each hit was tallied as one point. A combined total of thirty archers from both sides competed.

Prior to World War II, an event called the Japan-America Friendship Correspondence Archery Tournament was held.[100] The first of these tournaments was held in 1936. The American archers shot at Woodside in New York, and the Japanese side shot at the American School in Meguro in Tokyo. The event was held according to the point system with archers shooting at a 120-centimeter-diameter target from a distance of 36 meters. The Japanese team, consisting of archers such as Urakami Sakae (1882–1971), who was one of the most famous Japanese *kyūdō* archers of

---

99. R. P. Erumā, *Yōkyū*, trans. Suga Shigeyoshi (Tokyo: Fumaidō Shoten, 1969).

100. In such a competition, archers in different locations compete and the results are communicated to the competitors after the competition is over to determine the winner.

the twentieth century, defeated the Americans. With the rules changing bit by bit, this competition was held four times up until 1940.

After the end of World War II, spearheaded by people such as Suga Shigeyoshi (1889–?) and Onuma Hideharu (1910–1990), the Japan Archery Club was founded in 1947, the same year that the ANKF was established. Up until around the time of the seventh National Sports Festival[101] in 1952, members of this club, shooting Western bows, competed in the kyūdō competition together with kyūdō archers.

The Japanese translation of Zen in the Art of Archery was published in 1956. How did the kyūdō community react? One might think that everyone welcomed it wholeheartedly, but this is not so. While it is true that Awa Kenzō, who had since died, had been a famous teacher, in the kyūdō world at that time his group of disciples was no more than a single faction based in the Tōhoku and northern Kantō regions. Of course, it goes without saying that Awa's disciples would have welcomed Zen in the Art of Archery more than anyone else.

Immediately after Zen in the Art of Archery was published in Japan, reviews of it began to appear in Kyūdō, the official publication of the ANKF. The first such review was written by a kyūdō aficionado from the city of Kitaibaragi in the northern Kantō area who seems to have been under Awa's influence. He wrote, "When, compared to this foreigner's accomplishments, I reflect upon the spectacle of us Japanese groping in the dark, I am truly ashamed."[102] I think that we can consider this an early example of a Japanese kyūdō practitioner seeing his own ideal image reflected in a foreign mirror.

The year after its publication, an article giving a detailed introduction to Zen in the Art of Archery was serialized in the January and February 1957 issues of Kyūdō.[103] The author was Inoue Kasaburō (1881–1963), the president of the Nara Prefecture Kyūdō Federation. Inoue praised Herrigel's supreme equanimity in the face of death, saying, "Herrigel's lack of fear of death and calm spirit is similar to the great spirit of Japanese bushidō [the Way of the Warrior]." Inoue was an educator and a kyūdō practitioner who had been the director of the Yamato Institute of Japanese History, the

101. The largest national sports competition in Japan.

102. Kagai Rōsei, "Herigeru-hakase cho Yumi to zen (hōyaku) o yomite," Kyūdō 75 (August 1956): 38.

103. Inoue Kasaburō, "Herigeru-shi to yumi," Kyūdō 81 (January 1957):7–9; Inoue, "Herigeru-shi to yumi," Kyūdō 82 (February 1957): 18–21.

forerunner of today's Kashihara Institute of Archaeology. *Zen in the Art of Archery* was an extremely popular book among educators, and Inoue is a perfect example of the Herrigel-admiring intellectual.

As this was going on, the International Olympic Committee (IOC) held its general meeting in Sofia, Bulgaria in September of 1957 and decided to recognize archery as an official Olympic event beginning in 1964. Even though the site of the 1964 Olympics had not yet been decided, the *kyūdō* world was in a fever of excitement over this issue. It was seen as a great chance for *kyūdō* to take its place on the world stage. To make it possible for *kyūdō* to participate in the Olympics, the ANKF applied to become a member of FITA, and this request was granted in 1958. The ANKF had secured the right to be represented as the official Japanese archery organization.

Even so, the ANKF did not exclude Western archery. It established an international division and appointed Onuma, who was both well versed in Japanese archery and had a line of communication with the Western archery club, as a committee member. However, the president of the ANKF at that time, Chiba Tanetsugu (1894–1959), stated definitively that "the ANKF will, without hesitation, compete in Olympic archery using Japanese bows."[104]

In 1959, Tokyo was chosen as the site for the 1964 Olympics. Japan, the host of the Olympics where archery was going to be featured for the first time, was going to compete using Japanese bows and take home the gold medal—this sense of mission pervaded the atmosphere in the ANKF.

The fact that Western archery was increasing its accuracy by equipping its bows with all sorts of mechanical aids gave rise to the belief that Japanese archery could not avoid doing the same thing. Even *Kyūdō* introduced proposals for sights and a new design for a Japanese bow fitted with an arrow rest.[105] As *kyūdō* equipment began in this way to evolve along the lines of Western archery equipment, the ANKF also asked the Ministry of Education and the mass media to use the word *kyūdō* as the translation for "archery" rather than the term "Western archery."[106]

While this was happening, the Japan Archery Club was searching for a way to survive. It reconstituted itself as the Japan Archery Association

104. Masui Kenkichi, "Orinpikku kyūdō ni omou," *Kyūdō* 106 (March 1959): 26.
105. Kubo Tamon, "Monomi to hyōjun gu," *Kyūdō* 107 (April 1959): 30–31; "Shin an Nihon yumi o shisha," *Kyūdō* 119 (April 1960): 9.
106. "Ācherī no wayaku wa 'kyūdō' o shiyō," *Kyūdō* 110 (July 1959): 47.

(JAA), and Onuma, who was the vice president, called upon Kawakami Gen'ichi (1912–2002) of the Yamaha Corporation to be the president of the new organization. Kawakami himself had experience in *kyūdō* prior to World War II but had become dissatisfied with it, saying "the spiritual aspect was overemphasized, and from a technical point of view it was practically an empty shell."[107]

In August 1959, the ANKF sent two representatives to observe the World Archery Championships being held in Stockholm, Sweden. Their job was to search for ways to help Japan to be victorious at the Tokyo Olympics. Seeing its phenomenal accuracy up close with their own eyes, upon their return to Japan the two representatives excoriated Western archery in their report to the ANKF, saying, "Western *kyūdō* is recreational *kyūdō*"; "the only thing that is important is hitting the target"; and "it exhibits none of Japanese *kyūdō*'s moral and ethical beauty or the contemplative life of Eastern philosophy." Expecting the world to share the values that prevailed in Japan seems too nationalistically self-centered, but this report probably expressed the true feelings of the ANKF representatives. Still, it was obvious that *kyūdō* could not defeat Western archery using spiritual theory. The two representatives reported that in order to be victorious in the Olympics, "we must, after all, compete for supremacy in accuracy."[108]

That being said, however, the difference in accuracy between Western archery and *kyūdō* was simply too great. The results from the Stockholm tournament tell the story: considering only the men's 30-meter competition, which is closest to the 28-meter distance used in *kyūdō*'s close-distance competition, the champion's overall score was such that even hitting a target 16 centimeters in diameter (a *kyūdō* target is 36 centimeters in diameter) with 72 out of 72 shots would not be enough to win. Only the greatest Japanese archer, a veritable Robin Hood worthy of having his name enshrined in the annals of *kyūdō* history, could hope to deliver this kind of accuracy on a regular basis in a major competition. Not only that, Western archers compete at long distances not used in *kyūdō* competition, such as 70 and 90 meters.

Anyone could see that it would be next to impossible for *kyūdō* to defeat Western archery at the Olympics and bring home the gold medal. It was around this time that people began to openly express the opinion that

107. "Kawakami Genichi-shi tokubetsu intabyū," *Ācherī* 54 (December 1980): 32.

108. "Ōshū haken kyūdō shisetsu Murakami Akai ryō-shi no kichō hōkoku," *Kyūdō* 113 (October 1959): 26–27.

kyūdō and archery were different. One of the people in the forefront of this movement was a *kyūdō* practitioner named Ban Shōtarō (1892–1981), who staked out his position as follows: "Rushing to change the beautiful Japanese bow into a target shooting device can only be described as a self-inflicted desecration of our own pride. What value is there in winning an Olympic competition if it means losing sight of *kyūdō's* true nature?"[109]

In opposition to this line of argument, Uno Yōzaburō (1878–1969), the president of the ANKF at that time and a former chief justice of the Japanese Supreme Court, took issue with Ban's position, saying that the *tōshiya* at Sanjūsangendō in Kyoto that was so popular during the Edo period was a great sporting event, and that people who object to participating in the Olympics "do not understand the real nature of Japanese *kyūdō*."[110]

As the *kyūdō* world was in an uproar over the issue of the Olympics, a controversy arose in the magazine *Kyūdō* concerning a certain essay. In order to obtain a high rank in *kyūdō*, one must, after successfully passing a practical shooting test and a verbal interview, also pass an essay test. As a subject for the seventh-degree test, the January 1959 issue of *Kyūdō* featured the essay subject "Explain *shari kenshō*" and a sample essay answering this question.[111] *Shari kenshō* (seeing true nature through the shot) is one of the teachings that Awa preached. It had now become a subject for the essay test for the high rank of seventh degree. In a word, *shari kenshō* had been officially sanctioned by the ANKF.

However, there were some *kyūdō* practitioners who could not remain silent in the face of the increasing influence of a Zen-like slogan such as *shari kenshō*. One of these was Arita Mikio, director of the Fukui Prefecture Kyūdō Federation and a member of the editorial staff at the *Fukui* newspaper. Regarding the sample essay on *shari kenshō*, Arita maintained that Herrigel had by no means been preaching Zen teachings and said, "there is no conflict with *kyūdō* if one simply wishes to get a taste of Buddhist thought, but forcibly trying to give this idea general currency as a *kyūdō* doctrine is unreasonable in the extreme."[112] He went on to say that what was needed for the development of *kyūdō* was not esoteric and abstruse theory but science.

The author of the original sample essay took great issue with the edi-

109. Ban Shōtarō, "Genka kyūkai shiken," *Kyūdō* 120 (May 1960): 13.
110. Uno Yōzaburō, "Sōkai ni nozomite," *Kyūdō* 121 (June 1960): 5.
111. "Shari kenshō ni tsuite," *Kyūdō* 104 (January 1959): 28–29. .
112. Arita Mikio, "*Shari kenshō* (kadai ronbun) ni tsuite," *Kyūdō* 106 (March 1959): 21.

torial department of *Kyūdō* over the fact that it had printed Arita's rebuttal and he apparently submitted a refutation of it. In the April 1959 issue of *Kyūdō*, the editorial department expressed its regret over the publication of Arita's essay, said that it would not publish the original author's response to it, and tried to defend itself, asking for understanding from both parties.[113] One can sense how frantic the editorial department was to quench the unexpected fire that had been ignited.

However, the interest in this issue in *kyūdō* circles was great. Subsequently, the May and September 1959 issues of *Kyūdō* took it up again, but this time both sample essays adopted a favorable tone.[114] It seems from this that within the editorial department of *Kyūdō*, that is to say within the ANKF, the pro–*shari kenshō* faction was in the ascendancy.

The magazine *Kyūdō* is the best source of information about the *kyūdō* world, so I hope that I can be excused for quoting it so extensively. The March issue of 1960 featured an article entitled "Nihon kyūdō ni omou" (Thinking about Japanese *kyūdō*) by a German professor at Sophia University, Heinz Balkenhol.[115] It talked about how Balkenhol had begun practicing *kyūdō* after reading *Zen in the Art of Archery* and how *kyūdō* had taught him a lot about life. Balkenhol fits the classic pattern of the foreigner steeped in *Zen in the Art of Archery*, and the appearance of people like him bolstered the Japanese *kyūdō* world's confidence.

Let us return to the Olympics. Regardless of the superiority of Japanese archery over Western archery in the spiritual realm, spirit alone cannot win competitions. The ANKF had to find a way to leave their mark on the Olympics by studying Western archery techniques and competing using Western bows. In June 1960, the ANKF held the first Western Archery Shooting Technique Seminar with Onuma and Kawakami as instructors. At around the same time, *Kyūdō* featured an article by Kamei Toshio (1927–), a *kyūdō* fifth-degree-rank holder as well as an expert in Western archery, in which he went on at great length about the distinctive characteristics of both Japanese and Western archery.[116]

113. "Gakka tōan narabi ni kadai ronbun no keisai ni tsuite," *Kyūdō* 107 (April 1959): 47.

114. Tejima Toshiko, "Kadai ronbun 'shari kenshō' to sono hihan ni omou," *Kyūdō* 108 (May 1959): 27–29; Murata Usakichi, "Issen tai ichigun," *Kyūdō* 112 (September 1959): 18–20.

115. Haintsu Barugenhōru [Heinz Balkenhol], "Nihon kyūdō ni omou," *Kyūdō* 118 (March 1960): 34–36.

116. Kamei Toshio, "Wakyū to yōkyū," *Kyūdō* 123 (August 1960): 10–14.

The ANKF wanted to be victorious in the Olympics with *kyūdō*; if that was not possible, then it wanted to win using Western archery. With opinions like this swirling around, the controversy was suddenly brought to a complete halt in December 1960. Citing such reasons as the small number of participating countries and archery's low level of dissemination internationally, the Japanese Olympic Committee decided to remove archery as an event for the Tokyo Olympics.

The *kyūdō* community must have been crushed. Even Ban Shōtarō, who had not been shy about discussing the effects of Olympic participation in the pages of *Kyūdō*, used *kyūdō* technique as a figure of speech to describe how the wind had been taken out of everyone's sails, saying, "it felt like having the arrow fall off the string just as I was raising the bow to shoot."[117]

Kyūdō was not going to be able to participate in the Olympics—while this must have been a source of great chagrin, it was also an opportunity to rethink the issue of the tremendous difference between Japanese archery and Western archery that had been put on the shelf up to that point. As the *kyūdō* community was trying to find a plausible story to explain why *kyūdō* and Western archery were different, and to do this in a way that was not Japanese culture–centric and so could be understood by people around the world, the worldwide popularity of Herrigel's *Zen in the Art of Archery* was most serendipitous.

Confining ourselves only to the magazine *Kyūdō*, around this time article after article praising Herrigel and Awa began to appear: articles describing the *kyūdō* fever in West Germany and how foreigners living in Japan were taking up *kyūdō* after reading Herrigel (April 1962);[118] an essay by Awa's senior disciple Anzawa Heijirō entitled "Shadō seishin ni tsuite" (The spirit of the Way of Shooting; February 1963);[119] a submission from a reader entitled "*Yumi to zen o yonde*" (Reading *Zen in the Art of Archery*; October 1963);[120] and a roundtable discussion between Anzawa and Komachiya Sōzō (June–August, 1965).[121]

---

117. Ban Shōtarō, "Gorin fusanka to kyūkai kongo no katsudō," *Kyūdō* 130 (March 1961): 26.

118. "Nishi Doitsu ni okeru saikin no Nihon kyūdō netsu," *Kyūdō* 143 (April 1962): 38.

119. Anzawa Heijirō, "Shadō seishin ni tsuite," *Kyūdō* 153 (February 1963): 4–7.

120. Ōga Yohei, "*Yumi to zen o yonde*," *Kyūdō* 161 (October 1963): 38–39.

121. "Zadankai: Awa Kenzō-hakase to sono deshi Oigen Herigeru-hakase no koto o Komachiya-hakase ni kiku: Sono ichi," *Kyūdō* 181 (June 1965): 20–23; "Zadankai: Awa

In the final event, *kyūdō* had a place in the Olympics as a part of a joint demonstration of traditional Japanese *budō*, along with *sumō* and *kendō*. On October 15, 1964, the *hikime* ceremony, ceremonial shooting by a group at a single target (*hitotsu mato sharei*), a demonstration by senior archers, and a demonstration of traditional battlefield shooting were performed, adding a glorious page to *kyūdō* history.

The ANKF still hoped to one day be able to participate in the Olympics officially. In this connection, for the first time the ANKF sent a *kyūdō* archer along with the Western archery contingent to the World Archery Championships held in Holland in 1967. The *kyūdō* archer was not at his best, and he finished dead last out of a field of 129 archers. While the depth of the disappointment of the archer himself and all of those involved must have been unfathomable, reality is a harsh thing.

While this was happening, the JAA was searching for a way to get the right to represent Japan to FITA transferred from the ANKF to the JAA. In 1966, the AJAF was founded with the politician Aichi Kiichi (1907–1973) as president. The efforts of the AJAF bore fruit, and in 1968 it was decided that the right to represent Japan to FITA would be transferred from the ANKF to the AJAF. This, finally, was when *kyūdō* and archery became institutionally distinct.

As *kyūdō* was trying to merge with archery in reaction to the external pressure imposed by the Olympics, it was faced with the reality of the overwhelming competitive superiority of Western archery. In the final analysis it found its path to survival through disassociating itself from Western archery. This experience brought about a change in the nature of *kyūdō*. The tendency to disdain accuracy and to glorify a Zen-based spiritualism spread in the *kyūdō* world. Such things as arrow rests and sights, which had been permitted because of the challenge presented by Western archery, were banned in 1971.[122] Japanese archery took the opposite path from Western archery, which continued to add mechanical aids to improve accuracy, such as the stabilizer, the clicker, and the cushion plunger, one after the other.

On the other hand, the Japanese archery world borrowed certain con-

---

Kenzō-hakase to sono deshi Oigen Herigeru-hakase no koto o Komachiya-hakase ni kiku: Sono ni," *Kyūdō* 182 (July 1965): 4–8; "Zadankai: Awa Kenzō-hakase to sono deshi Oigen Herigeru-hakase no koto o Komachiya-hakase ni kiku: Sono san," *Kyūdō* 183 (August 1965): 4–7.

122. "Kyōgi kisoku chū 'tsuku' wa shiyō kinshi," *Kyūdō* 248 (January 1971): 14.

cepts and institutions from the *kyūdō* world as it developed. One example of this is the adoption of *kyūdō* terminology to describe Western archery techniques and equipment. For example, in Kamei Toshio's book *Illustrated Archery* (1970),[123] one can find such Western terminology as *stancing, set,* and *nocking* replaced by their respective *kyūdō* counterparts: *ashibumi* (setting the feet), *dōzukuri* (setting the torso), and *yugamae* (bow at the ready). Another example is the adoption by the AJAF of a rank examination system copied wholesale from the ANKF system in 1983. This testing system incurred the wrath of Kawakami, who had always distrusted the ANKF testing system, but it did rescue the AJAF from its financial problems.[124]

One of the things behind the successful separation of *kyūdō* and archery was probably the hope that as *Zen in the Art of Archery* gained popularity in Europe and America, *kyūdō* could spread to the rest of the world. The American martial arts magazine *Black Belt* featured an article entitled "Kyūdō: The Art of Emperors" and a complete translation of this article was printed in the April 1967 issue of *Kyūdō*.[125] As usual, it was a glorification of Herrigel. Even at the World Archery Championships in Holland where the *kyūdō* archer had suffered a humiliating defeat, the mayor of the hosting city mentioned *Zen in the Art of Archery* in his remarks at the reception, and every day the media would visit the Japanese contingent and ask about the spirit of *kyūdō* and Zen, which the leader of the Japanese team found deeply moving.[126]

Then, finally, in 1968, Herrigel's photograph graced the opening pages of the April and May issues of *Kyūdō*. In the same year, the May through July issues featured a discussion between Onuma Hideharu and Murakami Hisashi (a director of the ANKF), who had both gone to Europe to observe the *kyūdō* situation there. They reported that in Europe, Herrigel's *Zen in the Art of Archery* was exerting a decisive influence as more and more people read it.[127]

123. Kamei Toshio, *Zukai ācherī kiso riron to torēningu hō* (Tokyo: Yūzankaku, 1970).

124. Takayanagi Noriaki, "Kawakami Genichirō-sensei no omoide," *Ācherī* 258 (November 2002): 62–64.

125. Andī Adamusu [Andy Adams], "Kyūdō: teiō no geijutsu," trans. Takeichi Yoshio, *Kyūdō* 208 (April 1967), 4–11.

126. Watanabe Ojirō, "Dai nijūyon kai ācherī sekai senshuken taikai hōkoku," *Kyūdō* 208 (September 1967): 7–11.

127. "Kichō kyūdan: Yōroppa ni okeru Nihon kyūdō no hyōka," *Kyūdō* 216 (May 1968): 8–11; "Kichō kyūdan: Yōroppa ni okeru Nihon kyūdō no hyōka," *Kyūdō* 217 (June 1968):

In September 1969, Anzawa Heijirō led a group on a pilgrimage to Herrigel's gravesite, and descriptions of the trip were featured in the October and November issues of *Kyūdō* that same year.[128] I think it is safe to say that this completed the deification of Herrigel and solidified his reputation within the Japanese *kyūdō* community as the prophet of *kyūdō* to the world outside of Japan.

The voices of Europeans and Americans themselves further strengthened the tendency to consider *kyūdō* a mystical art, unlike Western archery. Takayanagi Noriaki (1936–), who participated in the World Archery Championships held in York, England, in 1971, reported that because of Herrigel many foreigners considered Zen and *kyūdō* to be one and the same.[129]

Among the Western *kyūdō* practitioners who were inspired by *Zen in the Art of Archery*, there were some who, hoping to scale the same heights Herrigel had climbed, devoted themselves to training day and night. Books like *One Arrow, One Life* (1988) by Kenneth Kushner[130] and *Zen in Motion* by Neil Claremon (1991)[131] show this tendency. In particular, Kushner trained at a Zen temple in Hawaii founded by Ōmori Sōgen while he studied *kyūdō* with Suhara Kōun and his group, and his desire to recreate Herrigel's experience for himself leaps out from the pages of his book.

An even more interesting book is *Illuminated Spirit* (1996) by the Americans Dan and Jackie DeProspero, a husband and wife who both practice *kyūdō*.[132] This book is primarily a biography of Onuma Hideharu, who was the DeProsperos' *kyūdō* teacher, published as a memorial to him. On one hand it describes him in mysterious terms, describing how, at the instant of his death, there was an earthquake, violent wind, and a thunderstorm followed by a rainbow; on the other hand it says nothing about Onuma's relationship with Western archery.

9–14; "Kichō kyūdan: Yōroppa ni okeru Nihon kyūdō no hyōka," *Kyūdō* 218 (July 1968): 7–10.

128. "Zadankai: Anzawa-hanshi ikkō hōō kichō dan: Zenpen," *Kyūdō* 233 (October 1969): 18–23; Zadankai: Anzawa-hanshi ikkō hōō kichō dan: Kōhen," *Kyūdō* 234 (November 1969): 28–32.

129. Takayanagi Noriaki, "Sekai ācherī senshuken taikai ni Nihon kyūdō o shōkai," *Kyūdō* 258 (November 1971): 26–29.

130. Kenneth Kushner, *One Arrow, One Life* (New York: Arkana, 1988).

131. Niel Claremon, *Zen in Motion* (Rochester, VT: Inner Traditions International, 1991).

132. Dan DeProspero and Jackie DeProspero, *Illuminated Spirit* (Tokyo: Kodansha International, 1996).

No one contributed more to the popularization of Western archery in Japan than Onuma. Half of the space in the *kyūdō* equipment shop he operated was devoted to archery. The DeProsperos, who lived at the Onuma home, could not possibly have been unaware of Onuma's deep relationship with archery. Was it necessary to suppress the fact that Onuma, the embodiment of the spiritual art of *kyūdō*, was also enthusiastic about Western archery?

Zen in the Art of Archery created the breeding ground for this kind of image manipulation. I cannot help but feel that the Japanese, even though they are fully aware that this kind of created image is an overidealization, have tried to proudly take advantage of the fact that foreigners hold them in high esteem.

The difference between *kyūdō* and archery is not self-evident. The two separated from one another only after the Tokyo Olympics. What would *kyūdō* and archery be like today if they had not separated but had found a way to coexist? We should be aware of the fact that *kyūdō* and archery, throwing away the various possibilities that could have opened up had they not separated, were created as opposing "social systems."

While the view of *kyūdō* as "spiritual" grew in foreign countries as a result of the influence of *Zen in the Art of Archery*, the *kyūdō* community in Japan was trying to merge with Western archery, which had been ridiculed as "recreational *kyūdō*." Perversely ironic is the only way to describe this. Finally, I want to point out again that the *Zen in the Art of Archery* boom gave an added boost to the separation of archery and *kyūdō*.

I KNEW IT! IT'S ZEN!

In the first half of the 1960s, as *kyūdō* was trying to merge with archery, the reputation of both Herrigel and the rock garden at Ryōanji became firmly established at about the same time among the Japanese and foreign intelligentsia. In closing, I would like to briefly summarize the spread of the Zen-Ryōanji-Herrigel myth using prominent statements from some of these intellectuals, who would not necessarily be expected to be particularly close to Zen itself.

As a supplement to his book *Antimémories* (1967),[133] the French author André Malraux (1901–1976) wrote a short essay called "The Challenge of

---

133. André Malraux, *Antimémoires* (Paris: Gallimard, 1967).

Japan."[134] This essay, added in response to the *seppuku* (ritual disembowelment) suicide of the novelist Mishima Yukio (1925–1970), is a discussion of Japanese culture, presented as a conversation between Malraux and a certain priest during Malraux's visit to Ryōanji in 1958. No one knows who this priest might have been; he is probably a fictional character created by Malraux. For Malraux too, this indecipherable rock garden was an easily recognizable symbol of Japanese culture.

The critic Roland Barthes, a French intellectual like Malraux, also touches on the rock garden. In his book *L'Empire des Signes* (The empire of signs; 1970) there is short prose piece called "The Zen Garden":

> No flowers, no footprints —
> Where is man?
> Is he in the transporting of the rocks?
> Or in the traces of the rake?
> Or in the work of writing?[135]

The photograph Barthes used to illustrate this piece, however, was not of Ryōanji but of the rock garden at Tōfukuji in Kyoto. The caption of the photograph reads "the garden at Tōfukuji in Kyoto, built in 1236." Tōfukuji was built in 1236, but in reality the rock garden there was made in 1939 by Shigemori Mirei. I do not know why Barthes used a photo of Tōfukuji rather than one of Ryōanji. I suspect he did not realize that the rock garden at Tōfukuji had been created so recently.

It is certain that Barthes was trying to explain the medieval Japanese garden, of which Ryōanji is the most representative example. He saw the rock garden without any trees or greenery as a Zen "sign" and was trying to decipher its *écriture*, or, symbolic meaning. However, contrary to Barthes's expectation, the rock garden had only become a Zen sign quite recently. Not only that, Barthes probably had no inkling that this had come about even later than 1939 when the rock garden at Tōfukuji was created.

Ryōanji makes an unusual appearance as the title of the musical work *Ryōanji*, written between 1982 and 1985 by the American composer John Cage (1912–1992). There were a number of steps in the process of writing *Ryōanji*. First of all, D. T. Suzuki gave a lecture at Columbia University in New York in 1949, where a large number of avant-garde artists were in

---

134. Malraux, *Antimémoires* (Paris: Gallimard, 1972, revised edition).
135. Roland Barthes, *L'Empire des Signes* (Geneva: Albert Skira, 1970), 102.

attendance, Cage among them. In addition to this, Cage was an old acquaintance of Isamu Noguchi's, and in 1947, two years before the lecture, they saw each other practically every day.[136] Cage was aware of Noguchi's sudden postwar infatuation with rock gardens, which probably piqued his interest in Ryōanji and lay behind his composition Ryōanji.

As though in concert with this trend among the Western intelligentsia to single out Ryōanji as a subject worthy of particular admiration, English-language statements from Japan regarding Ryōanji had come to coalesce around a certain theme. Here I would like to present three examples from English-language books written by Japanese authors and published from 1963 to 1965. I think that these statements show clearly that a standard description of the garden, which continues to be used to the present day, had come into being.

> The chief priest of the temple says the real value of the simplicity in this garden can be appreciated only when the secrets of Zen are mastered. It is said that those well-versed in Zen hear the sounds of waves breaking against the stones.[137]

> This form of expression is completely unlike that of conventional gardens; it is spare, abstract, conducive to meditation, and filled with the flavor and perplexities of Zen thought.[138]

> It is believed that in former days the garden was designed with the distant landscape in the background and with cherry trees planted in the garden. At least the former garden was surely different from the present one. However, landscapes and scenery change. Eliminating all plants and instead composing the garden with white sand and rocks, it now has boundless scope and eternity. The spirit of "Vajira" was sublimed into what the Zen Buddhists call "spiritual awakening."[139]

136. Ashton, Noguchi: East and West, 75.

137. Kyoto by Camera and Pen, comp. Asahi Press, Kyoto Branch, trans. Thomas I. Elliott and Yamaguchi Masuo (Kyoto: Tankō-shinsha, 1963), 139.

138. Nakane Kinsaku, Kyoto Gardens, trans. M. L. Hickman (Osaka: Hoikusha, 1965), 17.

139. Here's Kyoto in Living Color (Tokyo: Froebel-kan, 1970), 19. Vajira was one of the twelve divine generals protecting Yakushi, the Buddha of medicine and healing.

I would like to emphasize once again that on the whole, statements like this directly linking the rock garden at Ryōanji to Zen Buddhism were practically never heard until the 1950s.

There was one event that showed the Japanese conclusively that foreigners admired the rock garden at Ryōanji. This was the visit of Elizabeth II (1926–), Queen of England, and her husband Prince Philip, 3rd Duke of Edinburgh (1921–) to Ryōanji on May 10, 1975. The *Asahi* newspaper of May 11 described the visit as follows:

Stones and Zen—The Queen Loses Her Smile

Queen Elizabeth conversed with the stones. For a long time, she gazed at the beauty of Japan, at the soul of Japan, motionless—... to the Queen and the duke, who were seated on the veranda in chairs decorated with the chrysanthemum crest, Chief Priest Matsukura explained: "this is a religious and philosophical garden, not something to be simply enjoyed." As he enjoined them to "take their time and meditate," the Queen's radiant, ever-present smile instantly disappeared and she sat gazing at the stones without speaking for approximately ten minutes ... the Queen questioned Chief Priest Matsukura regarding the meaning of the character "the Void" that he had written and he replied: "this cannot be translated into a foreign language, but to express it in Christian terms, it means 'God.'" The Queen earnestly requested Chief Priest Matsukura's calligraphy as a keepsake, and later it was delivered to the Imperial Palace.[140]

Accompanying the article was a large photograph of the Queen gazing at the rock garden, seated on a chair that had been placed on the veranda of the abbot's quarters. Now that Ryōanji had been honored by the visit of "Her Brittanic Majesty," no one could argue with its exalted status. Not only that, but in response to Chief Priest Matsukura's urging, she had even conversed with the stones and the mass media had broadcast this exchange. What the garden was supposed to be had now been trumpeted throughout Japan. For the management of the temple, there could be no better publicity than this.

However, the reaction of the British media contingent that accompanied Queen Elizabeth differed considerably from that of the Japanese

140. "Ishi to Zen—egao kieta joō-sama" [Stones and Zen—the queen loses her smile], *Asahi Shinbun*, May 11, 1975. I am grateful to Dr. Katahira Miyuki for informing me about this article.

media. According to *The Times*, after visiting the old Imperial Palace in Kyoto and viewing a demonstration of *kemari* (an ancient aristocratic game where players kick a ball made from deerskin, trying to keep it airborne) the Queen visited the Nishi Honganji temple and then went to the Ise Grand Shrine by way of Nara.[141] *The Times* article contains not the slightest mention of Ryōanji whatsoever. It appears that *The Times* correspondents who accompanied the Queen decided that her visit to Ryōanji would be of no interest to their readers. Essentially, the "beauty" of Zen contained within Ryōanji was publicized only for domestic consumption, using the opportunity provided by the Queen's visit. The Japanese mass media made a big production out of something that *The Times* ignored.

However, there is no doubt that the rock garden at Ryōanji was held in high esteem in Europe and America at that time. In 1975, the same year as Queen Elizabeth's visit to Kyoto, the French historian Jacques Benoist-Méchin (1901–1983) offered the following panegyric in his book *L'Homme et ses Jardins ou Les Métamorphoses du Paradis Terrestre* (Man and his gardens, or the metamorpheses of earthly paradise; 1975):

> There exist in Japan many gardens other than Ryōanji, and even some that have been created more recently. However, none of these are as authentically and intrinsically Japanese. Above all, there is no other garden which so clearly expresses what the Japanese expect from their gardens: not really a broadened awareness of the universe, but rather a condensed vision of their own country, in order to be able to love it and to serve it still more, up to the point of "bearing the unbearable" to assure its survival.[142]

Benoist-Méchin himself never actually saw Ryōanji with his own eyes, nor did he ever visit Japan. He spun these words out of nothing but photographs and documents. That is, Benoist-Méchin's words can be considered a distillation of all of the various things about Ryōanji written in French and English. This is a classic example of how the reputation of a thing comes into being.

While this may be hard for the young readers of today to grasp, among "cultured" Japanese born prior to 1960, *Zen in the Art of Archery* was treated

141. Peter Hazelhurst, Queen Sees Japan's Most Holy Shrine," *Times* (London), May 12, 1975, 6.

142. Jacques Benoist-Méchin, *L'Homme et ses Jardins: ou Les Métamorphoses du Paradis Terrestre* (Paris: A. Michel, 1975), 98.

as something that everyone should know about. In his book *Dō no shisō*
(The idea of the way; 1978), the literary critic and scholar of French literature Terada Tōru (1915–1995) spent two chapters lauding *Zen in the Art of
Archery*. While Terada seemed to be uncomfortable with Herrigel's "It," he
rationalized this as follows:

> While I have misgivings about whether or not Master Awa used the "It" that
> is in our Japanese vocabulary when he said "It," what I want to say is this: is
> not this indeed the "Way?"[143]

To me, this seems like Terada is doing his best to convince himself in spite
of his misgivings about the term "It." Finally, Terada positioned *Zen in the
Art of Archery* as follows:

> It is truly ironic that out of all of the books that I devoured right and left to
> help me understand what the "Way" was, no other book gave me as strong
> an idea of what it might be.[144]

To Terada, it was precisely Herrigel's *Zen in the Art of Archery* that seemed to
explain the "Way." I think this sort of assessment is representative of the
manner in which cultured people spoke about Herrigel in the 1970s.

The critic Nishio Kanji wrote in great detail about Herrigel in his book
Kōi suru shisaku (Thoughts on action; 1982) in his critique of the nature of
Japanese "culturedness." Nishio said that "the innocence of enjoying garden variety East-West comparisons like comparative culture or comparative philosophy which require no actual experience"[145] is the best that cultured Japanese can do, and that there are no people in Japan like Herrigel
"who undertook a personal experiment requiring action."

The clinical psychologist Kawai Hayao (1928–2007) goes even further.
In his book *Kage no genshōgaku* (The phenomenology of shadows; 1976)
he says that the "It" of the "Target in the Dark" is a good example of the
concepts of "the revelation of the shadow" and "synchronicity" found in
Jungian psychology.[146] Herrigel and Awa's respective "shadows" were re-

---

143. Terada Tōru, *Dō no shisō* (Tokyo: Sōbunsha, 1978), 186.

144. Ibid., 172.

145. Nishio Kanji, *Kōi suru shisaku* (Tokyo: Chūō Kōronsha, 1982), 34.

146. Kawai Hayao, *Kage no genshōgaku* (1976; Tokyo: Kōdansha Gakujutsu Bunko, 1987),
290–95.

vealed simultaneously when Herrigel challenged Awa as to whether he could hit the target even if he were blindfolded and Awa responded by telling Herrigel to come to the training hall that evening; and then, on top of that, the miracle of the second arrow striking and breaking the nock of the first arrow occurred. According to Kawai, this is "synchronicity."

Kawai's interpretation obscures the major question of how truthful the account of the "Target in the Dark" actually is. However, if *Zen in the Art of Archery* is read not as an account of actual events but as a literary work, one cannot condemn interpretations like Kawai's out of hand.

Since the publication of *Zen in the Art of Archery*, a veritable multitude of intellectuals have cited Herrigel. Since a complete list of reference documents does not exist, one can only chance upon these quotes and citations when they appear in books and essays, which makes them hard to find. I am sure that there is a mountain of references to Herrigel that I have not seen.

Even though it is difficult to make a comprehensive list of documents that cite Herrigel, I would like to introduce one by a modern author. This is *Shintai kankaku o torimodosu* (Recovering our sense of the physical; 2000) by the scholar of pedagogy Saitō Takashi (1960−). In this book, Saitō repeats the myth by quoting Herrigel to explain the similarity between the "feeling of 'Let'" that D. T. Suzuki emphasized and the *hanare* (release) of *kyūdō*. Interestingly, in the same book and in the same chapter, Saitō refers to the rock garden at Ryōanji. Saitō is trying to explain the sense of balance that is omnipresent in Japanese culture:

> For example, the famous rock garden at Ryōanji has a number of stones of differing sizes arranged in exquisite balance. If one were to move the stones, they would convey a different feeling from the feeling of peacefulness they convey in their unmoved positions. At first glance, it seems like the stones at Ryōanji are placed arbitrarily without any rhyme or reason. However, the stones maintain a strict mutual balance, so much so that one gets the feeling that if one of the stones were moved it would be difficult to balance the stones without moving the others as well.[147]

My task here is to dissect Herrigel and the rock garden. From this book's point of view, statements like this dissect themselves. Of course,

147. Saitō Takashi, *Shintai kankaku o torimodosu* (Tokyo: Nihon Hōsō Shuppan Kyōkai, 2000), 179−80.

saying this does not necessarily detract from the overall worth of Kawai and Saitō's books.

It cannot be denied that Herrigel and Ryōanji are unique. However, the key point here is that when one searches for the diverse interpretations one might expect such uniqueness to have generated, one finds that there are none. Indeed, the situation is precisely the opposite: only a hackneyed cookie-cutter interpretation has been accepted. This is the interpretation that says that *Zen in the Art of Archery* and Ryōanji represent the true pinnacle of Japanese culture.

Why did the Japanese feel it was necessary to amplify the Zen interpretation of *kyūdō* and Ryōanji? Why was it necessary for diverse opinions, such as those that questioned whether or not *kyūdō* and Ryōanji were really Zen, to be suppressed until they disappeared? One possible answer to this can perhaps be found in the social and economic situation in which Japan found itself. It is common knowledge that after World War II, the Japanese had to rebuild their country from scratch. The 1960s saw an economic boom that gave Japan a firm footing on which to build economic independence, but from a cultural point of view, the Japanese were intent solely on imitating the West. In the midst of this situation, the Japanese discovered that Japan possessed a wonderful culture of which the West approved: "Zen."

Was it a good thing for the Japanese to have unquestioningly accepted the "Zen" that the West saw? This acceptance was heavily contaminated by D. T. Suzuki's approach, which connected all of the various aspects and expressions of Japanese culture to Zen, even if it was necessary to make this connection by brute force. Still, I cannot help but think that many Japanese were aware that Japanese culture was not synonymous with Zen to that extent.

However, now we come to the heart of the matter. To curry favor with the Western point of view, the Japanese went so far as to change their own view of their own culture. This gave birth in the 1960s to the phenomenon of forcing all of the interpretations of *kyūdō* and Ryōanji into the Zen mold.

A diverse culture is a strong culture. Zen was one element of a diverse Japanese culture. When foreigners turned their gaze on Japanese culture, the fact that Zen was there was surely one of Japanese culture's strengths. It is precisely because Zen was there that, when the Japanese realized foreigners were paying attention to it, they were able to build on it, all the while transforming the appearance of Japanese culture to suit the foreign view.

Koestler metaphorically called Zen "the tranquilizer pill of feudal Japan."[148] But he was wrong. If Japanese culture is seen as a living organism, Zen is not a medication taken from an outside source, nor is it something that has an effect only on the feudalistic aspects of Japan. Popular Zen is, rather, a self-generated narcotic that, coming into being as a response to the external stress Japan faced after World War II, gave Japan a feeling of euphoria about itself. "Japan's postwar endorphin" perfectly describes this kind of "Zen."

When a healthy organism self-generates a narcotic substance, this substance will be automatically broken down once it is no longer needed, and fresh secretions of the substance will cease. However, once the "Japanese culture = Zen" idea reached the level of ideology, its role in society became entrenched and the auto-dissolution mechanism ceased to function. This is, in a manner of speaking, something approaching a state of mental illness. As a result, the image of Japanese culture with all its diversity was forced into a stereotypical mold and has become cramped and stifling. And so it has seemingly become impossible to describe *kyūdō* and rock gardens as anything other than Zen.

It is the Japanese themselves who have created this stereotype by choosing from among the many available theories of Japanese culture only a single idea that conformed to a standardized taste. Stereotypes destroy cultural diversity and sap cultural vitality. It seems to me that we should construct a much more liberated image of Herrigel, Ryōanji, and, even more, of Japanese culture itself.

After all, aren't there are as many interpretations of a rock garden as there are people who see it?

148. Koestler, "A Stink of Zen," 16.

Postscript

Officially, my field is informatics. I used to work in circles concerned with engineering and I had little to do with the academic world that focused on the humanities. I suppose that a scholarly background like this does not make me particularly suited for writing this sort of book. However, it is my belief that all the things I have dealt with in this book are issues of informatics. How has Japanese cultural information been transmitted overseas? How has it then been reintroduced back into Japan? How has this changed Japanese culture itself? All of these issues are concerned with the creation and transmission of information.

Culture is dynamic. As cultural information goes back and forth between different entities, culture itself is born, changes, and dies. Random elements alone do not bring about this dynamism; the intention of the entity itself towards the information it receives acts selectively on determining the direction in which the situation will develop. As information goes back and forth and is either selected or rejected, at some point culture—which is originally born from the relationship between oneself and others—is reduced to being discussed from an essentialist perspective. I think this is a good abstract of the subject of this book.

While this dynamism is what creates and reorganizes culture, I do not mean to imply that this is limited to *kyūdō* or rock gardens. From the past to the present, all areas of culture—from high culture to subcultures—have been constantly undergoing this same process. For this reason, I believe that it is beneficial to question the origin of the commonly held opinion that "it is precisely such-and-such that represents Japanese culture." I am convinced that the concepts and methods of informatics can be useful now more than ever in analyzing this process.

I do not believe in forcing informatics into the constricted methodology of engineering. The kind of informatics that concentrates only on methods for analyzing and organizing information is also unsatisfying to me. I aspire to a more wide-ranging informatics, which can be useful in all of the various enterprises having to do with culture.

I believe that informatics should be a field of scholarship that embraces both science and the humanities. For this reason, I believe it is important to make the most of credible research results and to learn from sound methodologies, regardless of whether they come from science or the humanities. However, I am fairly certain that this style of mine will not be well received in academic circles.

Eight years have passed since I came to work at the International Research Center for Japanese Studies (IRCJS, or Nichibunken), an organization that conducts research in the humanities. At the center, I attend conferences and the like with researchers who come from completely different fields of specialization, and so I can observe the practices and conventions of a variety of academic disciplines.

While engineering is my field, it has been my experience that in engineering-oriented academic societies, the scholars who are well regarded are mainly those who produce artificial data based on unrealistic hypotheses and who can then create an elegant theory that can be applied only to that data. To put it another way, a low value is assigned to applied research, which is a desperate struggle with real-world data, which has no fixed form, and which is full of exceptions and "noise." Therefore, even if a beautiful new theory is born, without making an effort to apply it, researchers immediately turn their attention to creating a new theory. This makes it difficult for researchers like me who live in the world of the humanities with its "dirty" data.

Having said this, however, this does not mean that academic societies focusing on the humanities are therefore easier to approach. Such societies are splintered into too many small areas of specialization, making them seem much more like fraternities centered on a small number of authoritative figures than academic societies. If one of these authorities takes a dim view of a researcher, his papers will not be published in the society's journal and he will not be recommended for a university post. As a result, young researchers are forced into dependence upon these authorities. In addition, individuals and groups jealously guard information in order to prevent outsiders from using it in their research.

From this book's standpoint, this is a problem. Apparently, a great deal of information on Awa Kenzō exists. However, only an extremely limited number of researchers are permitted to see this information. This is very different from Germany and the United States, where the information on Herrigel and Acker is extremely well organized and is available to any researcher who asks to see it. Public institutions such as universities keep orderly archives as well as accurate records of the people who previously belonged to those institutions.

This creates a manifest difference between the foundation supporting research into the humanities in Japan on the one hand and Europe and the United States on the other. Universities and research institutes in Japan have practically no concept of the archive. In most cases there are only fragmentary records left by previous members of the institution. In addition, Japanese researchers tend to keep their information close to the vest and are passive about sharing it widely—that is, about publicizing their trade secrets.

Researchers also make little effort to explain their most recent results in words that can be understood by people who are not specialists in those fields. This is true both in the sciences and the humanities. As a result, the wisdom that has been so painstakingly assembled never circulates beyond the confines of its field, making it difficult in the extreme for research results to be compared across disciplines and new meta-level knowledge to be discovered from them. On top of that, all over Japan everyone is now working harder than ever to guard their information, citing such things as protection of intellectual property as reasons.

For people like me who are trying to do interdisciplinary research, this is an extremely difficult environment in which to work. For the advancement of scholarship, it is imperative to create an environment where both primary and secondary source documents — the foundation of research — can circulate freely so that as many researchers as possible can discuss the same data.

My fifteen years of experience with *kyūdō* is what allowed me to develop an awareness of the problem that I have discussed in this book. While I do not have sufficient experience in *kyūdō* by any means, I have been practicing *kyūdō* five times longer than Herrigel did. My teacher, the late Inagaki Genshirō, was a teacher of a traditional school of *kyūdō* that is said to date back to the fifteenth century. In theory and practice, he was the complete opposite of Herrigel and Awa. That is to say, I have experienced with my own body what non-Zen *kyūdō* is like.

However, I was faced with the difficult problem of how to explain this experience to people who have never picked up a bow and arrow. No matter how much I may contradict Herrigel and Awa from the standpoint of my own *kyūdō* experience, this can easily be dismissed as nothing more than a simple difference in our respective *kyūdō* styles, a difficult charge for me to answer. Rather than treat how Herrigel had been received in Japan as a *kyūdō* problem, it was necessary to look at it with fresh eyes as a question of Japanese cultural characteristics in a broad sense. The same can be said of Ryōanji.

I publicly presented the kernel of the Herrigel theory put forth in this book for the first time at an internal seminar at the IRCJS shortly after I transferred there; I believe it was in the spring of 1997. It took me a full eight years to do the necessary research, uncover unpublished material, and finally shape everything into the Japanese edition of this book. Perhaps it was fate that I was able to publish this research in a single volume in Japanese on the fiftieth anniversary of Herrigel's death.

The main points put forth in this book have already been published in the following papers, which I authored. None of these papers appeared in publications that would attract a general readership, but it is precisely in these low-key kinds of publications where the most recent research results are often to be found.

- "Shōwa shoki no beikoku jin kyūdo ka uiriamu akkā ni tsuite" (William Acker, an American *kyūdō* practitioner of the early Shōwa period), *Budōgaku kenkyū* 31:1 (1998): 1–9 [in Japanese]

- "The Myth of Zen in the Art of Archery," *Japanese Journal of Religious Studies* 28/1–2 (2001): 1–30
- "Oigen Herigeru no shōgai to nachisu: shinwa to shite no yumi to zen (2)" (The myth of *Zen in the art of archery*, Part 2: Herrigel and the Nazis), *Nihon kenkyū* 24 (2002): 201–226 [in Japanese]
- "'——— to zen' no kicchu na sekai" (The kitschy world of *Zen in/and the art of . . .*), *Nichibunken* 28 (2002): 31–35 [in Japanese]
- "Kyūdō to ācherī no bunki ten" (Kyūdō and archery: the parting of the ways), *Budō* (July 2004): 102–110 [in Japanese]

Before I proceed to the acknowledgements, I want to emphasize one thing. While I have discussed various opinions regarding Zen in this book, I have not written anything about Zen itself. Zen is a spiritual culture with a long history. To say that I am ill-equipped to discuss the teachings of Zen is to vastly understate the case. I myself find the stoic side of Zen attractive in a certain sense. In addition, I think that proper respect must be paid to a religious practice with such a long history. For these reasons, I thought it behooved me to be careful about venturing any opinion about Zen itself. For the same reason, I have said practically nothing regarding *kyūdō* theory. I hope that one day I will be able to tackle such profound issues as Zen and *kyūdō* head on, but I doubt if I will ever be able to manage it.

I am greatly indebted to many people for their help in bringing this book to completion. First, I want to thank the late Professor Inagaki Genshirō, Professor Irie Kōhei of the Martial Arts Research Group of the University of Tsukuba, Professor Mori Toshio of the *Kyūdō* Research Group of the University of Tsukuba, and all of the members of the *Kyūdō* Research Group for their warm friendship and great help on questions of *kyūdō* history and techniques.

For my research into Herrigel in Germany, I received very valuable suggestions from Professor Wolfgang Schamoni of the Japanese Studies Department of the University of Heidelberg, his wife Ms. Akisawa Mieko, and my colleague at the IRCJS, Professor Inaga Shigemi. Ms. Madea Izumi, who lives in Germany, also assisted greatly with my research there.

For my research in Germany I am indebted to the staffs of the German National Archives, the University of Erlangen Archives and the University of Heidelberg Archives. As helpful as all of these archives were, to this day I still remember the excitement I felt when I came upon the Herrigel materials in the archives of the University of Heidelberg. The moment I laid eyes on them, I could see that for research into Herrigel's life, they were of absolutely the first order. When I asked the person in charge about them I was told they had yet to be examined by anyone. For a researcher, having the data for which he had been searching fall into his hands in virgin condition is an experience that may or may not come along even once in a lifetime.

I want to take this opportunity to simply thank the gods of good fortune for smiling on me. At the same time, I want to say that I felt that it was my mission to make public both where these valuable materials are kept and the gist of the information they contain. I do not know how well this book accomplishes that mission, but it is my hope that researchers who come after me will be able to analyze these materials even more closely and draw out new knowledge or counter-arguments from them.

I want to thank Professor William Bodiford of the University of California, Los Angeles; Professor Paul Swanson of the Nanzan Research Center for Religious Culture of Nanzan University; and Mr. Earl Hartman, a translator and longtime *kyūdō* practitioner, for noticing my first paper on Herrigel, "The Myth of Zen in the Art of Archery," and taking the trouble to translate it into English. Thanks to their efforts, my thesis has had something of an impact among *kyūdō* practitioners and students of religion in the English-speaking world. The English version of my thesis first appeared in the *Japanese Journal of Religious Studies* as well as in two other publications and has been translated into Italian. In addition, the entire September 2004 edition of *Zanshin*, the house organ of the German *Kyūdō* Federation, was devoted to the German response to my paper. Unfortunately, I had already submitted the manuscript for this book for publication by the time I received a copy of the magazine, so I was not able to use any of the information it contained in the preparation of this book.

I want to thank the staff of the Seikei Gakuen Archives for their help in my research on Ōhazama Shūei. In Japan, where real archives are few and far between, the existence of this archive was a great help.

I also want to thank Ms. Yoshimura Reiko of the Smithsonian Freer Gallery of Art in the United States for her help in my research into their documents on William Acker. The Acker materials in the Freer Gallery's archives were first-rate, with all of the material organized and maintained in a very comprehensive manner. I can only call it a stroke of luck that I was blessed with such complete documentation.

I am indebted to the staff of the IRCJS library for their help in researching and procuring various documents. Their prompt and meticulous service is unmatched and was a great help to me. As I pointed out in the footnotes, Dr. Katahira Miyuki, who came to the IRCJS as a graduate student, told me about the existence of various documents on the history of gardens. Ms. Okaya Junko also was a great help at various stages of this book's preparation.

Every time I publish a book, I realize once again that for interdisciplinary research there is no better research environment that the IRCJS. This is because it is filled with experts from all sorts of fields to whom I can address questions whenever I come across something that I do not understand. My colleague and expert in garden history, Professor Shirahata Yōzaburō, looked through the rough draft and gave me advice on a number of points. I began my research and writing on garden history knowing nothing and teaching myself as I went along, so I was relieved to find that there was little difference between Professor Shirahata's views and my own impressions regarding the garden history field. Another colleague of mine, Professor Inoue Shōichi, a specialist in the history of architecture, also looked over the first draft and gave me much valuable advice. I have always been impressed with Professor Inoue's unique point of view and the rigorous and thoroughgoing way he searches for data. When he commented that my draft was "interesting," I was as happy as a child.

Finally, I want to express the utmost gratitude to members of my family who warmly supported their husband and father in his staring match with his computer.

Yamada Shōji
January 2005

Translator's Afterword

For as long as I can remember I have loved bows and arrows. Growing up, Robin Hood was my hero, and every chance I got, I was out with my bow shooting at things. Other kids worshipped rock stars, but not me; playing the guitar was all well and good, I supposed, but really: was there anything cooler than being able to split an arrow at a hundred paces? My childhood and high school years were one long attempt to not just imitate Robin Hood but to *become* him. Oh, for a stout bow of yew and a grey goose shaft!

So when I read Eugen Herrigel's *Zen in the Art of Archery* when I was eighteen, I naturally fell instantly and completely under its spell. I was elated to discover that, in a sense, Robin Hood was not just a fictional character after all. But Herrigel's Master was clearly on a more superhuman level altogether: not only did he split his own arrow, *he did it in the dark without even aiming!* Not even Robin Hood had done that.

So this is how you learn how to hit your own arrow, I

thought. You don't need to rely on anything as mundane as aiming or technique; all you have to do is become enlightened and let "It" do everything for you! Well, who would not want to learn this kind of magic? All I had to do was apprentice myself to an enlightened Zen sage. According to Herrigel, Japan was bursting at the seams with them, so I thought that if Herrigel could do it, I could, too.

Thus, when I had the opportunity to go to Japan in 1972 at the age of twenty to practice *kendō*, which I had taken up in high school, I was already determined to seek out a *kyūdō* master. Armed with the arcane knowledge provided by Herrigel and D. T. Suzuki's *Zen and Japanese Culture*, I was confident that I was fully prepared for complete immersion in the rarefied world of Zen archery, where physical skill was seen not as a goal but rather as the Devil's temptation, a veritable obstacle to the pursuit of Truth.

However, what I found was not what Herrigel had described. Expecting to be gruffly dismissed by an inscrutable Master, I was shocked, and somewhat disappointed, when he accepted me as a student with not even so much as a raised eyebrow (you mean *anyone* can become an initiate into the mysteries?). Practice was simplicity itself: stand like this, breathe like this, hold the bow like this, draw the string like this, don't panic. Where were the abstruse *kōans*, the cryptic hints, the veiled references to a mysterious spiritual realm beyond understanding that only the pure of heart could hope to enter? My teacher never once talked to me about Zen, enlightenment, or meditation. He just patiently corrected my technique and told me to keep shooting until I got it right.

To make things worse, I discovered that to advance in rank one had to learn how to hit the target and that there were even tournaments with winners and losers. Competition was fierce. To top it all off, the people who practiced *kyūdō* were not Zen sages at all but regular, everyday people, many of whom (my teacher included) carefully marked down hits and misses in their daily practice journals. Needless to say, I was horrified. With the arrogance of youth, I consoled myself with the thought that even if everyone else had abandoned the True Way, I would never do so. So I redoubled my efforts to "Zennify" my *kyūdō* practice, interpreting everything through the lens Herrigel had provided.

Fortunately, reality has a way of showing one the truth of things so long as one has the sense to get one's nose out of a book and pay attention to what it is one is actually doing. As I continued to practice, and as I became more fluent in Japanese and so could have real discussions with my teachers and fellow practitioners and read books on my own, I eventually came to the inevitable conclusion: Herrigel had simply gotten it wrong. Real *kyūdō* just was not what he had said it was. *Kyūdō* does, indeed, have a deep spiritual dimension. But Herrigel, saddled with a dualistic Western mind and obsessed with otherworldly mysticism, had misunderstood it.

Thus, when I was given the opportunity to translate Professor Yamada's first paper on this subject, "The Myth of Zen in the Art of Archery," I was elated to discover that someone else had reached many of the same conclusions about Herrigel to which I had come, but, unlike me, had the scholarship to back up his conclusions and the ability to explain them in a clear and lucid way. I also discovered that Professor Yamada's *kyūdō* teacher, Inagaki Genshiro, and one of my own teachers, Murakami Hisashi, had been fellow disciples of that giant of *kyūdō*, Urakami Sakae, who was a contemporary of Herrigel's own teacher, Awa Kenzō. Indeed, the world is a small place.

It has been thirty-five years since I took up the bow under Herrigel's influence. I have yet to put it down. I suppose that I owe Herrigel something of a debt: had it not been for his book, I might never have known about *kyūdō* at all. However, it was only a bridge to something better; once crossed, the traveler moves on, his eyes always ahead. Over the years I have discovered that the true Way of the Bow is a far more worthwhile endeavor than anything that Herrigel could have imagined. I want to thank Professor Yamada for giving me the opportunity to translate his book, and I hope that those who have read it found it as interesting and "enlightening" as I did.

Earl Hartman
Palo Alto, California
March 2007

Appendix: Herrigel's Defense

The fact that during the last five months of the war I served as rector of the University of Erlangen suggests my inclusion in group II (activists, militarists, profiteers). I can present evidence that this legal assumption does not apply to me.

I. How I Became Rector

In the spring of 1944, university rectors were informed that those among them who had been in office for more than two years were to expect their gradual replacement and should name successors suitable for the post. The then rector Prof. Dr. Wintz informed *Reichsminister* (Imperial Minister) Rust in a private letter (the content of which he would later reveal to me during a conversation) about the following: He, Wintz, felt prepared and capable to remain in office. However, if this was thought to be inappropriate because of the six years he had already been in office, he could only name his prorector (vice rector)—that was me—who had been entrusted with the duties of the named office for six years and who was therefore familiar with affairs in such a difficult time as the present one. This letter by Prof. Wintz remained—as far as I have learnt—without reply and it seemed as if everything would remain as before. Surprisingly, however, in the beginning of November a decree by the Minister of the Sciences (*Reichswissenschaftsminister*) arrived, announcing the abdication of Prof. Wintz and my appointment as rector. That meant I was being proclaimed rector without the usual appraisement by the head of the association of lecturers (*Gaudozentenbundsführer*), the head of district, and the head of province. If these party authorities had been asked beforehand, I would certainly not have been chosen because I was still a provisional party member only (without membership book). Moreover, I was still on bad terms with the then *Gaudozentenbundsführer*, Dr. H. A. Molitoris, who had repeatedly tried to procure my discharge as prorector for the present rector, Dr. Wintz.

I could have rejected my appointment as rector under some pretext. But this would have resulted in the appointment of someone who ensured that he was willing to dance to the tune of the *Gaudozentenbundsführer* and the head of province. And this—which I was convinced of by long-term experience—would have had an extremely unfavorable effect on university matters. In such a desperate situation and to prevent this, I held it my duty to assume the position of rector, being determined to avert what might imperil the existence of the university in the last minute (cf. attachment no. 11).[1] Whoever served as prorector during the war years as I did, moreover in a situation when Germany was on the brink of disaster, could indeed not have wanted to become rector out of ambition or a craving for recognition, because instead of honor and appreciation he faced stress, work, and bitter disappointment.

II. How I Administered the Office of Rector (From November 19, 1944, to April 16, 1945)

1. As soon as I had been installed as rector, the district head, Mr. Gross, demanded the delivery of the [ceremonial] robes of the professors for the collection of textile fibres. He rang me up regarding this matter literally

---

1. The complete text for the numbered attachments referred to in parentheses is not included here. These attachments were all written by different people in support of Herrigel's words.

every second day and even made the head of the united women of the district (*Kreisfrauenschaft*) try to persuade me. Moreover, my former rector urgently pointed out that it was our duty to sacrifice the robes, which had become "ridiculous." Although the rectors of other universities had already set a good example, I did not surrender. The university thus is still in possession of its robes today.

2. In December 1944 the provincial authorities (*Gauleitung*) informed me that there were about 3,000 refugees from the Saar area to be accommodated. There was no choice but to make use of a great number of rooms in the students' dormitory. During the meetings I opposed this plan vehemently, arguing that in practice this would lead to the closing down of the university. I succeeded in preventing the requisition of Erlangen for the refugees.

3. After a heavy air raid on Nuremberg in January 1945, the provincial authorities again demanded room for 2,500 people whose homes had been destroyed. Again the university was in danger of having to close its gates. I entered a protest in Nuremberg and finally succeeded by pointing out that the University of Erlangen was one of the few universities in Germany left intact, but I had to put up with offending and tactless remarks about the "intellectual who acted heartlessly toward comrades (*Volkgenossen*) in bitter need."

4. In the end, Erlangen was to take in about 3,000 Silesian refugees. This time, the provincial authorities did not bother to ask, but simply informed me that in the present situation Erlangen could no longer be spared. I had no choice but to ask Prof. Dr. Volz (faculty of natural sciences) to lodge a complaint in Berlin with the commissioner for the management of the stream of refugees and to give him two extensive reports as documents, one of which was written by Mayor Dr. Ohly and the other one by me. Prof. Volz returned with the order that the provincial head had to accommodate the refugees in his province without using the facilities of the city and the university of Erlangen. It was only then that the head of the province withdrew his decree. Obviously the provincial authorities were on bad terms with me afterwards. I did not care, however. My main concern was that I had saved the university from great harm. As witnesses for points 2–4 I can name: the former mayor, Dr. Ohly, Prof. Dr. Volz, and the former head of student housing, Mr. H. Moessner.

5. Around the end of February, the then commander of the Erlangen militia (*Volkssturm*), Lt. Col. Hans Ritter von Schmidt came to see me and discuss the situation—at first in a very careful manner because we knew

each other only superficially. The militia, he elaborated, was so poorly armed that they would not be able to make any impact in the event of an armed attack. He took the occasion to inquire what I as rector of the university thought about the decreed defense of Erlangen. I replied that, on the one hand, I had to take into account the 8,000–9,000 injured and ill people lying in the military and civilian hospitals and that, on the other hand, I was opposed to any defense of Erlangen in respect to Erlangen's status as a university town. When Herr von Schmidt asked me in return whether I would allow him to make use of this opinion against a superior department I gave my consent without hesitation.

A few weeks later, during a second meeting, Herr von Schmidt explained to me that by higher authority one did not necessarily insist on a defense of Erlangen. Apparently, however, only the head of district Mr. Gross would insist determinedly on a defense at whatever price. I then asked Herr von Schmidt whether he had some reliable men who would dispose of the head of district (*Kreisleiter*) if necessary—that was "to kill" him. Herr von Schmidt believed that he could be positive about this. To make short work of him seemed the only and legitimate way out of this situation.

During a third meeting in April, we discussed the threat that came from the party's youth organization (*Hitlerjugend*) in case they still possessed arms and explosives. Three days after this last meeting, Herr von Schmidt was arrested by the secret police (*Gestapo*) and sentenced to death after a short trial. The circumstances under which he escaped death cannot be explained here. I thus did not speak against the defense of Erlangen while the U.S. troops stood before its gates but already weeks before, and I therefore knew precisely which fate I faced if my opinion became known before the occupation of the city.

Witness: Herr von Schmidt (cf. attachment no. 16)

In this connection I have to point out that it was not during the last months of the war that I came to the conclusion that the Thousand-Year Reich was coming to an end, but years before, as may be seen from a remark I made to a former student when she visited me for a confidential appointment: "Just wait—it will all change!" (cf. attachment no. 8). I was therefore indeed an "activist," however, not for but against Hitlerism.

Finally, I would like to stress that during my time as rector I did neither hold a public nor a private meeting. I did this on purpose because otherwise I would have been forced to employ the usual Nazi phraseology that was against my convictions and intentions.

I have not suffered a nameable disadvantage from the dangerous meetings with Herr von Schmidt. But suppose the occupation of Erlangen by U.S. troops had been postponed for a few weeks for some reason—who knows what would have happened to me. In the long run my convictions could not have escaped official notice.

III. My Attitude as Rector during the Last Months of the War Was Consistent with My General Attitude during the Years 1933–45

1. I did not apply for party membership voluntarily, but was called upon to join in autumn 1937. As I was dean of the faculty of philosophy since 1936, a refusal to join the party would have had very adverse effects, taking into account the utterly strained relationship between the University of Erlangen and the then head of province Mr. Streicher—not so much for myself but for the university (I was full professor since 1929 and therefore could not expect an "improvement" of my position [by joining the party]). The plan to make Erlangen the third Bavarian university to be closed down had not been put *ad acta* yet. I knew only too well from my time as prorector what effort it had cost to prevent this and to secure the continuing existence of the university. Which conviction I held in private can be seen by the fact that my wife was not a party member of any of the Nazi organizations and did not allow herself to be deployed by them. With my consent, she determinedly rejected any cooperation whenever she was asked to do so, arguing that she was the wife of the prorector.

2. It is self-understood that I, as a man who had gotten to know the world extending to the Far East, by principle had to dismiss racism and above all racial hate. This was expressed in the fact that I

   a. had the Jewish physician Dr. Mosé (Hindenburgstrasse 6 ½) as my doctor from 1930 until his hasty move to Vienna.
   b. in January 1934 admitted a Jewish student named Aron Cohn for a PhD and did grant him the grade "very good" (cf. PhD book of the faculty).
   c. in 1942, in spite of adverse decrees and at my own risk, gave permission to a first-grade Jewish half caste, who had been discharged from service at the front, to continue his studies and, moreover, did give him RM [Reichsmark] 500 at his disposal (cf. attachment no. 3).

d. in spite of the strict rules, did not remove any books by Jewish philosophers from the philosophical library (cf. attachment no. 3).

e. treated the teachings of Jewish philosophers as extensively and approv-
ingly as those of non-Jewish philosophers (cf. attachments no. 2, 3, 5, 7).

f. ignored the examination in philosophy of life (*Weltanschauung*) that was
provided by law for state examinations and examined, as can be seen in
the examination records, as of old the history of philosophy only (cf. attachment no. 3).

3. In my lectures and tutorials I took great pains to apply utmost objectivity and not to give any space to the Nazi ideology (cf. attachments no.
2, 3, 5, 7, 8, 17, 21, 23, 28). Never did I did exploit my lectures and presenta-
tions about Japan and East Asia for propaganda, although this would have
suggested itself (cf. attachments no. 3, 5, 9).

4. As rector as well as prorector, I did not in any single case let my de-
cisions be influenced by the political convictions of the civil servants and
employees (cf. attachments no. 2, 4, 11, 12, 13).

a. I thus for example supported Prof. Dr. Brenner being made head of
English Studies, although the head of district was opposed to that idea
(cf. attachment no. 10).

b. In the very same sense I adopted the cause of Prof. Dr. R. Zocher, whom
the head of the union of lecturers, Dr. H. A. Molitoris, had initially refused to include in the new system of lecturers (cf. attachment no. 12).

c. Likewise I recommended the very able furnace feeder Mr. Hintz for pro-
motion to foreman, although I knew that he was regarded, as was later
confirmed in print, as "intolerable" (cf. attachment no. 4).

d. Adversely, I refused to make a lecturer whose performance was regarded
nonsufficient a member of staff, although the former head of staff Mr.
Klein determinedly pleaded for him at the Bavarian Ministry of Cultural
Affairs (cf. attachment no. 12).

5. I have always granted the civil servants, employees, and students
the right of free speech and I have neither rejected nor denounced anti-
fascist or defeatist remarks — as would have been my duty (cf. attachments
no. 6, 7, 8).

6. During my six-year term as prorector, as can be proven, I did not accept a single penny for compensation. In accordance with the regulations,

I received reimbursement for expenses only during official trips. I covered all private expenses while on duty from my own pocket, although I could also have credited them to myself.

As rector I received only the traditional allowance for special expenditures which any rector receives and otherwise no bestowment—least from the side of the party.

IV. Cooperation with the Military Government

After the occupation of Erlangen I contacted the military government in my function as rector. Immediately, I became subject to two interrogations, a brief one by the military police and a more extensive one by the then governor Major Adair. As the military government apparently gradually came to the conclusion that my genuine efforts to follow their orders and create an atmosphere of trust were not to be doubted, they put me through a third interrogation of two and one-half hours, which took place in the office of Major Adair and was conducted by two high-ranking officers of the general headquarters in the presence of Lt. Kimpel.

The result was that on orders of the military government, I was appointed prorector on May 31, 1945, and was entrusted with the management of the administration (cf. attachment no. 14). I thus worked with the military government until the appointment of a new rector and prorector, that is until December 5, 1945. This was the moment when my dismissal, which was stipulated by military laws no. 51 and no. 8, respectively, could not be postponed any longer. Lt. Kimbel explained to me that the request by the military government of Erlangen to allow me to remain in office in spite of this law, because of the result of my interrogation, had not been replied to as yet. I therefore could no longer remain in office.

His successor, Major Lundeen, also promised to attend to my case. This even more so as, referring to the announcement of my dismissal, the military government had informed the rector's office of the university that it intended to take steps in my matter (cf. attachment no. 15). Major Lundeen thought that my case could perhaps be settled by the beginning of the summer term of 1946.

During my last visit in March he informed me that unfortunately the military government could not do anything for me because the settlement of all such cases had been transferred to the German authorities.

On October 14, 1946, Lt. Kimbel stopped on his way in Erlangen and had me come to the military government's office, where he inquired about the present state of affairs. Again he expressed his conviction that my case was an exception that fell under the terms of the laws no. 51 and 8 not in substance, but due to general procedures.

(Translated by Prof. Dr. Hans-Peter Rodenberg, University of Hamburg)

Kanji for Personal Names

Abe Jirō 阿部次郎 (1883–1959)
Aichi Kiichi 愛知揆一 (1907–1973)
Akamatsu Kaname 赤松要 (1896–1974)
Akisato Ritō 秋里籬島
Amano Teiyū 天野貞祐 (1884–1980)
Anzawa Heijirō 安沢平次郎 (1887–1970)
Aono Hisao 青野寿郎
Arita Mikio 有田三樹男
Asagai Kōichirō 朝海浩一郎 (1906–1995)
Ashikaga Yoshimasa 足利義政 (1436–1490)
Awa Kenzō 阿波研造 (1880–1939)
Ban Shōtarō 伴鐘太郎 (1892–1981)
Chao-chou 趙州 (778–897)
Chiba Tanetsugu 千葉胤次 (1894–1959)
Chikurin'bō Josei 竹林坊如成
Chun Yaosui 陳姚最
Confucius 孔子 (551 BC–479 BC)

Domon Ken 土門拳 (1909–1990)
Eyama Masami 江山正美 (1906–1978)
Fujii Jintarō 藤井甚太郎 (1883–1958)
Fujikake Shizuya 藤懸静也 (1881–1958)
Fujiki Kunihiko 藤木邦彦 (1907–1993)
Fujita Keizō 藤田敬三 (1894–1985)
Fujiyoshi Jikai 藤吉慈海 (1915–1993)
Furuta Ryōichi 古田良一 (1893–?)
Gamō Ujisato 蒲生氏郷 (1556–1595)
Giten Genshō 義天玄承 (1393–1462)
Hakuho Eryō 伯蒲恵稜 (1544–1628)
Hani Gorō 羽仁五郎 (1901–1983)
Hara Setsuko 原節子 (1920–)
Harada Jirō 原田治郎 (1878–1963)
Hasegawa Saburō 長谷川三郎 (1906–1957)
Heki Danjō Masatsugu 日置弾正正次 (ca. 1444–1502)
Higo Kazuo 肥後和男

Hikojirō 彦二郎
Hiraizumi Kiyoshi 平泉澄 (1895–1984)
Hisatsune Shūji 久恒秀治 (1911–)
Hisamatsu Shin'ichi 久松真一 (1889–
    1980)
Honda Toshitoki 本多利時 (1901–1945)
Honda Toshizane 本多利実 (1836–1917)
Horiguchi Sutemi 堀口捨己 (1895–1984)
Hosokawa Katsumoto 細川勝元 (1430–
    1473)
Ichikawa Kojirō (Nobumitsu) 市川虎四郎
    (信光) (1846–1925)
Ienaga Saburō 家永三郎 (1913–2002)
Ikeda Masuo 池田満寿夫 (1934–1997)
Imakita Kōsen 今北洪川 (1816–1892)
Inatomi Eijirō 稲富栄次郎 (1897–1975)
Indō Masatsuna 印東昌綱 (1877–1944)
Inobe Shigeo 井野邊茂雄
Inoue Kasaburō 井上嘉三郎 (1881–
    1963)
Inoue Yasushi 井上靖 (1907–1991)
Ishihara Ken 石原謙 (1882–1976)
Itazawa Takeo 板澤武雄 (1895–1962)
Iwanami Shigeo 岩波茂雄 (1881–1946)
Iwasaki Tsutomu 岩崎勉 (1900–1975)
Kamei Toshio 亀井俊雄 (1927–)
Kanamori Sōwa 金森宗和 (1584–1656)
Kanō Jigorō 嘉納治五郎 (1860–1938)
Kanō Masanobu 狩野正信 (1434–1530)
Katsu Kaishū 勝海舟 (1823–1899)
Katsumoto Seiichirō 勝本清一郎 (1899–
    1967)
Kawahara Shunsaku 河原春作
Kawai Hayao 河合隼雄 (1928–2007)
Kawakami Gen'ichi 川上源一 (1912–
    2002)
Kimiya Yasuhiko 木宮泰彦
Kimura Shizuo 木村静雄
Kimura Takeyasu 木村健康 (1909–1973)
Kimura Tatsugorō 木村辰五郎
Kinoshita Kazuo 木下一雄 (1900–?)
Kinoshita Seitarō 木下成太郎 (1865–
    1942)
Kishiro Shūichi 木代修一

Kita Ikki 北一輝 (1883–1937)
Kita Reikichi 北昤吉 (1885–1961)
Kitada Kōzō 北田宏蔵 (1899–)
Kitagawa Momoo 北川桃雄 (1899–
    1969)
Kitawaki Noboru 北脇昇 (1901–1951)
Kiyohara Sadao 清原貞雄 (1885–1964)
Kiyonori of Yoshii-zumi 吉井住清則
Kobayashi Fumio 小林文夫
Kobori Enshū 小堀遠州 (1579–1647)
Kobori Sōhaku 小堀宗柏
Kōda Shigetomo 幸田成友 (1873–1954)
Kodama Kōta 児玉幸多 (1909–
    2007)
Kokushō Iwao 黒正巖 (1895–1949)
Komachiya Sōzō 小町谷操三 (1893–
    1976)
Komiya Toyotaka 小宮豊隆 (1884–1966)
Konishi Shirō 小西四郎 (1912–1996)
Kotarō 小太郎
Kūkai 空海 (774–835)
Kuki Shūzō 九鬼周造 (1888–1941)
Kurata Chikatada 蔵田周忠 (1895–
    1966)
Kurita Mototsugu 栗田元次 (1890–
    1955)
Kuroita Katsumi 黒板勝美 (1874–1946)
Kurokawa Dōyū (Michisuke) 黒川道祐
    (?–1691)
Kuruma Samezō 久留間鮫造 (1893–
    1982)
Lin Kun 劉昆
Maeda Toshiie 前田利家 (1538–1599)
Matsukura Shōei 松倉紹英 (1908–1983)
Matsumoto Hikojirō 松本彦次郎 (1880–
    ?)
Matsuo Toshirō 松尾俊郎 (1897–1979)
Matsuzaki Hisakazu 松崎寿和 (1913–
    1986)
Miki Kiyoshi 三木清 (1897–1945)
Minamoto no Tametomo 源為朝 (1139–
    1170)
Minamoto no Yorimasa 源頼政 (1104–
    1180)

Mishima Yukio 三島由紀夫 (1925–1970)

Miura Hiroyuki 三浦周行 (1871–1931)

Mizuno Kinzaburō 水野欣三郎

Mori Katsumi 森克己 (1903–1981)

Mori Osamu 森蘊 (1905–1988)

Morikawa Kōzan 森川香山

Morisue Yoshiaki 森末義彰 (1904–1977)

Moriya Kyōgo 守屋恭吾

Mu Qi (Japanese, Mokkei 牧谿; act. thirteenth century)

Muchaku Dōchū 無着道忠 (1653–1744)

Murakami Hisashi 村上久

Murō Saisei 室生犀星 (1889–1962)

Mutai Risaku 務台理作 (1890–1974)

Mutō Makoto 武藤誠 (1907–1995)

Naganuma Kenkai 長沼賢海 (1883–?)

Naitō Tōichirō 内藤藤一郎 (1897–1939)

Nakae Chōmin 中江兆民 (1847–1901)

Nakajima Matsuchi 中島待乳 (1850–1938)

Nakamura Ichirō 中村一良

Nakamura Kōya 中村孝也 (1885–1970)

Nakamura Naokatsu 中村直勝 (1890–1976)

Nakane Kinsaku 中根金作 (1917–1995)

Naramoto Tatsuya 奈良本辰也 (1913–2001)

Naruse Mukyoku 成瀬無極 (1884–1958)

Nasu Toshisuke (Munekazu) 那須容和 (1901–1978)

Nasu no Yoichi 那須与一

Natsume Sōseki 夏目漱石 (1867–1916)

Needham, Rodney (1923–)

Nishida Naojirō 西田直二郎 (1886–1964)

Nishikawa Issōtei 西川一草亭 (1878–1938)

Nishimura Keishin 西村恵信 (1933–)

Nishio Kanji 西尾幹二 (1935–)

Nishioka Toranosuke 西岡虎之助 (1895–1970)

Nishiyama Matsunosuke 西山松之助 (1912–)

Noguchi, Isamu 野口イサム (1904–1988)

Ōba Hideo 大庭秀雄 (1910–)

Obi Hanji 小尾範治

Ōe Seiichi (Seishirō) 大江精一 (精志郎) (1897–?)

Ōe Seizō 大江精三 (1905–?)

Ogasawara Heibei Tsuneharu 小笠原平兵衛常春 (1666–1747)

Ogasawara Nagakiyo 小笠原長清

Ōhazama (Ōhasama) Shūei (Schuej, Chikudō) 大峽 (大巌) 秀榮 (竹堂) (1883–1946)

Ōhira Zenzō (Shabutsu) 大平善蔵 (射仏) (1874–1952)

Oikawa Giemon 及川儀右衛門

Okakura Kakuzō (Tenshin) 岡倉覚三 (天心) (1862–1913)

Okazaki Aya'akira 岡崎文彬 (1908–1995)

Okuda Masatomo 奥田政友

Ōmori Kingorō 大森金五郎

Ōmori Sōgen 大森曹玄 (1904–1994)

Ono Masa'aki 小埜雅章 (1947–)

Onuma Hideharu 小沼英治 (1910–1990)

Ōsaki Ryūen 大崎龍淵

Osaragi Jirō 大佛次郎 (1897–1973)

Ōuchi Hyōe 大内兵衛 (1888–1980)

Ōyama Heishirō 大山平四郎 (1917–?)

Ozawa Eiichi 小澤榮一 (1910–?)

Ozu Yasujirō 小津安二郎 (1903–1963)

Ryū Chishū 笠智衆 (1904–1993)

Ryū Susumu 龍粛 (1890–?)

Saitō Hishō 斎藤斐章 (1867–1944)

Saitō Katsuo 齋藤勝雄

Saitō Takashi 齋藤孝 (1960–)

Sakamoto Tarō 坂本太郎 (1901–1987)

Sakurai Yasunosuke 櫻井保之助

Sano Kiichi (Tōemon) 佐野輝一 (藤右衛門) (1928–)

Sano Masanori 佐野正則

Sasakawa Rinpū 笹川臨風 (1870–1949)

Sasaki Kōzō 佐々木剛三 (1928–)

Sasaki Nobutsuna 佐々木信綱 (1872–1963)

Seijirō 清二郎
Sesshū 雪舟 (1420–1506)
Shaku Sōen 釈宗演 (1860–1919)
Shaku Sōkatsu 釈宗活 (1871–1954)
Sharaku 写楽
Shiba Kazumori 芝葛盛 (1880–1955)
Shibata Jisaburō 柴田治三郎
Shiga Naoya 志賀直哉 (1883–1971)
Shigemori Kanto 重森完途 (1923–1992)
Shigemori Mirei 重森三玲 (1896–1975)
Shiken Saidō 子建西堂
Sōami 相阿弥 (?–1525)
Suga Shigeyoshi 菅重義 (1889–?)
Sugano Jirō 菅野二郎
Suhara Kōun 須原耕雲 (1917–)
Suzuki, Daisetsu (Daisetz) T. 鈴木大拙 (1870–1966)
Suzuki Munetada 鈴木宗忠 (1881–1963)
Takahashi Satomi 高橋里美 (1886–1964)
Takasaki Tatsunosuke 高崎達之助 (1885–1964)
Takayanagi Mitsutoshi 高柳光寿 (1892–1969)
Takayanagi Noriaki 高柳憲昭 (1936–)
Takeda Bokuyō (Tsunejirō) 武田朴陽 (常次郎)
Takeuchi Rizō 竹内理三 (1907–1997)
Tamura Tsuyoshi 田村剛 (1890–1979)
Tanaka Sansetsu 田中三雪
Tatsui Matsunosuke 龍居松之助
Tatsui Takenosuke 龍居竹之介
Tatsuno Yutaka 辰野隆 (1888–1964)

Terada Tōru 寺田透 (1915–1995)
Tōkai Sekimon 東海石門
Tokugawa Yoshimune 徳川吉宗 (1684–1751)
Tomita Yoshirō 富田芳郎
Tono Takuma 戸野琢磨 (1891–1985)
Toyama Eisaku 外山英策
Toyota Takeshi 豊田武 (1910–1980)
Toyotomi Hideyoshi 豊臣秀吉 (1537–1598)
Tsubouchi Shōyō 坪内逍遙 (1859–1935)
Tsugawa Masahiko 津川雅彦 (1940–)
Ueno Isaburō 上野伊三郎 (1892–1972)
Uno Yōzaburō 宇野要三郎 (1878–1969)
Uozumi Sōgorō 魚澄惣五郎 (1889–1959)
Urakami Sakae 浦上栄 (1882–1971)
Wakamori Tarō 和歌森太郎 (1915–1977)
Wakimoto Sokurō 脇本十九郎 (1883–1963)
Wasa Daihachirō 和佐大八郎
Watanabe Yosuke 渡辺世祐 (1874–1957)
Xie He 謝赫
Yamada Mumon 山田無文 (1900–1988)
Yamaguchi Seishi 山口誓子 (1901–1994)
Yamamoto Yū 山本尤 (1930–)
Yamaoka Tesshū 山岡鉄舟 (1836–1888)
Yanagi Muneyoshi 柳宗悦 (1889–1961)
Yanagida Seizan 柳田聖山 (1922–2006)
Yoshida Shigekata 吉田重賢 (1463–1543)
Yoshida Shigemasa 吉田重政 (1485–1569)
Zhang Yanyuan 張彦遠

Kanji for Japanese Terms

ashibumi 足踏

Ashikaga period 足利時代

Bishū 尾州

bonseki 盆石

bōshi kazari 帽子飾り

budō 武道

bunraku 文楽

busha 武射

bushidō 武士道

Butokuden 武徳殿

Butokukai 武徳会

buyō 舞踊

chanoyu 茶の湯

chigaidana 違い棚

Chikurin-ha 竹林派

daimyō 大名

Dai Nippon Shagakuin 大日本射覚院

Daisen'in 大仙院

Daishadōkyō 大射道教

Daitokuji 大徳寺

Daiunzan 大雲山

dan 段

dandan ashi ga deru 段々足が出る

dōgu 道具

dōraku 道楽

Dōsetsu-ha 道雪派

dōsha 堂射

dōtaku 銅鐸

dōzukuri 胴造

Edo period 江戸時代

Engakuji 円覚寺

Enpukuji 円福寺

eshajōri 会者定離

Fukōin 普広院

Genpei War 源平合戦

Ginkaku 銀閣

gozan 五山

hanare 離れ

harakiri 腹切り

hatamoto 旗本

Heian period 平安時代

Heike monogatari 平家物語

Heki-ryū 日置流

Higashiyama culture 東山文化

Higashiyama period 東山時代

hikime 蟇目

hitotsu mato sharei 一的射礼

hōjō 方丈

Honda-ryū 本多流

Hōryūji 法隆寺

hosha 歩射

hyakusha-gake 百射がけ

hyappatsu hyakuchū 百発百中

hyappatsu seisha 百発聖射

ikebana 生け花

Insai-ha 印西派

inuōmono 犬追物

Ippakutei 一白亭

Ise Grand Shrine 伊勢神宮

Ishidō Chikurin-ha 石堂竹林派

issha zetsume 一射絶命

Iwanami Bunko 岩波文庫

Iwanami Shoten 岩波書店

Jōmon period 縄文時代

jūjutsu 柔術

kabuki 歌舞伎

kai 会

kaiyūshiki 回遊式

Kamakura period 鎌倉時代

Kan'ei era 寛永時代

kangyōjō 勧業場

karesansui 枯山水

kata 型

Katsura Detached Villa 桂離宮

kemari 蹴鞠

kendō 剣道

kenshō 見性

Kinkaku 金閣

kisha 騎射

Kishū 紀州

kōan 公案

Kōdōkan 講道館

Kokedera 苔寺

kōjiya 麹屋

kokoro 心

Kyōyōchi pond 鏡容池

kyū 級

kyūdō 弓道

kyūjutsu 弓術

makiwara 巻藁

Manpukuji 万福寺

Matsuo Grand Shrine 松尾大社

Meiji period 明治時代

Meiji Restoration 明治維新

menkyo kaiden 免許皆伝

Momoyama culture 桃山文化

mondō 問答

mu no bi 無の美

Muromachi period 室町時代

Myōshinji 妙心寺

Nihon shoki 日本書紀

Nijō Castle 二条城

Nishi Honganji 西本願寺

noh 能

nue 鵺／鵺

Ogasawara-ryū 小笠原流

ōgi 奥義

Ōkura-ha 大蔵派

Ōnin War 応仁の乱

orei 御礼

Otokoyama Hachimangū 男山八幡宮

ōyakazu 大矢数

raku ware 楽焼

reisha 礼射

Reiun'in 霊雲院

Rengeōin 蓮華王院

renshi 錬士

Rikugien 六義園

Rinzai sect 臨済宗

Rokumei Hall 鹿鳴館

Rokuonji 鹿苑寺

Ryōanji 龍安寺／竜安寺

Ryōbō-kai／Ryōbō Kyōkai 両忘会／両忘協会

Ryōgen'in 龍源院
Ryōkōin 龍光院
Saigen'in 西源院
Saihōji 西芳寺
Sakon'emon-ha 左近衛門派
Sanjūsangendō 三十三間堂
San'nai Maruyama site 三内丸山遺跡
Sekka-ha 雪荷派
sen 銭
sensei 先生
shadō 射道
shakkei 借景
shaku 尺
shari kenshō 射裡見性
shazen kenshō 射禅見性
shidare zakura 糸桜
shinden zukuri 寝殿造り
Shingon 真言
shōgi 将棋
shoin 書院
shoin zururi 書院造り
Shōkintei 松琴亭
Shōkokuji 相国寺
Shōren'in 青蓮院
Shōwa period 昭和時代
shūseki 醜石

sumie 墨絵
sumō 相撲
Taishō period 大正時代
Takarazuka Theater 宝塚劇場
Takuboku-ryō 択木寮
tanka 短歌
tatami 畳
Tenryūji 天龍寺
Tōfukuji 東福寺
tokonoma 床の間
Tokudaiji 徳大寺
tora no ko watashi 虎の子渡し
tōshiya 通矢
tsubo 坪
tsugiya 継矢
Tsūtenkaku 通天閣
uekiya 植木屋
ukiyoe 浮世絵
Weishu 魏志
yabusame 流鏑馬
Yakushiji 薬師寺
Yamato-ryū 大和流
Yayoi period 弥生時代
yugamae 弓構え
Zokutōan 続燈庵

Bibliography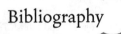

"Ācherī no wayaku wa 'kyūdō' o shiyō." *Kyūdō* 110 (July 1959): 47.

Acker, William R. B. *Japanese Archery*. Rutland, VT and Tokyo: Tuttle, 1965. Originally published with Nasu Munekazu as *Fundamentals of Japanese Archery* (Kyoto: Shikisha, 1937).

————. Personal File. Collection of Smithsonian Freer Gallery of Art.

————. *Some T'ang and Pre-T'ang Texts on Chinese Painting*. Westport, CT: Hyperion Press, 1954.

————. *The Wall-Paintings of Horyuji*. Baltimore: Waverly Press, 1943.

Adamusu, Andī [Adams, Andy]. "Kyūdō: teiō no geijutsu." Translated by Takeichi Yoshio. *Kyūdō* 208 (April 1967): 4–11.

Akisato Ritō. *Miyako meisho zue*. Kyoto: Yoshinoya Tamehachi, 1780.

————. *Miyako rinsen meishō zue*. Kyoto: Ogawa Tazaemon, 1799.

Amano Teiyū. "Haideruberuku gakuha no hitobito." *Risō* 87 (1938): 38–43.

Amanuma Shun'ichi, and Shigemori Mirei. *Kyōto bijutsu taikan: Teien*. Tokyo: Takayamadō Shoten, 1933.

Anzawa Heijirō. "Shadō seishin ni tsuite." *Kyūdō* 153 (February 1963): 4–7.

Arita Mikio. "Shari kenshō (kadai ronbun) ni tsuite." *Kyūdō* 106 (March 1959): 21.

Arsone, Sarah. *Zen and the Art of Changing Diapers*. Los Angeles: Sarah Arsone, 1993.

Ashton, Dore. *Noguchi: East and West*. New York: Knopf, 1992.

Ban Shōtarō. "Genka kyūkai shiken." *Kyūdō* 120 (May 1960): 12–16.

————. "Gorin fusanka to kyūkai kongo no katsudō." *Kyūdō* 130 (March 1961): 26–27.

Bardin, Matt, and Susan Fine. *Zen in the Art of the SAT: How to Think, Focus, and Achieve Your Highest Score.* Boston: Houghton Mifflin, 2005.

Barthes, Roland. *L' Empire des Signes.* Geneva: Albert Skira, 1970.

Barugenhōru, Haintsu [Balkenhol, Heinz]. "Nihon kyūdō ni omou." *Kyūdō* 118 (March 1960): 34–36.

Benoist-Méchin, Jacques. *L'Homme et ses Jardins: ou Les Métamorphoses du Paradis Terrestre.* Paris: A. Michel, 1975.

Benz, Ernst. *Zen in westlicher Sicht.* Weilheim: O.W. Barth-Verlag, 1962.

Boldt, Laurence G. *Zen and the Art of Making a Living: A Practical Guide to Creative Career Design.* New York: Arkana, 1993.

Bradbury, Ray. *Braddoberi ga yattekuru.* Translated by Ogawa Takayoshi. Tokyo: Shōbunsha, 1996. Originally published as *Zen in the Art of Writing* (Santa Barbara, CA: Joshua Odell Editions, 1989).

Brownell, Lauren Cassel. *Zen and the Art of Housekeeping: The Path to Finding Meaning in Your Cleaning.* Avon, MA: Adams Media, 2008.

Chaline, Eric. *Zen and the Art of Travel.* Naperville, IL: Sourcebooks, 2000.

————. *Zen and the Art of Well-Being.* Naperville, IL: Sourcebooks, 2001.

Claremon, Niel. *Zen in Motion.* Rochester, VT: Inner Traditions International, 1991.

Condor, Josiah. *Landscape Gardening in Japan.* Tokyo: Kelly & Walsh, 1893.

Cosin, Elizabeth M. *Zen and the Art of Murder.* New York: St. Martin's Press, 1998.

————. *Zen and the City of Angels.* New York: St. Martin's Minotaur, 1999.

Creekmore, Charles. *Zen and the Art of Diabetes Maintenance.* Alexandria, VA: American Diabetes Association, 2002.

Crum, W. R., L. D. Griffin, D. L. G. Hill, and D. J. Hawkes. "Zen and the Art of Medical Image Registration: Correspondence, Homology, and Quality." *NeuroImage* 20 (2003): 1425–37.

DeProspero, Dan, and Jackie DeProspero. *Illuminated Spirit.* Tokyo: Kodansha International, 1996.

Domon Ken, Yamaguchi Seishi, and Fukuyama Toshio. *Saihōji, Ryōanji.* Tokyo: Bijutsu Shuppansha, 1959.

Enomiya-Lassalle, Hugo M. *Zen-Unterweisung.* Munich: Kösel, 1988.

Erumā, R. P. *Yōkyū.* Translated by Suga Shigeyoshi. Tokyo: Fumaidō Shoten, 1969.

Eyama Masami. "Daisen'in teien kōsei ni kansuru Dynamic Symmetry teki kenkyū." *Zōen zasshi* 3:2 (1936): 97–107.

————. "Ryōanji teien no kōsei ni tsuite." *Zōen zasshi* 30: 2 (1966): 2–6.

————. "Taisū teki kinsei ni yoru Ryōanji teien no kōsei ni tsuite." *Zōen zasshi* 2:2 (1935): 101–14.

Farias, Victor. *Heidegger and Nazism.* Edited by Joseph Margolis and Tom Rockmore. Translated by Paul Burrell, Dominic Di Bernardi, and Gabriel R. Ricci. Philadelphia: Temple University Press, 1989. Originally published as *Heidegger et le Nazisme* (Lagrasse: Editions Verdier, 1987).

Faust, August. "Vorbemerkung des Herausgebers." In *Zen: der lebendige Buddihismus in Japan*, by Ohasama Schuej, x–xiii. Gotha: Verlag Friedlich Andreas Perthes, 1925.

French, Hal. *Zen and the Art of Anything*. New York: Broadway Books, 1999.

Froug, William. *Zen and the Art of Screenwriting: Insights and Interviews*. Los Angeles: Silman-James Press, 1996.

Fujiyoshi Jikai. "Ōbei zengyō angya." *Zen bunka* 14 (1959): 40–47.

"Gakka tōan narabi ni kadai ronbun no keisai ni tsuite." *Kyūdō* 107 (April 1959): 47.

The Gateless Barrier: The Wu-men Kuan (Mumonkan). Translated and with commentary by Robert Aitken. New York: North Point Press, 1990.

Gendai kyūdō kōza, 2nd ed. Vol. 6, *Kyūdō bunka hen*. Tokyo: Yūzankaku, 1982.

Glockner, Hermann. *Heidelberger Bilderbuch*. Bonn: H. Bouvier u. CO. Verlag, 1969.

Gülberg, Niels. "Eugen Herrigels Wirken als philosophischer Lehrer in Japan (1)." *Waseda-Blätter* 4 (1997): 41–66.

———. "Eugen Herrigels Wirken als philosophischer Lehrer in Japan (2)." *Waseda-Blätter* 5 (1998): 44–60.

Haietto, Girubāto [Hyatt, Gilbert]. "Zen no shinpi." Translated by Kobori Sōhaku. *Zen bunka* 7 (1957): 23–29.

———. "Zen no shinpi." Translated by Kobori Sōhaku. *Zen bunka* 9 (1957): 7–13.

Hakue. *Sanshū myōseki shi* (1702). *Shinshū Kyōto sōsho*, 2nd ed., vols. 15 and 16, edited by Noma Kōshin. Kyoto: Rinsen Shoten, 1976.

Hale, Gill. *Zen and the Art of Gardening*. Naperville, IL: Sourcebooks, 2000.

Hamilton, Bruce Taylor. *Human Nature, the Japanese Garden of Portland, Oregon*. Portland, OR: Japanese Garden Society of Oregon, 1996.

Harada Jiro. *The Gardens of Japan*. London: The Studio Limited, 1928.

Hasegawa Saburō. "Noguchi Nippon." *Bijutsu techō* 33 (1950): 58–60.

Hearn, Lafcadio. "In a Japanese Garden." In *Glimpses of Unfamiliar Japan*. New York: Houghton Mifflin, 1894.

Here's Kyoto in Living Color. Tokyo: Froebel-kan, 1970.

Herrigel, Eugen. "Die Aufgabe der Philosophie im neuen Reich." *Pfälzische Gesellschaft zur Förderung der Wissenschaften* (1934): 26–32.

———. Correspondence/Papers. Collection of Bundesarchiv, Berlin.

———. "Entnazifizierung." Unpublished typed transcript (ca. 1947). In Herrigel and Schopfer's family history file, collection of Universität Archiv Heidelberg.

———. "Das Ethos des Samurai." *Feldpostbriefe der Philosophischen Fakultät* 3 (1944): 2–14.

———. Herrigel and Schopfer Family History Papers. [?]. Collection of Universität Archiv Heidelberg.

———. "Kyūjutsu ni tsuite." Translated by Shibata Jisaburō. *Bunka* 3:9 (1936): 1007–34. Tōhoku Teikoku Daigaku Bunkakai. Originally published as "Die Ritterliche Kunst des Bogenschiessens" (*Nippon, Zeitschrift für Japanologie* 2:4 [1936]: 193–212.)

———. *The Method of Zen*. Translated by Richard F. C. Hull. New York: Pantheon Books, 1960. Reprint, London: Arcana, 1988. Originally published as *Der Zen-Weg*. Compiled by Hermann Tausend (Munich: Otto Wilhelm Barth-Verlag, 1958).

————. *Nationalsozialismus und Philosophie*. 1935. Collection of Universitätsbibliothek Erlangen-Nürnberg.

————. *Nihon no kyūjutsu*. Translated by Shibata Jisaburō with an essay (1940) by Komachiya Sōzō and an afterword (1941) by Shibata Jisaburō. Tokyo: Iwanami Shoten, 1941. Reprinted with a new afterword by Shibata Jisaburō. Tokyo: Iwanami Bunko, 1982. Originally published as "Die Ritterliche Kunst des Bogenschiessens" (*Nippon, Zeitschrift für Japanologie* 2:4 [1936]: 193–212.)

————. "Die Ritterliche Kunst des Bogenschiessens." *Nippon, Zeitschrift für Japanologie* 2:4 (1936): 193–212.

————. "Die Tradition im japanischen Volks = und Kulturleben." In *Kulturmacht Japan*, edited by Richard Foerster, 14–15. Vienna: Die Pause, 1942.

————. *Yumi to zen*. Translated by Inatomi Eijirō and Ueda Takeshi with forewords by Gusty L. Herrigel (1955), Komachiya Sōzō, and Inatomi Eijirō. Tokyo: Kyōdō Shuppan, 1956. Originally published as *Zen in der Kunst des Bogenschiessens* (Munich: Otto Wilhelm Barth-Verlag, 1948).

————. *Zen in the Art of Archery*. Translated by Richard F. C. Hull with a foreword by D. T. Suzuki and a preface by Eugen Herrigel. New York: Pantheon Books, 1953. Reprint, without the author's preface, New York: Vintage Books, 1999. Originally published as *Zen in der Kunst des Bogenschiessens* (Munich: Otto Wilhelm Barth-Verlag, 1948).

Herrigel, Gusty L. *Der Blumenweg*. Munich: Otto Wilhelm Barth, 1958.

Hisamatsu Shin'ichi. *Zen and the Fine Arts*. Translated by Tokiwa Gishin. Tokyo: Kōdansha International Ltd., 1971. Originally published as *Zen to bijutsu* (Kyoto: Bokubisha, 1958).

————. "Zen no sekaiteki shimei." *Zen bunka* 17 (1959): 7–19.

Hisatsune Shūji. *Kyōto meien ki: Chūkan*. Tokyo: Seibundō Shinkōsha, 1968.

————. "Ryōanji sekitei no kachi." *Geijutsu shinchō* 4:11 (1953): 152–158.

Horiguchi Sutemi. *Niwa to kūkan kōsei no dentō*. Tokyo: Kashima Shuppankai, 1965.

Humphreys, Christmas. *Zen Comes West*. London: George Allen & Unwin Ltd., 1960.

Ienaga Saburō. *Ichi rekishi gakusha no ayumi*. Tokyo: Sanseidō, 1977.

————. *Nihon bunkashi*. Tokyo: Iwanami Shinsho, 1959.

————. *Shin Nihon shi*. Tokyo: Fuzanbō, 1947.

————. *Shin Nihon shi*. Tokyo: Sanseidō, 1952.

Ikeda Masuo. "Ikite iru ishi." In *Nihon no teien bi*. Vol. 4, *Ryōanji*, edited by Inoue Yasushi and Sen Sōshitsu, 50–58. Tokyo: Shūeisha, 1989.

Ikokujin no mita bakumatsu Meiji Japan. Tokyo: Shin Jinbutsu Ōraisha, 2003.

Inatomi Eijirō. "Herigeru sensei no omoide." In Herrigel, *Yumi to zen*, 11–31. Tokyo: Kyōdō Shuppan, 1956.

Inoue Kasaburō. "Herigeru-shi to yumi." *Kyūdō* 81 (January 1957): 7–9.

————. "Herigeru-shi to yumi." *Kyūdō* 82 (February 1957): 18–21.

Inoue Yasushi. *Utsukushii mono to no deai*. Tokyo: Bungei Shunjūsha, 1973.

"An Interview with R. J. Zwi Werblowsky: ZEN." *Center Magazine* 3: 2 (March/April 1975): 61–70.

Ippakutei: The Ceremonial Tea House & Garden. Washington, DC: The Embassy of Japan, n.d.

Ishihara Ken. "Haideruberuku daigaku no omoide." *Risō* 87 (1938): 25–32.

Kagai Rōsei. "Herigeru-hakase cho *Yumi to zen* (hōyaku) o yomite." *Kyūdō* 75 (August 1956): 37–38.

Kamei Toshio. "Wakyū to yōkyū." *Kyūdō* 123 (August 1960): 10–14.

———. *Zukai ācherī kiso riron to torēningu hō*. Tokyo: Yūzankaku, 1970.

Karasz, Alex. *Zen and the Art of Dodgeball*. Charleston, SC: BookSurge, 2006.

Katahira Miyuki. *"Nihon teien" zō no keisei to kaishaku no kattō: eigo ken no manazashi to Nihongawa no ōtō (1868–1940)*. Kanagawa: Sōgō Kenkyū Daigakuin Daigaku Hakase Ronbun, 2004.

Kataoka Kenzō. *Kyōto meisho annai*. Kyoto: Fūgetsu Shōzaemon, 1899.

Kaufman, Stephen F. *Zen and the Art of Stickfighting*. Lincolnwood, IL: Contemporary Books, 2000.

Kawai Hayao. *Kage no genshōgaku*. Tokyo: Shisakusha, 1976. Reprint, Tokyo: Kōdansha Gakujutsu Bunko, 1987.

"Kawakami Genichi-shi tokubetsu intabyū." *Ācherī* 54 (December 1980): 32–33.

Kehoe, Brendan P. *Zen and the Art of the Internet: A Beginner's Guide*. Englewood Cliffs, NJ: PTR Prentice Hall, 1992. Translated by Nishida Takeshi as *Shoshinsha no tame no intānetto* (Tokyo: Toppan, 1993).

"Kichō kyūdan: Yōroppa ni okeru Nihon kyūdō no hyōka." *Kyūdō* 216 (May 1968): 8–11.

"Kichō kyūdan: Yōroppa ni okeru Nihon kyūdō no hyōka." *Kyūdō* 217 (June 1968): 9–14.

"Kichō kyūdan: Yōroppa ni okeru Nihon kyūdō no hyōka." *Kyūdō* 218 (July 1968): 7–10.

Kita Reikichi. *Tetsugaku angya*. Tokyo: Shinchōsha, 1926.

Kitagawa Momoo. *Sekitei rinsen*. Tokyo: Chikuma Shobō, 1952.

Koestler, Arthur. *The Lotus and the Robot*. Danube edition with a new preface by the author. London: Hutchinson, 1966.

———. "A Stink of Zen: The Lotus and the Robot (II)." *Encounter* 15:4 (1960): 13–32.

Komachiya Sōzō. "Herigeru-kun to yumi" (1940). Reprinted in Herrigel, *Nihon no kyūjutsu* (1982), 69–100.

Komiya Toyotaka. "Ryōanji no niwa." *Geijutsu shinchō* 1:9 (1950): 56.

Koshōshi. *Kyō habutae oridome* (1689). In *Shinshū Kyōto sōsho*, 2nd ed. Vol. 2, edited by Noma Kōshin, 313–586. Kyoto: Rinsen Shoten, 1976.

Kubo Tamon. "Monomi to hyōjun gu." *Kyūdō* 107 (April 1959): 30–31.

Kuck, Loraine E. *The Art of Japanese Gardens*. New York: John Day, 1940.

———. *One Hundred Kyoto Gardens*. London: Kegan Paul, Trench Trubner, 1936.

———. *The World of the Japanese Gardens*. New York and Tokyo: Weatherhill, 1968.

Kuitert, Wybe. *Themes, Scenes, and Taste in the History of Japanese Garden Art*. Amsterdam: J.G. Gieben, 1988.

Kurata Chikatada. *Burūno Tauto.* Tokyo: Sagami Shobō, 1942.

————. "Ryōanji sonota." In *Kindaiteki kakudo,* 263–73. Tokyo: Shinyūdō Shoten, 1933.

Kuroita Katsumi. *Kōtei kokushi no kenkyū kakusetsu ge.* Revised edition. Tokyo: Iwanami Shoten, 1936. Originally published as *Kokushi no kenkyū.* (Tokyo: Bunkaidō Shoten, 1908).

————. *Shintei Nihon rekishi.* Tokyo: Yoshikawa Kōbunkan, 1906.

Kurokawa Michisuke. *Saga kōtei* (1680). In *Kurokawa Michisuke kinki yūran shikō,* edited by Kamimura Kankō, 41–67. Kyoto: Junpūbō, 1910.

————. *Tōzai rekiranki* (1681). In *Kurokawa Michisuke kinki yūran shikō,* edited by Kamimura Kankō, 95–115. Kyoto: Junpūbō, 1910.

————. *Yōshūfu shi* (1682). *Shinshū Kyōto sōsho,* 2nd ed. Vol. 10, edited by Noma Kōshin. Kyoto: Rinsen Shoten, 1968.

Kushner, Kenneth. *One Arrow, One Life.* New York: Arkana, 1988.

"Kyōgi kisoku chū 'tsuku' wa shiyō kinshi." *Kyūdō* 248 (January 1971): 14.

Kyoto by Camera and Pen. Compiled by the Asahi Press, Kyoto Branch. Translated by Thomas I. Elliott and Yamaguchi Masuo. Kyoto: Tankō-shinsha, 1963.

Kyōto Rinsen Kyōkai. *Shinban suishō Nihon no meien: Kyōto Chūgoku hen.* Tokyo: Seibundō Shinkōsha, 1978.

Kyōto-shi Hensanbu. *Keika yōshi: Jō.* Kyoto: Kyōto-shi Sanjikai, 1895.

Kyōto-shi Sanjikai. *Heian tsūshi* 2:42. Kyoto: Kyōto-shi Sanjikai, 1895.

————. *Kyoto, Japan (with 120 illustrations)/compiled by the Kyoto City Council.* Kyoto: K. Azumae, 1903.

Kyōto-shi Ukyō-ku Ryōanji. *Sōami chikuzō Ryōanji hōjō no teien (tsūshō toranoko watashi).*

Lee, Charles C. *Zen and the Art of Foosball: A Beginner's Guide to Table Soccer.* Lincoln, NE: Writers Club Press, 2002.

Lewis, Steven. *Zen and the Art of Fatherhood: Lessons from a Master Dad.* New York: Plume, 1997.

Linssen, Robert. *Essais sur le Bouddhisme en général et sur le Zen en particular.* Paris: La Colombe, 1954. Translated by Diana Abrahamas-Curiel as *Living Zen* (London: George Allen & Unwin, 1958). Reprinted with a preface by Christmas Humphreys, New York: Grove Press, 1960.

————. *le Zen.* Verviers: Gérard, 1969. Originally published as *Essais sur le Bouddhisme en général et sur le Zen en particular* (Paris: La Colombe, 1954).

Malraux, André. *Antimémoires.* 1967. Revised edition, Paris: Gallimard, 1972.

Masui Kenkichi. "Orinpikku kyūdō ni omou." *Kyūdō* 106 (March 1959): 26–27.

Matsukura Shōei. "Ryōanji konjaku monogatari." *Zen bunka* 64 (1972): 41–45.

————. "Tōzenkō." *Zen bunka* 22 (1961): 53–63.

McLaughlin, Joseph. *Zen in the Art of Golf.* New Philadelphia, OH: Pale Horse Press, 1991.

McPhail, Mark Lawrence. *Zen in the Art of Rhetoric.* New York: State University of New York Press, 1996.

Meier, Kenneth J., Warren S. Eller, Robert D. Wrinkle, and J. L. Polinard. "Zen and the Art of Policy Analysis: A Response to Nielsen and Wolf." *Journal of Politics* 63:2 (2001): 616–29.

Miki Kiyoshi. *Miki Kiyoshi zenshū*. Vol. 1. Tokyo: Iwanami Shoten, 1966.

The Miyako Hotel Guide to Kyoto and the Surrounding Districts. Kyoto: Nishimura Jinbei, 1908.

Mizuno Kinzaburō. "Ryōanji no sekitei to kashiopea za." *Zen bunka* 91 (1978): 52–54.

———. *Zen to geijutsu no setten*. Tokyo: Kondō Shuppansha, 1983.

Momoi Tōu. *Kyūai zuihitsu* (1781–1788). In *Nihon zuihitsu taisei dai 2 ki*. Vol. 12, edited by Nihon Zuihitsu Taisei Henshūbu, 1–285. Tokyo: Yoshikawa Kōbunkan, 1974.

Moore, Abd al-Hayy. *Zen Rock Gardening*. Philadelphia and London: Running Press, 2000.

Mori Osamu. "Ryōanji teien no kenkyū." *Gasetsu* 33 (1939): 791–807.

———. "Ryōanji sekitei ni tsuite." *Zen bunka* 64 (1972): 48–54.

Morse, Edward S. *Japanese Homes and Their Surroundings*. New York: Harper & Bros., 1885.

Murata Usakichi. "Issen tai ichigun." *Kyūdō* 112 (September 1959): 18–20.

Murō Saisei. *Murō Saisei zenshū*. Vol. 5. Tokyo: Shinchōsha, 1965.

———. *Nihon shijin zenshū*. Vol. 15, *Murō Saisei*. Tokyo: Shinchōsha, 1967.

Murphy, Bernadette. *Zen and the Art of Knitting*. Avon, MA: Adams Media, 2002.

Mutai Risaku. "Ryūgaku jidai no Takahashi Satomi-san." In *Shisaku to kansatsu: Wakai hitobito no tame ni*, 170–79.

———. *Shisaku to kansatsu: Wakai hitobito no tame ni*. Tokyo: Keisōshobō, 1968.

Mutō Makoto. "Geijutsu to shite no teien: Ryōanji no niwa to Saihōji no niwa." *Heishi* (Spring 1932): 38–44.

Naitō Tōichirō. *Hōryūji hekiga no kenkyū*. Osaka: Tōyō Bijutsu Kenkyūkai Ōsaka Shibu, 1932.

Nakamura Naokatsu. *Kyō no miryoku*. Kyoto: Tankō Shinsha, 1959.

Nakane Kinsaku. *Kyō no meien*. Tokyo: Hoikusha, 1963.

———. *Kyoto Gardens*. Translated by M. L. Hickman. Osaka: Hoikusha, 1965.

———. *Nihon no niwa*. Kyoto: Kawahara Shoten, 1963.

———. "Ryōanji no ikezoko no ikō to sekitei no sakutei nendai ni tsuite." *Zōen zasshi* 21:4 (1958): 1–8.

———. "Ryōanji teien." *Shin kenchiku* 32:10 (1957): 65–66.

Naramoto Tatsuya. *Kyōto no niwa*. Tokyo: Kawade Shinsho, 1955.

———. "Ryōanji zuisō." *Zen bunka* 64 (1972): 55–58.

Nasu Munekazu, and William R. B. Acker. *Fundamentals of Japanese Archery*. Vol. 1. Kyoto: Shikisha, 1937.

Nasu Toshisuke, and Betty Hornish. *A Syllabus on Japanese Archery*. Kyoto: Kyoto American School, 1949.

Needham, Rodney. *Exemplars*. Berkeley: University of California Press, 1985.

Nenkan jinbutsu jōhō jiten. Tokyo: Nichigai Asociētsu, 1982.

"Nihon ni okeru gaijin no Nihon kyūdō nyūmon." *Kyūdō* 143 (April 1962): 38.

"Nishi Doitsu ni okeru saikin no Nihon kyūdō netsu." *Kyūdō* 143 (April 1962): 38.

Nishida Naojirō. *Nihon bunkashi josetsu*. Tokyo: Kaizōsha, 1932.

————, and Suzuki Shigetaka. *Nihon to sekai.* Tokyo: Teikoku Shoin, 1956.

Nishikawa Issōtei. "Kyōdō seisaku no niwa Ikkyūji no niwa to Daisen'in no niwa." *Heishi* (Autumn, 1931): 39–42.

Nishio Kanji. *Kōi suru shisaku.* Tokyo: Chūō Kōronsha, 1982.

Niwa Keisuke. *Kyoto.* Kyoto: Kyoto Exhibitor's Association to the Japanese-British Exhibition, 1910.

————. *The Official Catalogue.* Kyoto: Kyōto Shōhin Chinretsusho, 1910.

"Niwa o kataru zadankai." *Heishi* (Special Spring issue, 1935): 1–17.

Noguchi Isamu. *Isamu Noguchi: A Sculptor's World.* London: Thames & Hudson, 1967.

Ōga Yohei. "Yumi to zen o yonde." *Kyūdō* 161 (October 1963): 38–39.

Ohasama, Schuej [Ōhazama Shūei]. *Zen: der lebendige Buddhismus in Japan.* Edited by August Faust. Foreword by Rudolf Otto. Gotha: Verlag Friedlich Andreas Perthes, 1925.

Ōhazama Shūei. "Rirekisho." Unpublished handwritten manuscript. Collection of Seikei Gakuen Shiryōkan, 1931.

Okazaki Aya'akira. "Ryōanji sekitei e no ichibetsu." *Zōen zasshi* 2:2 (1931): 50–52.

Okuda Masatomo. "Sekitei no sugao." *Zen bunka* 64 (1972): 63–65.

Olson, Carl. *Zen and the Art of Postmodern Philosophy.* New York: State University of New York Press, 2000.

Ōmori Sōgen. *Ken to zen.* Tokyo: Shunjūsha, 1966.

————. "Zen to kyūdō." 1968. Reprinted in *Gendai kyūdō kōza*, 2nd ed., Vol. 6: *Kyūdō bunka hen.* Tokyo: Yūzankaku, 1982, 159–75.

Ono Masa'aki. "Ryōanji hōjō nantei II: Shōzen." *Rinsen* 320 (1980): 3–5.

————. *Bessatsu taiyō: Kyō no niwashi to aruku kyō no meitei.* Tokyo: Heibonsha, 2003.

Oppenheimer, Marina. "Zen and the Art of Supervision." *Family Journal: Counseling and Therapy for Couples and Families* 6:1 (1998): 61–63.

"Ōshū haken kyūdō shisetsu Murakami Akai ryō-shi no kichō hōkoku." *Kyūdō* 113 (October 1959): 26–27.

Ōyama Heishirō. *Nihon teienshi shinron.* Tokyo: Heibonsha, 1987.

————. *Ryōanji sekitei nanatsu no nazo o toku.* Tokyo: Kōdansha, 1970.

————. "Ryōanji sekitei ni kansuru nana shō (ge)." *Zen bunka* 67 (1972): 66–71.

Pascale, Richard Tanner. "Zen and the Art of Management." *Harvard Business Review* 56:2 (1978): 153–62.

Pastore, Michael. *Zen in the Art of Child Maintenance.* Dayville, CT: Zorba Press, 1993.

Payne, Peter. *Martial Arts: The Spiritual Dimension.* London: Thames & Hudson, 1981.

Petersen, Will. "Stone Garden." *Evergreen Review* 1:4 (1957): 127–37.

Phillips, Larry W. *Zen and the Art of Poker.* New York: Plume, 1999.

A Photographic Diary of the Visit of the Garden Club of America to Japan. Tokyo: Beikoku Teien Kurabu Shōtai Iinkai, 1935.

Pirsig, Robert M. *Zen and the Art of Motorcycle Maintenance.* New York: Morrow, 1974. Translated by Igarashi Yoshikatsu and Kodama Mitsuhiro as *Zen to ōtobai shūri gijutsu* (Tokyo: Merukumāru, 1990).

Pretniss, Chris. *Zen and the Art of Happiness*. Los Angeles: Power Press, 2006.

Pursglove, Paul David, ed. *Zen in the Art of Close Encounters: Crazy Wisdom and UFOs*. Berkeley, CA: The New Being Project, 1995.

Ross, Nancy Wilson, ed. *The World of Zen*. New York: Vintage Books, 1960.

"Ryōanji sekitei." *Shin kenchiku* 32:10 (1957): 61.

Sabat, Jack M. *Zen and the Art of Street Fighting*. Berkeley, CA: Frog Ltd., 1996.

Saitō Katsuo. "Ryōanji no ishigumi 'toranoko watashi' no kaibō." *Teien* 5:8 (1923): 6–9.

———. " 'Ryōanji niwa ni taisuru ichi shiken' o yomite." *Teien* 24:1 (1942): 32–33.

Saitō Takashi. *Shintai kankaku o torimodosu*. Tokyo: Nihon Hōsō Shuppan Kyōkai, 2000.

Sakurai Yasunosuke. *Awa Kenzō: ōinaru sha no michi no oshie*. Sendai: Awa Kenzō Sensei Seitan Hyakunensai Jikkō Iinkai, 1981.

Sandifer, Jon. *Zen and the Art of Cooking*. Naperville, IL: Sourcebooks, 2001.

Sankey, Jay. *Zen and the Art of the Monologue*. New York: Routledge, 2000.

———. *Zen and the Art of Stand-Up Comedy*. New York: Routledge, 1998.

Sasaki Kōzō. "Ryōanji sekitei no nazo." *Geijutsu shinchō* 22:9 (September 1971): 122–27.

Scholem, Gershom. "Zen-Nazism?" *Encounter* 16:2 (1961): 96.

Sharf, Robert H. "The Zen of Japanese Nationalism." *History of Religions* 33:1 (1993): 1–43.

"Shari kenshō ni tsuite." *Kyūdō* 104 (January 1959): 28–29.

Shibata Jisaburō. "Kyūhan e no yakusha kōki kara" (1941). Reprinted in Herrigel, *Nihon no kyūjutsu* (1982), 101–5.

———. "Shinpan e no yakusha kōki." Reprinted in Herrigel, *Nihon no kyūjutsu* (1982), 107–22.

Shields, Patricia M. "Zen and the Art of Higher Education Maintenance: Bridging Classic and Romantic Notions of Quality." *Journal of Higher Education Policy and Management* 21:2 (1999): 165–72.

Shiga Naoya. *Shiga Naoya zenshū*. Vol. 5. Tokyo: Iwanami Shoten, 1999.

Shigemori Mirei. "Nihon teien no kanshō hō (2)." *Rinsen* 2 (1935): 56–59.

———. *Nihon teienshi zukan*. Vol. 4. Tokyo: Yūkōsha, 1938.

———. "Ryōanji to Daisen'in no sekitei bi." *Shiseki to bijutsu* 17:4 (1947): 142–50.

———, and Shigemori Kanto. *Nihon teienshi taikei*. Vol. 7, *Muromachi no niwa (3)*. Tokyo: Shakai Shisōsha, 1971.

"Shin an Nihon yumi o shisha." *Kyūdō* 119 (April 1960): 9.

Shintei gishi wajin den hoka san pen. Tokyo: Iwanami Bunko, 1951.

Shoshanna, Brenda. *Zen and Art of Falling in Love*. New York: Simon & Schuster, 2003.

Shulman, Neville. *Zen in the Art of Climbing Mountains*. Rutland, VT and Tokyo: Tuttle, 1992.

Sonnenblick, Jordan. *Zen and the Art of Faking It*. New York: Scholastic Press, 2007.

Stabinsky, Miron, and Jeremy Silman. *Zen and the Art of Casino Gaming: An Insider's Guide to a Successful Gambling Experience*. n.p., Summit Publishing, 1995.

Suzuki Daisetsu. "Gendai sekai to zen no seishin." *Chūō kōron* (August 1961): 64–77.

———. "Herigeru *Yumi to zen* e no jobun" (1953). Reprinted in *Suzuki Daisetsu zenshū zōho shinpan*. Vol. 35.

———. "A Reply from D. T. Suzuki." *Encounter* 17:4 (1961): 55–58.

———. *Suzuki Daisetsu zenshū zōho shinpan*. Vol. 20. Tokyo: Iwanami Shoten, 2001.

———. *Suzuki Daisetsu zenshū zōho shinpan*. Vol. 35. Tokyo: Iwanami Shoten, 2002.

———, and Hisamatsu Shin'ichi. "Taidan: Amerika no zen o kataru." *Zen bunka* 14 (1959): 16–29.

Suzuki Makoto. *Nihon jin no teien kan*. Tokyo: Tōkyō Nōgyō Daigaku Zōen Gakka, 1997.

Taitō Shodōin, ed. "Kyoto Ryōanji no niwa." *Shodō* 2:9, n.d. Reprinted in 1986 by Tōyō Shodō Kyōkai.

Takayanagi Noriaki. "Sekai ācherī senshuken taikai ni Nihon kyūdō o shōkai." *Kyūdō* 258 (November 1971): 26–29.

———. "Kawakami Gen'ichi-sensei no omoide." *Ācherī* 258 (November 2002): 62–64.

Tamura Tsuyoshi. *Art of the Landscape Garden in Japan*. Tokyo: Kokusai Bunka Shinkokai, 1935.

———. "Nihon teien ni okeru hiraniwa no ishō." *Zōen kenkyū* 17 (1936): 1–8.

———. *Zōen gairon*. Tokyo: Seibidō Shoten, 1918.

———. *Zōengaku gairon*. Tokyo: Seibidō Shoten, 1925.

Tanaka Sansetsu. "Ryōanji niwa sōken." *Teien* 24:12 (1942): 514–15.

Tatsui Matsunosuke. *Gardens of Japan*. Tokyo: The Zauho Press, 1935.

———. *Japanese Gardens*. Tokyo: Maruzen Co., 1934.

———. "Kyōto no meien o mite." *Teien to fūkei* 14:10 (1932): 316–17.

———. *Nihon meien ki*. Tokyo: Takayamabō, 1924.

Tatsui Takenosuke, and Ono Kazunari. "Nakane Kinsaku-shi no 'Ryōanji sekitei sakutei nendai' kōshō ronbun ni taisuru gimon." *Zōen zasshi* 22:1 (1958): 5–8.

Taut, Bruno. *Houses and People of Japan*. Tokyo: The Sanseido Co. Ltd., 1937. Translated by Hideo Shinoda as *Nihon no kaoku to seikatsu* (Tokyo: Iwanami Shoten, 1966).

———. *Nihon Tauto no nikki 1933 nen*. Translated by Shinoda Hideo. Tokyo: Iwanami Shoten, 1975.

Tejima Toshiko. "Kadai ronbun 'shari kenshō' to sono hihan ni omou." *Kyūdō* 108 (May 1959): 27–29.

Terada Tōru. *Dō no shisō*. Tokyo: Sōbunsha, 1978.

Terajima Ryōan. *Wakan sansai zue* (1712). In *Tōyō bunko*. Vols. 447, 451, 456, 458, 462, 466, 471, 476, 481, 487, 494, 498, 505, 510, 516, 521, 527, 532. Tokyo: Heibonsha, 1985–1991.

Tōkai Sekimon. "Ryōanji zen jūshoku Matsukura Shōei oshō no senge o itamu." *Zen bunka* 110 (1983): 126–28.

Tōkyō Daigaku Bungakubunai Shigakkai, ed. *Nihon shi*. Tokyo: Yamakawa Shuppan, 1951.

Toyama Eisaku. *Muromachi jidai teienshi*. Tokyo: Iwanami Shoten, 1934.

———. "Ryōanji teien no dentōteki setsumei o haisu (ge)." *Kokka* 35: 2 (1925): 58–64.

————. "Ryōanji teien no dentōteki setsumei o haisu (jō)." *Kokka* 35:1 (1925): 26–30.

Tsugawa Masahiko. "Watashi to Ryōanji." In *Daiunzan Ryōanji*. Kyoto: Saikōsha, n.d.

Uno Yōzaburō. "Sōkai ni nozomite." *Kyūdō* 121 (June 1960): 4–5.

Usuta Zan'un. *Kokumin no Nihon shi dai 7 hen: Muromachi jidai*. Tokyo: Waseda Daigaku Shuppanbu, 1923.

Valentine, Alonzo M. Jr. "Zen and the Psychology of Education." *Journal of Psychology* 79 (1971): 103–10.

Van Tonder, Gert J., Michael J. Lyons, and Yoshimichi Ejima. "Visual Structure of a Japanese Zen Garden," *Nature* 419 (2002): 359–60.

Victoria, Brian A. *Zen at War*. New York and Tokyo: Weatherhill, 1997.

Wakimoto Sokurō. "Ryōanji no niwa." *Gasetsu* 5 (1937): 49–67.

Watanabe Ojirō. "Dai nijūyon kai ācherī sekai senshuken taikai hōkoku." *Kyūdō* 208 (September 1967): 7–11.

Watts, Alan W. *Beat Zen, Square Zen, and Zen*. San Francisco, CA: City Lights Books, 1959.

————. "The Democratization of Buddhism." In *Zen and the Beat Way*, 63–88. Boston: Tuttle, 1997.

————. *The Spirit of Zen*. London: Murray, 1936.

————. *The Way of Zen*. London: Thames & Hudson, 1957.

Watts, Mark. Intoduction. In Alan Watts, *Zen and the Beat Way*. Boston: Tuttle, 1997.

Yamada Mumon. "Kokoro no kiyoki mono." *Zen bunka* 65 (1972) : 4–7.

————. "Zeni to zen." In *Mumon hōwashū*, 63–85. Tokyo: Shunjūsha, 1963.

Yamamoto Hikaru. "Kyōto meien kanshōkai kansō." *Teien* 18:1 (1936): 18–19.

Yamamoto Kakuma. *The Guide to the Celebrated Places in Kiyoto & The Surrounding Places for the Foreign Visitors*. Kyoto: Niwa, 1873.

Yamamoto Yū. *Nachizumu to daigaku*. Tokyo: Chūkō Shinsho, 1985.

Yamashina Dōan. *Kaiki* (1729). In Nakamura Yukihiko, Nomura Takatsugu, and Asō Isoji, eds. *Nihon koten bungaku taikei*, vol. 96. 375–498. Tokyo: Iwanami Shoten, 1965.

Yanagida Seizan. *Zen to Nihon bunka*. Tokyo: Kōdansha Gakujutsu Bunko, 1985.

Yoshii Tsunetarō. *Illustrated Guide to Kyoto & Its Suburbs: with Map, an Entirely New Work*. Osaka: T. Nakashima, 1891.

"Zadankai: Anzawa-hanshi ikkō hōō kichō dan: Kōhen." *Kyūdō* 234 (November 1969): 28–32.

"Zadankai: Anzawa-hanshi ikkō hōō kichō dan: Zenpen." *Kyūdō* 233 (October 1969): 18–23.

"Zadankai: Awa Kenzō-hakase to sono deshi Oigen Herigeru-hakase no koto o Komachiya-hakase ni kiku: Sono ichi." *Kyūdō* 181 (June 1965): 20–23.

"Zadankai: Awa Kenzō-hakase to sono deshi Oigen Herigeru-hakase no koto o Komachiya-hakase ni kiku: Sono ni." *Kyūdō* 182 (July 1965): 4–8.

"Zadankai: Awa Kenzō-hakase to sono deshi Oigen Herigeru-hakase no koto o Komachiya-hakase ni kiku: Sono san." *Kyūdō* 183 (August 1965): 4–7.

"Zadankai: Zen no kokusai-sei ni tsuite." *Zen bunka* 29 (1963): 34–41.

Index